The 3-Wheelers Almanac

RECOMMENDATION

This book is published with the recommendation of the Michael Sedgwick Trust

Founded in memory of the famous motoring researcher and author
Michael Sedgwick (1926-1983),
the Trust is a registered charity to encourage new research
and the recording of motoring history.
Suggestions for future projects, and donations, should be sent to
The Honorary Secretary of the Michael Sedgwick Memorial Trust,
20 High Street, Milford-on-Sea, Lymington, Hampshire, SO41 0QD England

The 3-Wheelers Almanac

John Cleve Graham

A Bajaj in Katmandu 1994. Picture by the author

BOOKMARQUE PUBLISHING
Minster Lovell • Oxfordshire

First published December 1997
Reprinted February 1998

© John Cleve Graham 1998

All rights reserved.
No part of this book may be reproduced or transmitted in any form or by any means, electronic or mechanical, including photocopying, recording or by any information storage or retrieval system, without prior permission from the publisher or copyright holder.

ISBN 1-870519-44-2

British Library Cataloguing in Publication Data
A catalogue record for this book is available from the British Library

Cover photos: *front* Peel Trident *back* Messerschmitt KR200
Hillman Imp with a motorcycle rear! spotted by the author in Australia

Set in Bookman
Published by Bookmarque Publishing • Minster Lovell • Oxon
Printed and bound by A. Rowe Ltd

ACKNOWLEDGEMENTS

Information for the listing of this A-Z of 3-wheeled vehicles has been gleaned from more than 20 years of searching old magazines and newspapers, from visits to museums and swap meets, from writing to editors of car magazines, and to secretaries of one-make clubs, gleaning for-sale notices, talking to people at rallies, as well as in the street – even if I was overseas a language barrier did not prevent me from obtaining an interesting account, one way or another... I am indebted to all those whom I encountered on the long journey to gather this material

Thank goodness for motoring and motorcycle magazines, old and new, from all over the world, when and wherever they could be read, bought or borrowed to assist in the search for information.

My thanks to the staff of the National Motor Museum, Beaulieu, in England, who made dozens of photocopies in answer to my queries from many thousands of miles away here in Australia.

And to the odd friend who did not think that I was barmy!

After all these years of compiling this listing I was then left with the problem of finding a publisher, so finally my thanks go to Brian Heath of The Michael Sedgwick Memorial Trust who pointed me in the direction of John Rose of Bookmarque who, in his wisdom or otherwise, decided to take it on.

BIBLIOGRAPHY

The Light Car HMSO

The Birth of the British Motor Car T R Nicholson

Floyd Clymer's Scrap Books

The Illustrated Encyclopaedia of Automobiles

The Encyclopaedia of Commercial Vehicles

American Cars since 1775

The History of Motorcycles

*The Motor Museums of Europ*e William Stobbs

Fairthorpe Cars John Allan

J C Graham
Batemans Bay, 2536, Australia
Author: *This is Papua New Guinea*
Regular contributor of photos and articles to numerous magazines

INTRODUCTION

The idea of a vehicle moving under its own power goes back to ancient times. Among Egyptian sculptures is a relief of a royal chariot ascending the heavens, borne upon a cloud. In both Greek and Roman art there are representations of mystic chariots moving by invisible powers.

The birth of the motor car has been recorded by many experts, masses of books have been printed about the subject and many arguments have been had over a pint, but few words have been said about how the humble vehicle on three wheels had come to appear in so many early prints and publications – mostly they are written-off as an oddity, and the enthusiasts of them as crackpots or maybe just a little strange.

Technically, there are many reasons why vehicles have had three wheels – one of the obvious is steering. In the early days coaches had four wheels with the front pair pivoted in the centre on a beam axle. With a horse attached there was little trouble in going in a straight line, and if one got stuck in a hole the horse pulled you out. If you were making a sharp turn the front wheels were small enough to go under the coach and you were never going fast enough to get into difficulty. The horse took care of that.

Once our intrepid inventor had worked out how to convert steam into power and make the bulky engines small enough to turn the long held dream of self-propulsion into reality, he then found that gravity needed to be taken into consideration.

Leonardo Da Vinci had already worked out that a single wheel on a central pivot was the way to go. Cugnot had tried to improve on this by attaching a steam engine to the single front wheel but found gravity got in the way. Gurney tried a different tack; he put two small wheels together at the end of a shaft where the horse used to be, but he found that when going downhill the heavy coach had a habit of taking over (gravity again).

It was soon realised that the single wheel at the front taking some of the vehicles weight with the bulky engine near the back wheels was the way to go. It was not until he found that the engine needed to be close to the road that the gravity problem seemed to be satisfied.

Even in those early 1800s we had the diehards who insisted that there had to be a wheel at each corner or it was not a proper vehicle. Many tried but it took a chap by the name of Ackermann to work out a means of turning two front wheels without a central pivot. The problem was it was a complicated procedure which added to the cost of the vehicle.

As technology advanced so did the cost of vehicles. But the masses needed to be catered for, and cheap motoring was available only in the so-called cyclecars. By moving a single wheel to the back, one was able to utilise motorcycle engines and the simple chain-drive. That concept has enabled motoring even today to be available to the populace of many countries.

This book is not the story of 3-wheeled motoring but a collection of all the people and their cars (and trucks) that had something to do in getting those strange, sometimes odd looking vehicles to the masses. I have had a lot of fun over twenty years gathering these facts together. They are as accurate as I have been able to make them at the time of gathering the information, and I am mindful of the potential minefield of this subject which no person has ever attempted before in this A-Z format. But there is a lot of material still sitting out there waiting to be discovered.

So here goes.

It was in 1335 that the first record of a self-propelled vehicle emerged. Guido da Vigevano sketched his version of a wind-powered cart – it was never built but the drawings of it still exist.

In the 1480s, Leonardo da Vinci (born 1452) built a clockwork model of a tricycle with a tiller steering single front wheel, which incorporated a differential supplying power to a live rear axle.

In 1649, a German, Johann Hantsch of Nuremberg, had a dream and built a carriage with three wheels, a single seat, and a clockwork motor that was able to travel for short periods at three leagues an hour. It was a success and toured all over Germany and was later sold to Prince Charles Augustus of Sweden. Possibly the first successfully powered, passenger carrying 3-wheeler and maybe Hantsch was the first 'used car salesman'!

In 1672 a Belgian priest serving in China, Father Ferdinand Verbiest, had an idea for a steam powered vehicle and built a working model that looked something like a steam kettle on wheels (two in front and one behind). Steam came out of the spout, hit a paddle wheel and through a series of gear-wheels propelled the vehicle forward in a straight line (until the steam stopped).

Between 1705 and 1712, a couple of Englishmen, Thomas Newcomen and Thomas Savery, devised a steam engine which was later improved by James Watt. This really got things going.

In the late 1760s, Nicholas Joseph Cugnot had adapted a method, worked out by a Mr Papin, of transmitting power to a wheel when he built his steam powered artillery carriage, demonstrated at the Paris Arsenal on 23rd October 1769. The single motor wheel was up front with a conical boiler on an outrigger which made steering almost impossible. The long timber chassis had two rear wheels but no springs – little wonder he had the first recorded motor accident. You can still see the dints if you pop into the National Museum in Paris. It sits next to a 3-wheeled steam-powered omnibus built by Amédée Bollée in 1873.

By the 1800s steam had come of age and in England was being used to power both stationery and portable engines. Trevithick's steam carriages of 1786 to 1801 were 3-wheelers but far ahead of their time. We had to wait until 1855 before the Boydell Endless Railway Company came up with the ancestor to the caterpillar track: at this stage it was wide slabs of timber attached to a wide steel wheel, again a 3-wheeler with a single steering wheel in front. No person had yet worked out how to have two wheels in front and allow them to steer without a central pivot, all satisfactory when a horse was 'pulling' a carriage but with a steam engine 'pushing' the contraptions along, they had a tendency to turn under the vehicle and all came to an abrupt stop. Ackermann steering was not going to come into fashion for another forty years.

Rickett came up with reliability in 1858 to 1865 with what we could call a small mobile steam train engine that had been adapted to a carriage with three wheels, passengers sat in armchair comfort protected by a phaeton hood. Journeys of 150 trouble-free miles were completed at the terrifying speed of 12 mph. By now English bureaucrats were getting into the fray and slapped on a speed limit of 10mph in the country and 5mph in the city. This was in 1861.

In 1868, Ravel, a Frenchman used liquid oil fuel to power a steam engine to drive his tricycle around Paris. Sadly the machine was destroyed in the Franco-Prussian war.

Vehicles were getting lighter and moved toward personal transport, even to self-drive vehicles. Catley and Ayres from Yorkshire built a neat wagonette just 8ft 6ins long, weighing 19cwt, and able to carry the driver and four passengers at the unheard speed of 20mph. Its single front wheel was tiller steered. In 1869 they could outstrip the coppers on their bicycles any time.

By 1878 things were moving fast. The steam engines were smaller, so small that Mr A. B. Blackburn had one that was oil-fired and hidden under the seat of his back-to-back 4-seater. He was such a stickler for tradition that he had the single front wheel steered by horse reins instead of the customary tiller.

Other forms of power were on the horizon: electricity was replacing the gas lamps while storage batteries were adapted to power motors to take the place of horses. Magnus Volk built a 3-wheeler in 1887 that was his pride and joy. He would parade along Madeira Drive in Brighton viewing his other creation, the tram line and the new electric tram cars.

In Germany, Benz had been experimenting with the new fangled petrol-powered engines and built a road-going passenger vehicle especially to take this engine. In 1885 he launched his 3-wheeler, so easy to drive that in 1888 his wife and sons borrowed it to make one of the first long distance journeys in what is recognised today as the first mass-produced motor car and the birth of a marque still regarded as one of the most prestigious on the road.

About the same time a Frenchman, De Dion, started building trikes powered by his own version of the petrol engine, an engine so popular it was exported all over the world and became the power that started many a motor manufacturer to his place of fame.

While in America Charles Duryea was building 3-wheelers that would welcome the birth of the American motor industry.

Back in England, it was November 14, 1896 fast approaching the 1900s, vehicles were moving faster and faster and the bureaucrats had to up the speed limit and everybody celebrated with a race that was not a race, so they called it the Brighton Run. Today it is celebrated each year with some of the actual vehicles that originally took part, many of them were 3-wheelers.

Also in 1896, Herbert Austin built a couple of 3-wheelers and took them out on a test run, he promptly built a 4-wheeler and launched the British automotive industry.

In 1904, butcher John Weller joined up with an engineer called John Portwine to design a delivery trike that was to change the lives of the delivery boys for ever. It became the flagship for the Post Office, it was bought in quantity for deliveries by the famous general store, Harrods – even the railways wanted their fleets. This was the A.C., a 3-wheeler that was built to last. Some are still around today over 90 years later and can be seen at the odd rally.

Then came the 1914-18 war. The Germans had the Phanomen, a 3-wheeled truck with the engine as part of the single front wheel. The Panmobile went to war in their hundreds and were used as ambulances. This was the war that gave a dint to the 'us and them', it also made thousands of drivers want their own transport: a motorcycle was ok for courting but the wife wanted something better. A sidecar was open to the elements, but a proper car was too expensive – come in the cyclecar. It was cheap and was light in weight, under 8cwt, and you could register it as a motorcycle if it had three wheels.

Cyclecars came and went, but the Morgan seemed to be here for ever, from 1909 to 1952 when it became respectable and sprouted a fourth wheel (it did add a fourth in 1934 but Morgan were sensible and kept building their 3-wheelers for another 18 years).

Along came another war, this was a global stoush that broke up the Empire and opened up new markets for 3-wheeled transport. The Italians came up with the Vespa that has endured since 1947 and has been exported in various forms all over the world and is still being built in its thousands in many other countries. This was the year that began my interest that has finally resulted in this book.

As a downy faced member of BCOF, I was stationed in the rural reaches of Japan. Walking from the RAAF base to the town of Iwakuni, my mate and I hitched a ride on a small 3-wheeled motorcycle-based truck, its load was lovely and soft, the driver was surly and still clothed in part of his army uniform. On reaching our destination I found out that we had been riding on a load of silkworms and had probably ruined much of his stock. With much bowing we handed over a tin of Players, some soap and a bar of chocolate; this was the local currency and from the beam on his face I think he would have given us the motorcycle.

On demob, I needed transport and in a country that was critically short of anything new, everything was imported from the old dart. I was offered a 3-wheeled Morgan with a Ford engine or a Morris 8 Ute with a canvas hood. I wished I could have taken the Morgan but with our gravelled country roads, no space for my very large tool box as well as camping gear, the Ute came first in a very unequal competition.

In the 1950s Morgan dropped the 3-wheeler and concentrated on four wheels, as the waiting list was longer. Reliant went soldering on, shrugging of bankruptcy, mergers and takeovers, adding new models and exporting. The 1950s also saw a surge in bubble cars, there was still a shortage of 'proper cars' in England as they were all being exported.

Europe was trying to get back into production, and small was the way to go. Messerschmitt and Heinkel hit the market from Germany, the Isetta from Italy, and the English came up with the Bond and the Berkeley.

In the 60s the bubble burst as the Mini stormed in. A 4-wheeler not much bigger than the bubble cars and with room for four and no increase in price. In the movies the bad boys loved it for racing up and down steps and rushing through storm water drains, the boys in blue loved it with souped up engines, it was fast. The Isle of Man made a flank attack, they launched the Peel, possibly the world's smallest passenger car with three wheels, it had a handle on the back to help you get out of potholes, reverse was just grab the handle, lift, then point in the direction you wished to go.

With the 1970s came DIY: buy a set of plans and build your own 3-wheeler, better still buy the pieces and put it together yourself. They came in all shapes and sizes but started out looking like upmarket 1930s Morgans but after the release of the Bond Bug they became wedge-shaped escapees from Dr Who or Star Wars.

By the 1980s the Japanese dominated the motorcycle world and the art of mating a superbike, without its front wheel, to a fibreglass ground hugging 2-seater cabin up front became an art. Some might look like they came from Disneyland. The big boys like Ford and GMH added their own style to the show, just for look, not for sale.

With the 1980s and the 1990s it was speed, alternative power and fuel consumption. Rocket powered 3-wheelers blasting along faster then the speed of sound: the Budweiser Bullet hit 1178.78km/h. In Australia we have a race for Solar-powered cars – 3000 kilometres where 3-wheelers exceed 100km/h. And then there are flimsy 3-wheelers with lightweight jockeys and minute 25cc petrol engines trundling around a race track doing 4000km per gallon.

So what's in store for the year 2000? It is getting harder to build or register a 3-wheeler in the likes of Australia, while Greece has made it known it wants all 3-wheelers off the roads, yet India goes on building cars as in a time warp. Bajaj, the Vespa of the 1960s, are still built in their thousands and gaining converts, and the Indian-built Tempo/Hanomag is still going great guns. China is still building commercial trikes based on Japanese designs and competes with India for Third World markets. Nepal, located between the two of them is crowded with imported 3-wheelers of all shapes and sizes. So, no matter how hard the bureaucrats try, the 3-wheeler has been with us in some form for three hundred years, I don't think they will be rid of it for some time yet.

John Cleve Graham

ABC Tricar   1968-1973   GB

Believed to be the first 3-wheeler to be based on the Mini. Originally called a Trimini, the prototype was based on the front end of a Mini with the rear chopped away but retaining the floor plan. This was stiffened with a subframe to accept one of the original Mini rear wheels. Add a fibreglass open 2-seater body with a pram hood, similar to the 1930's Morgan, and we have a potent little machine. About 25 units were built.

ABI   1971   GB

The ABI could be called unique – a marine plywood monocoque body/chassis was mated to a standard Mini front subframe. With the engine exposed, lights mounted on waist-high mudguards and the body enclosed in stylish fibreglass, the vehicle had a slight resemblance to a 1930s Morgan. Antique Automobiles Ltd of Baston, Peterborough, offered the ABI in a body/chassis kit form.

AC (Auto-Carrier)   1900-1920   GB

John Weller (a very able engineer) and John Portwine (a very wealthy butcher) were an unlikely combination for the birth of a car industry that is still in evidence today. Dabbling in the 4-wheeled category, John Weller built a tourer of advanced design for the 1903 Motor Show. However, the two Johns identified a need for a small, fast, reliable delivery vehicle, which would be economical to maintain and easy to drive. In 1904 the Auto-Carrier was introduced and orders poured in from the Post Office, from Harrods, from the Railways and many of the large stores in the London area. The first vehicles had a sizeable goods compartment mounted on the 2-wheeled front axle, while the single rear wheel was driven through a 2-speed gearbox (mounted on the wheel itself) by a chain from a single cylinder air-cooled engine, rated at 5.6hp. Running at very low speeds, the engine, fuelled from a 2-gallon petrol tank, was able to give the machine a range of 80 to 100 miles.

By 1907 a new assembly line was producing the AC Sociable using the same mechanical layout (the driver sat at the back over the engine but with the passenger seat taking the place of the delivery box). Tiller steering mounted on the side of the vehicle was still used but the passenger compartment was fully enclosed. Later the driver moved in beside the passenger. Civilian car production ceased when the factory was put on a war footing in 1914 but enough vehicles were adapted to equip the 25th County of London Unit with machine guns and ammunition carriers. Production was resumed in 1919 for a short period, but ceased in favour of the 4-wheeled vehicles. These sturdy Auto-Carriers and Tri-Cars were maintained well into the late 1930s and still appear at rallies in various forms today.

AC Cars   1913 to date   GB

From the same factory that produced the Auto-Carrier and the AC Tricar at the start of this twentieth century, AC Cars Ltd went on to produce touring cars starting with the 4-cylinder, 10hp single seat tourer of 1913 and culminating in the classic AC 428 fastback, one of the most powerful, luxurious and expensive cars available today. However, 3-wheelers were not forgotten. After the Second World War, they were again produced in their thousands in the form of the AC Acedes, a small vehicle suitable for the incapacitated; a square-nosed fibreglass body with a pram hood provided full weather protection, a big door gave easy access, and the controls were hand operated. Unlike the early ACs these had a single front wheel that allowed a small turning circle and easy manoeuvrability.

In 1953 the AC Petite, a modern-looking fibreglass 3-wheeler with wide doors and comfortable seating for two came into its own as a petrol miser during the Suez Canal crisis. 5,000 were made in a 24 month period but production tailed off in 1958. Built for reliability and not for speed, the AC Petite can still be seen pottering round some of the English country villages today. Power was a single cylinder 346cc 2-stroke engine producing 8.5hp at 3,500rpm. A top speed of 45mph gave about 60 mpg. A few vans were made on the Petite chassis but proved not to be popular. Further notes are listed under AC (Auto-Carrier).

AC Donington 1982 GB
A professionally built 'one-off' clothed in aluminium and based on Mini parts.

Acam Nica 1984-1987 Italy

Acoma Mini Comtesse 1976-1980 France
An early French micro car which at one stage was selling at the rate of 3,000 per year. A single-seater with a polyester bodywork, a single front wheel and a folding gullwing door. A 50cc Motobecane motor supplied the power. It was the covered motor scooter for the office worker. In 1978 a fourth wheel was added and the three wheel production was reduced and finished by 1980.

Addax 1974-1980 France
More information is listed under Vitrex Riboud.

Addison 1906 GB
Built in Liverpool this Tri-Car had a 6.5hp engine of 2 cylinders and featured engine controlled variable-lift inlet valves.

Ade 1932-1933 Germany
Using a format that is still popular today, the Ade was a 3-wheeled commercial with a front platform and a single driven rear wheel, with no protection for the driver. Power was the Ilo 2-stroke engine with a choice of 200cc, 350cc or 400cc capacity. All controls were on the handlebars as befits its motorcycle ancestry.

Adi 1950 Germany
The Adi had the unusual feature of having its 120cc motor placed above (driving by chains) the single front wheel of this bench seat three person vehicle. The driver sat in the middle. Top speed was rated at 50km/h.

Adler 1886 Germany
Adler, of Frankfurt-am-Main, was a well-established bicycle manufacturer when the proprietor, Heinrich Klyer, turned to horseless carriages in 1886. The factory had been supplying wheels to the Benz Company when an Aachen engineer, Max Cudell, wanted a batch of tricycles built with Dion-Bouton engines. These were successful and Klyer decided to start his own production. After experimenting with 3 wheels, a number of prototypes were built. Production of the Adler, a 4-wheeled copy of Louis Renault's Voiturette, began in 1900. More information under Cudell.

Advance 1906-1908 GB
Coming from the Advance Motor Company of Northampton, a firm of motorcycle makers, this was a tricar along conventional lines with the passenger in front. It

used a 6hp (later 9hp) water-cooled engine driving through a 3 forward and reverse gearbox with shaft-drive to a final chain-drive to the single rear wheel. Control of ignition, air and throttle were all located on the steering column. In 1907 an air-cooled motor was added to the tricar line.

Aerial **1899** **GB**
The Aerial Cycle Company announced at the Stanley Cycle Show a Motor-Tricycle made entirely by British labour with British capital. Using a 1.75hp petrol engine it was reported as 'fitted with a lamp of electric ignition'. 3-wheeled commercials were also marketed under the Aerial name in the 1930s with the two front and one rear wheel layout.

Aermacchi **1947-1970** **Italy**
A series of 3-wheeled commercial vehicles from the Macchi Aircraft factory. Using a flat-twin 750cc engine, underslung in a tubular backbone frame with shaft-drive through 8 forward and 2 reverse gears to the two rear wheels. A fully enclosed cabin housed the office end while a variety of tray, tip or enclosed van bodies were available with capacities up to 1.5 tons.

In 1950 a larger version with a 18hp, 973cc 2 cylinder air-cooled diesel engine was announced. The company was acquired by Harley-Davidson in 1960 and renamed Aermacchi Harley-Davidson SpA. In 1960 another takeover saw the company renamed AMF-Harley-Davidson Varese SpA. The motor vehicle division was sold to Fratelli Brennan in 1970 and all 3-wheelers continued in production under the name of Bremach. More information under that name.

Aerocarene **1947** **France**

AF Grand Prix **1971-1980** **GB**
The AF Spider was built from 1971–72 to be followed by the AF Grand Prix, 1972-80, a much improved 3-wheeler available from A T Fraser Ltd of Sleaford, Lincs.

Airmobile **1937** **USA**
Paul Lewis of Lewis American Airways Inc, Rochester, New York and Denver, Colorado, conceived the idea in 1930 of a futuristic automobile to be built in metal using methods just entering the aircraft manufacturing industry. Utilising an aerodynamically-styled model created by John Tjaada, designer of the Lincoln-Zephyr, the firm of Doman and Marks began construction on the 3-wheeled, front wheel drive Airmobile Sedan in 1936. The completed prototype was pronounced road ready in April 1937. Driven some 45,000 miles throughout the United States in a promotional tour, the Airmobile proved to be a technical success with speeds of 80mph and average fuel consumption of 43.6 mpg. Promoted as a low cost mass produced people's car, the boat-tail rear end with the single wheel totally enclosed, did not appeal to the financial world and production backing was not forthcoming. Just the one Airmobile Sedan was built – this has been restored to showroom condition by Harrah's Automobile Museum in Nevada.

Aisa **1952-1957** **Spain**
From Actividades Industriales, SA, Barcelona, builders of small touring motor-cycles, came a light delivery tricycle, powered by a 197cc Hispano-Villiers air-cooled engine driving the single rear wheel, via a 3 speed gearbox. Coil sprung suspension was used.

A.K.-Ellas   **1968 to date**   **Greece**
From Nikaia, Piraeus, a ultra-light tricycle powered by a Sachs 50cc engine. Later models were to have a Kazal 50cc power unit. A 2-seat fibreglass cab is fitted and automotive controls and hydraulic brakes used. Vehicle has been restyled every few years.

Akitsu   **1952**   **Japan**
A 3-wheeled delivery truck using the front of a large motorcycle with a dropside tray of generous proportions added to the rear. Shaft-drive to the two rear wheels.

Alba   **1919-1930s**   **Germany**
Alfred Brauch formed the Alba-Werk at Stettin-Mohringen, supplying a single cylinder 1.5hp engine that could be fitted to a bicycle frame. He soon progressed to making his own 2-wheelers and it was not long before he added a 3-wheeled parcel car to the line up. Using a standard motorcycle to almost the rear hub, he added a 2-wheeled axle, powered by either a 196cc or a 250cc single cylinder ohv vertical Alba motor. A weatherproof box was mounted on elliptical springs between the rear wheels and a frame to hold empty boxes was placed on top. With cycle guards on all wheels and a sprung saddle, this was a smart looking vehicle. It was still listed with improvements in 1934.

Albrecht   **1950-1951**   **Germany**

Aleu   **1954**   **Spain**

Alexis Tri-Car   **1900**   **GB**
3.5hp and 6hp tricars built by Taig Motors, Alexandria, Scotland in early 1900s.

Alfaro   **1953-1957**   **Spain**
A 3-wheeled van with a load capacity of 400kg, built by the motorcycle firm of Construcciones Mecanicas Alfaro, Santa Perpetua de la Moguda, Barcelona.

Alfi   **1922-1928**   **Germany**
The Alfi Automobile GmbH. of Berlin produced electric vans and trucks. An exception was its unique 3-wheeled goods carrier in 1927. The single front wheel was coupled to a DKW engine and a large steering wheel all as one unit. Just turn the lot 180 degrees and one could be going backward as fast as going forward!

Alge   **1927-1937**   **Germany**
Motoren und Fahrzeugfabrik, Alfred Geissler, Knauthain near Leipzig, were the manufacturers of a trivan, built along motorcycle lines with one front wheel and a rear box or platform. Power was from a Villiers 6hp or 10hp 2-stroke engine.

Alldays and Onions   **1898**   **GB**
This used what was becoming the standard form of 3-wheeler, the passenger or cargo box sitting between the two front wheels and the driver over a 3hp engine placed just in front of the single rear wheel, with final drive by chain.

Allard   **1899-1902 & 1949**   **GB**
Allard and Co of Coventry started production of motorised tricycles in 1899 and later merged with Rex in 1902. Vehicles were produced under the names of Rex,

Rexette and Airettes until 1906. The Allard name was used on a short lived 3-wheeled car in 1949: a futuristic, all curves, fibreglass 2-seater, the 'ultimate economy car' – just 12 were made. The company is better known for its 4-wheeled sports cars. See Rex/Rexette for more information.

Allard Clipper   1953-1955   GB

The Clipper was a weird looking car designed by David Gottleib and in fact was one of the first vehicles fitted with a plastic body. Single front wheel steering, while drive from a 346cc Villiers engine was to one of the two back wheels only. Plagued by problems in its two years of production, numbers were low and few survive.

All Cars Charly   1974-1985   Italy

First presented by a firm called Autozodiaco in 1974, the Charly was a plastic 2-seater with a body composed of straight lines, a single front wheel and a fully enclosed cabin. Power came from a Minarelli 49cc engine. In 1978 a change of owners meant a change of name also to All Cars Snuggy, with a 50cc Morini engine. A convertible version, painted khaki, named Snuggy Tobrouk, was introduced with a 250cc engine as an option, and a top speed of 85km/h. Many were exported to Germany. All production ceased in 1985.

Alpha   1927-1936   Spain

Alpino   1952-1960   Italy

Alpino SpA, Stradella, Pavia, makers of a light 3-wheeled commercial vehicle based on continental classic lines using a 2-stroke single cylinder engine and 3-speed gearbox. The 200kg model was chain-driven by a 49cc motor while the heavier 'Golia' had a 300kg load capacity and was powered by a 125cc engine using shaft-drive to its two rear wheels.

Alta   1967-1980s   Greece

In continuous production since 1967 the Alta could be classed as the most successful 3-wheeled light truck ever built in Greece. The Alta 700 was designed, engineered and built locally, using a box section chassis fitted with a rear-mounted BMW 2-cylinder horizontal engine producing 35hp and driving through an integrated gearbox. A modern spacious 2-seater cabin made of fibreglass and a payload of 800kg were included in the specifications. A variety of bodies including tray, dropside and lockable van were available.

In 1970, using the name of Alta, a 3-wheeled passenger car was made under licence from the German Fuldamobil, a vehicle that had been popular there some 20 years earlier. This was a plastic bodied 2-seater with car-like dimensions, two front wheels and a single rear wheel which took power from the rear mounted 198cc Sachs engine. Some BMW 700s were made under licence in the 1980s.

Alvis   1955-1958   Spain

This was a delivery tricycle with engines available in 125cc and 175cc. The builders, Tallares 'Alvis' de Construcciones Mechanicas, Barcelona, had no connection with the famous British car maker of the same name.

American Thunder Tryke   1993 to date   USA

The King of Slopers, a trike that will blow you away, from its inclined front wheel heading a long and massive chassis, the extended handlebars (reminiscent of the tiller steering of olden days), to a small block Chevrolet engine with shaft-drive to the extra-wide rear wheels and tyres. Tandem seating on rally-type highbacks with four-point safety harness and a roll-over-bar and side pipes help with protection as the top speed is a mind-blowing 200 plus mph! With a completed price of $25,000, sales are reported as buoyant.

American Tri-Car   1912   USA
Built by the Tricar Company of America, Denver, Colorado. A passenger vehicle but no production numbers noted.

Amica   1970s-1980s   ?
Imported into Holland, a fibreglass 3-wheeled 2-seater with an enclosed cabin, car type controls and a single front wheel. It was powered by a 50cc single cylinder engine with variable drive to the rear axle.

Andre Py   1899   France

Anglian   1905-1907   GB
Built in Beccles, Suffolk, the Anglian was a tricar powered by a de Dion engine: a 3.5hp single cylinder or a coupled twin of 5hp.

Anglo-American   1899-1900   GB
The Anglo-American factory was based in York and produced a conventional motor tricycle, using an engine of their own manufacture as well continental imports rated at 2hp.

Ape   1947 to date.   Italy
Piaggio/Co Spa, Genoa. From aircraft to motor scooters this Italian firm has become most successful in its field. Marketing scooters under the well-known name of Vespa (Wasp), the first commercial vehicles were basically a Vespa scooter front end mated to a 2-wheeled delivery box rear end. Power was from the 125cc 2-stroke engine (under the driver's seat), through a 4-speed gearbox via chain to the back axle, with torsion bar suspension. Called the Ape (Bee) the vehicle was rapidly improved and by 1960 had an enclosed cab, electric starter, 169cc motor and a variety of body styles, with payloads from 2 to 12cwt. Still in production and exported to many corners of the world.

API Rickshaw   1955 to date   India

Arabia   1928-1930s   Japan
Built by Nishiura, using imported JAP engines of 750cc and local engines of 350cc.

Argoe   1924-1927   Germany
A Berlin firm which built both 2-wheelers and commercial trikes that used 198cc or 246cc 2-stroke single cylinder engines.

Argson   1930s   GB
The Stanley Engineering Co Ltd of Egham, Surrey, were well-known as makers of gasoline and electric tricycles for invalids. The Argson was a 3-wheeled parcel carrier with a single front wheel. Power came from a Villiers 2-stroke engine with an Albion 3-speed gearbox and a single chain-drive to the nearside rear wheel.

Load capacity was 2cwt. Vehicles could be purchased as a chassis priced at only £45 and a variety of bodies could be obtained or built to your own requirements.

Argson Electric   1930s   GB
Also built by the Stanley Engineering Co Ltd of Egham, Surrey, this was the road going carriage suitable for the disabled. A low walk through floor, a large armchair type seat, tiller steering and controls to suit the driver. Pram hood and weather protection were optional.

Ariel   1898-1967   GB
The Ariel name can almost be traced back to the birth of the wheel – the wire spoked wheel. Invented by James Starley and William Hillman in 1870, the tensioned wire spoke wheel was to revolutionise the bicycle industry. Starley and Hillman went on to build a lightweight Penny-farthing bicycle called the Ariel. Amalgamating with the Westwood Manufacturing Company of Birmingham in 1896, they moved into powered transport in 1898 with a quadricycle powered by a de Dion engine mounted behind the rear axle. It proved not very stable so a tricycle followed in 1899. This was solid and reliable with its de Dion engine mounted in front of the back axle and was often seen towing a passenger trailer. In 1902 a 2-wheeled motorcycle appeared, and these machines were to become the mainstay of the factory until 1966 when the Ariel 3 appeared, a futuristic moped with the 50cc engine mounted between the two rear wheels and clothed in a fibreglass engine bay. The front section of the frame was hinged to allow the rider to lean into corners as though he were on a 2-wheeler. Sadly by 1967 the Ariel name had sunk under the invasion of the Japanese super bikes.

Arielette   1904   GB
See Ariel for more information.

Armadale   1906-1907   GB
This was classed as the 'perfect 3-wheeler' and was built by Toboggan Motors of London. It featured a infinitely variable friction-drive and had a pressed steel chassis, an unusual feature on a tricar of that period.

Arola   1976-1983   France
Designed by Daniel Manon, the Arola had a simple polyester and fibreglass body making use of a lot of clear plastic in its fully enclosed design. Power was from a 47cc single cylinder Sachs 2-stroke engine that pushed this single front wheel 3-wheeler along at 40km/h, or a little faster if a strong wind was pushing the slab rear end along. At one stage production was 300 per month. A 4-wheeled version with a 125cc BCB engine was offered later.

Arsenal   1898-1899   GB
Built at St Albans, Hertfordshire, this was a Bollée-like tricycle with a 3.5hp engine. Tiller steered, it was reputed to be able to carry two or three people.

Arzens L'Oeuf   1942   France
Possibly the world's first bubble car, Paul Arzens designed and built this little car during the war. The egg-shaped body was made from hand-formed aluminium while the curved side-doors and windscreen were made of Plexiglass, a new product at the time (probably from crashed aeroplanes). Power came from batteries

and was transmitted to the single rear wheel. After the war a 125cc engine was installed and the vehicle was used by its owner/builder until his death in 1990.

Asahi Iwasaki   1930s   Japan
A commercial trike with the cargo box between the two rear wheels. Engine was 750cc and cargo capacity 400kg. About 1,200 units were produced in 1937.

Ashton-Evans   1919-1928   GB
This was a 4-wheeler masquerading as a 3-wheeler. Built in Birmingham by Ashton-Evans Motors Ltd, their first effort at motor transport after a generation of building railway locomotives. This unusual vehicle had a tubular trussed frame accommodating a 10/15hp 4-cylinder engine. Power to the rear wheels was by cardan shaft-drive to a simple bevel and crown wheel, directly to the short back axle, with the rear wheels only 8ins apart. A sporty 2-seater open body made this a good looking car. The company went on to make cars of the normal four wheel variety in 1920 before it closed in 1928.

Asia   1930s   Japan
A cargo trike using the front end of a motorcycle powered by a 744cc engine.

Aster   1906-1907   USA
A tricar built by Aster and Company of New York.

Astro 111   1969   SA
Another dream car from Chevrolet; a long wedge-shaped body ending in a bubble capsule for two. The rear wheels were on outriggers and totally enclosed, while the single front wheel was actually two wheels, just inches apart and totally hidden, well back from the long nose. Built as a show car it had no engine, although it was planned to install a gas-turbine some time in the future. A similar shape was used by the Trimuter in 1980 and by the Trylon in 1989.

Atom/Atomota   1955   GB
The early Atom and Atomota cars built by Don (of Pathfinder fame) Bennett's Fairthorpe company were thought by some, even a well-known motoring historian, (mistakenly) to have been 3-wheeled. Certainly powered by motorcycle engines, yes, but with 3 wheels, no. All were 4-wheeled. See Fairthorpe for more information.

Atomette   1922   GB
A diminutive 3-wheeler built by Allan Thomas, using standard car type format, the Atomette came from Wolverhampton and was powered by a 343cc Villiers 2-stroke engine located just in front of the single rear wheel. Drive was by chain through a Burman 3-speed gearbox and final-drive by belt. Vertical windscreen, side by side seating without doors or other weather protection, and a slab sided body with wire spoke wheels completed this 2.5cwt car.

Attica   1968   Greece
A 3-wheeled cyclecar from Vioplastic S A, Moschaton, Athens, and built under licence from Fuldamobil in Germany, they also built the Delta Cargo Tricycle. A number of 4-wheeled vehicles were also built at these factories. For more information look under Fuldamobil and Delta Cargo Tricycle.

Audenis 1930-1936 Spain
Built by Franscisco Audenis, a former racing driver at the Motor Palace Audenis S.A., Barcelona, this was a delivery tricycle with the unusual arrangement of the engine over the single front wheel, driven by an arrangements of chains. The added weight gave good traction but was heavy on the steering.

Aurora 1904 GB
Built on motorcycle lines the Aurora Tri-Motor was powered by a 3.5hp engine.

Aurore 1897-1900 Hungary
The first Hungarian car was built by Janos Csonka in 1897. Early vehicles were 3-wheelers and marketed under the names of Aurore and Csonka. A number of vehicles are still in existence in the Haris Testverek Motor Museum in Budapest.
More information under Csonka.

Austin 1896 GB
Herbert Austin, in 1896, many years before he was to form the Austin Motor Company (1905), built two experimental 3-wheelers. The first, with a rear mounted flat twin engine driving the single rear wheel, and similar to the Leon Bollée car of the day, had the innovation of a gate gearchange, shaped like an E. The second, and much improved, was a two or four passenger vehicle with a single front wheel using the same type of engine as his first model. This second model was exhibited at the 1896 National Cycle Show at the Crystal Palace and was catalogued for sale at £110 for the 2-seater or £150 for the larger version seating four.
    In June of 1898, Austin was to make a successful journey of 250 miles at an average speed of 8mph in one of these vehicles. This journey probably caused him to build his first 4-wheeler under the name of Wolseley in 1899.
More information see Wolseley.

Austral (1) 1899-1914 France
'One of the most up-to-date tricars in the Paris Motor Show of 1905' was how the *Motor Cycle* magazine greeted the unveiling of the Austral. Available as a passenger or goods vehicle, the frame was somewhat similar to the 3-wheeled delivery bicycles of the day. The passenger seat or delivery box was positioned between the two steerable front wheels, the 3.5 hp air-cooled engine placed behind the box and in front of the driver, who sat on a saddle, bicycle style. From the engine the drive was taken through a leather-faced friction clutch to a gearbox giving 2 speeds, whence a cardan-shaft ran to a system of bevel gearing on the rear wheel.
    The Austral was also known to have a 4.5hp motor and 3-speed gearbox while the previous year's models were propelled by a an Aster water-cooled engine with belt drive to the rear wheel.
    By 1910 the Austral La Trivoiturette had reached a degree of luxury – steering wheel, hood, and well-padded seating for both driver and passenger. The 8-9hp twin cylinder engine was closer to the rear wheel and now under the driver's seat. Passenger seat or delivery box was still in the front while a substantial pram hood with straps to the front mudguards gave some degree of weather protection.

Austral (2) 1905-1914 GB
For information look under Bozier.

Austral (3) 1930-1932 France
The Austral was a parcel van with a single front wheel, powered by a single

cylinder engine mounted under the seat and driving the rear wheels, via a single chain through a Sturmey-Archer gearbox. Manufacturers were from the long established motorcycle firm of Ets, Austral, Puteaux, Seine.

Autobambi 1950-1956 Spain
From the well-known motorcycle firm of Manufacturas Mechanicas Aleu, SL, Esparraguera, Barcelona, came a line of 3-wheeled mini cars, light vans and trucks powered by 125cc M. M. Aleu single cylinder 2-stroke engines.

Auto-Bob 1914-1915 America
A scaled down 3-wheeled cyclecar with a 3-5hp engine and intended as a plaything for 10 to 15 year olds with parents owning large estates. Built by Jack Hickman of East Pittsburgh, Pennsylvania.

Autocar 1897 USA
The Autocar Company of Pittsburgh and Ardmore, Pennsylvania, built two cars in 1897 believed to be 3-wheelers, before building 4-wheelers until 1911.

Autocarrier 1907-1920 GB
Originally listed under the name AC and first marketed in 1904 the firm became Autocarriers Ltd, West Norwood, in 1907 and had a reorganisation and a move to become Autocarriers (1911) of Thames Ditton, Surrey. Adding to the information listed under AC, fleets of Autocarriers were in use with the Great Western and London and South Western Railways, Associated Newspapers and Carr's biscuits.

A large export market was established with vehicles going to China, Argentina, Spain and Portugal. They were sold in numbers to Europe with the main markets in France and Italy. A number of vehicles were marketed in London by F. B. Goodchild & Co, under the name of Goodchild Carrier. Production ceased in 1920 in favour of a 4-wheeled cargo carrier called the Autocarrier Junior.

Auto Electric 1924-1939 GB
Built by the Murphy Cars and Trucks Ltd at the Cordwallis Works, Maidenhead, Berks. The first vehicle, introduced in early 1925, was called 'The Errand Boy on Wheels'. A large box up front able to carry 8cwt of goods while the driver was perched over the single rear wheel. Power came from a 1.5hp Langham 40-volt electric motor. Batteries were carried amidships beneath the frame.

An invalid carriage was added to the range in 1933 while the company went on to produce internal works trucks of 10/15cwt and 20/25cwt capacities. All civilian production ceased in 1939 when the company was put on a war footing with the outbreak of the Second World War.

Autoette 1952-1957 USA
Built by the Autoette Electric Car Company of Long Beach, California, this was a 3-wheeler used as a golf cart and for other commercial enterprises.

Autogear (1) 1897 USA
The Autocar Company of Ardmore, Pennsylvania, built their first vehicle, a tricycle, in 1897. The one cylinder air-cooled engine and differential was mounted directly in front of the back axle and drove the rear wheels. This vehicle is preserved in the Franklin Institute Museum in Philadelphia. The second vehicle built was a 4-wheeler in 1898, produced until a change over to trucks in 1911.

Autogear (2) 1922-1923 GB
Coming from Leeds in Yorkshire, the Autogear had a Blackburne 10hp air-cooled V-twin engine coupled to a single front wheel in a complex cradle that also steered. In 1923 production moved to Dublin with a name change to Leprechaun.

Autolette 1905-1907 Holland
The Rotterdam firm of S Bingham and Co had built bicycles since 1890 and progressed to automobiles in 1903 with the importation of the Oldsmobile. In 1905 they started to produce motorcycles and tricars with 3.5hp to 4.5hp engines. The tricar was of a modern concept for the day with a steering wheel, armchair seating for the driver and a passenger seat between the two front wheels although still maintaining the motorcycle concept. 1906 showed much improvement with the engine under the driver's seat and fully enclosed. Power had been increased to 5.5hp. The passenger compartment was now 2-seater and lights had been installed. Production of 3-wheelers stopped in 1907. A 4-wheeled cyclecar had been built under the same Autolette name for the years 1906 and 1907 using both 5hp single and 7hp twin cylinder engines.
   At the end of 1907 production of 3- and 4-wheeled vehicles halted and the firm reverted back to bicycles and motorcycles.

Auto-Lux 1937 & 1945-1950 Italy
Built following the usual commercial 3-wheeled style in vogue in Italy, with two driven rear wheels, handlebar steering and an enclosed cab. This parcel mover was powered by an electric motor and battery pack that required recharging each night. Although production began in 1937 it was not until the end of the Second World War that they were made in any quantity.

Automirage 1976-1985 Italy
Mirage 3 was one of the most basic microcars available in Italy. Slab sided, wedge shaped body (described as 'driver and small passenger occupancy'), side opening doors with sliding windows, with power coming from a 50cc moped engine driving a single rear wheel. The vehicle enjoyed a large export market and was available in a brilliant red, blue or yellow fibreglass body. Production came from one of Italy's largest buggy manufacturers.

Auto Mouche 1921 France
First 3-wheeler from motorcycle firm Monet-Goyon. See listing under this name.

Auto-Mower (Auto-Truck) 1921-1947 GB
Established in 1922, the Auto-Mower Engineering Co Ltd of Norton Street Phillip, Bath, Somerset, made motor mowers and motor rollers but added a commercial 3-wheeler to the production line in 1925. Sold as the Auto-Truck, it was powered by a 550cc single cylinder Blackburne oil-cooled engine driving the single front wheel. For reverse the whole engine/wheel unit was turned 360 degrees. The design was purchased by R A Lister and Sons Ltd and is still in production in various forms for work on estates and in factories. Another vehicle was produced in 1954 called the Nippy Carrier, a 3-wheeled 10cwt truck with a 500cc JAP single cylinder engine driving the rear wheels. After a run of just six vehicles the project was dropped.
   Another specially-built vehicle, the Auto-Tractor, was built to order for the timber industry and produced in small numbers. Powered by a Ford 4 cylinder engine, 48 units had been completed when production ceased in 1947.

Automotette 1898-1899 France
Powered by a 3hp horizontal single cylinder engine and dual-ratio belt-drive this light 3-wheeled carriage was tiller steered.

Auto Riksha 1980s India
Believed to come from the Bajaj factory. More information under Bajaj.

Auto-Tractor 1945-1947 GB
For more information see under Auto-Mower.

Auto Tri 1898-1900 USA
Built by C. W. Kelsey at the Auto Tri Company's plant at Chestnut Hill, Pennsylvania, this 3-wheeled one cylinder car was a prototype and probably the vehicle used by Kelsey as a base for his venture into manufacture of the Motorette and other cars under the Kelsey name some years later.
More information under Kelsey and Motorette.

Auto-Tri-Car 1914 USA
A 3-wheeler built by A. E. Osborn in New York.

Autotrix 1913 GB
A 6hp or 8hp twin cylinder powered this 3-wheeled cyclecar of limited production.

Avia 1956 to date Spain
The first motor vehicle built by aircraft firm Aeronautic Industrial SA, of Madrid, was a light 3-wheeler, powered by a 197cc Hispano-Villiers single cylinder engine. They soon changed to a medium-sized 4-wheeler truck and it is still in production.

Avolette 1956-1957 France
Another of the Brütsch-inspired microcars this was one of the better efforts. A fibreglass 2-seater body made in two shells on a simple T-shaped tubular steel backbone chassis, with car type controls, a steering wheel and a wrap-round windscreen. Power came from a 175cc Ydral single cylinder air-cooled engine with enclosed chain-drive to the single rear wheel. Top speed was advertised at 100km/h with a petrol consumption of 3 litres per 100km. Reports indicate that some vehicles have been sighted with 125cc and 150cc Lambretta engines. See notes on Brütsch for more information.

Avon 1902-1910 GB
A 3-wheeled car built in Bristol, England. It used a large steering wheel and car type bodywork with a 3.75hp engine with the unusual feature of twin radiators placed one either side of the driver's seat. Its 3-speed gearbox was controlled by a Bowden cable with drive to the single rear wheel.

Avon Trimobile 1903-1912 GB
Using a tubular frame chassis with a 5.5hp single cylinder motor driving the axle by chain. Available as a 2-seater car or a 4cwt van. Built by Avon Motor Manufacturing Co Ltd, Keynsham, Bristol. More information under Trimobile.

Ayrton-Perry 1882 GB
An electric tricycle with a very limited range, powered from a bank of 10 batteries.

It used a very small rear wheel for steering and was unique in the use of electric lighting and had a speed of 8 mph.

Badal   **to date**   **India**
Produced by Sunrise Auto Industries of Bangalore, this is a very good looking 4-seater of generous proportions. Its Italian designed engine sits well behind the rear axle, while up front the single wheel is hidden under a stubby car type bonnet.

Badsey Bullet   **1979-1983**   **South Africa**
First built in South Africa, the prototypes had a motorcycle engine located up front just behind the two front wheels. Driving the single rear wheel was a long chain passing through a tunnel which divided the two lay-back seats. Later versions had shaft-drive, all located in a sturdy steel frame chassis covered by a wedge-shaped fibreglass body. Entry was by a lift-up canopy with individual wrap-around windscreens. This fun machine quickly migrated to America (1983 to date) where it was improved and became the Badsey Fun Machine. In its original guise it is thought a limited number only were built.

Badsey Fun Machine   **1984 to date**   **USA**
Coming from the same home as the Badsey Bullet, in Anaheim, California, the home of Disneyland. Clothed in a fibreglass body, the twin front wheels are derived from Formula race car design and there all resemblance to the usual tricar design ends. This is a genuine 3-wheeled motorcycle clothed in a space-age body. Steering is by the usual motorcycle handlebars with the driver and passenger sitting in tandem and out in all the weather. A wedge-shaped front, a cross between a Formula 1 race car and a spaceship from Star Wars provides ample storage space as well as protection from the elements.

A Yamaha 550 Vision 4-stroke V-twin puts ample power to the single back wheel for long distance highway cruising. The Badsey Fun Machine has taken on a cult following.

Bajaj   **1950 to date**   **India**
Built in India under licence from the Vespa/Piaggio motor scooter manufacturers of Italy. These vehicles are available in a variety of bodies including vans, pick-up trucks and many passenger versions. They are sold all over Asia and can be seen trundling along roads with loads far in excess of the makers specifications. Almost all the vehicles in Nepal are 3-wheelers with the Bajaj Taxi dominating the scene, while in Jakarta more than 30,000 'Red Terrors', many of them more than twenty years old, still ply the streets.

Using a 150cc air-cooled single cylinder 2-stroke engine, a 4-speed forward and reverse gearbox, chain-drive is to the two rear wheels. The cabin is roofed but otherwise open to the elements with a canvas blind put in place on rainy days. Steering is by handlebars with a throttle and gear-change using twist grips. Rear wheel hydraulic brakes are operated from a foot pedal while a lever-type handbrake is under the instrument console.

In 1963 Bajaj took over the German Tempo/Hanomog range of 3-wheelers and are still constructing medium-size trucks and taxis in the style of the 60s. In 1985 the Hindalco State-run Aluminium Co and the Bajaj Auto Co announced that they had developed an all-aluminium 3-wheeler closed body car that was to go into immediate production. However, as India had the highest cost of aluminium production in the world production was always doubtful.

Baldet Bluebird 1950 GB

Bambi 1960 Chile
The Fuldamobil built under licence – the Bambi name was also used in Norway and Argentina. For more information look under that name.

Bamby 1983 GB
The original Bamby was an updated Peel with innovations built by Alan Evans of Hull. The 49cc Minarelli engine, through an automatic transmission, was able to push the 235lbs all-up weight plus driver along at a reasonable speed at 100 mpg. Design changes replaced the gullwing door with a conventional side-hinged door, and motors were upgraded to Yamaha or Suzuki moped units. This was an overpriced vehicle and with about 50 units produced the project went into liquidation. More information under Peel.

Bandini 1993 GB
For more information look under Berkeley.

Barcino 1960-1966 Spain
Delivery tricycles made by Talleres Metalurgicos Barcino, of Barcelona. These vehicles were powered by a variety of engines including 125cc, 175cc and 197cc.

Bard 1899-1900 GB
Built by George Hand's Bard Cycle Company at Bard, in England, these Grappler-tyred motor tricycles were on show at the Stanley Fair in 1899. Hand went on to build the Calthorpe 4-wheelers.

Barker 1920s GB
Conventional style 3-wheeler using a water-cooled 961cc V-twin with shaft-drive to the single rear wheel.

Barnes 1904-1906 GB
Built by Goerge A Barnes of Lewisham, his early vehicles were a single bucket seat trike with a specially designed frame with a low centre of gravity. The 4hp water-cooled motor was placed just behind the front axle and drove the single rear wheel via your choice of belt or chain.. The steering wheel was equipped with finger tip controls for spark and petrol while an Opperman 3-speed gearbox had a foot operated clutch. Later reports had the Barnes much improved and able to carry passengers. Built in Deptford in Kent, these tricars used engines of the firm's own manufacture with a choice of twin cylinder units of 6hp, 8hp, or a much improved 12hp 4 cylinder water-cooled monster mounted in a lengthened 6ft 10ins frame under a modern-looking louvred bonnet that gave the machine a very sporting appearance. An optional extra seat could be mounted in front of the engine.

Baronet 1881 GB
Built by A. H. Bateman & Company of East Greenwich for the designer, Sir Thomas Parkyns of Beckenham, Kent. A 3-wheeled steam-driven tricycle with the boiler fired by a liquid fuel burner. The tiny 2-cylinder engine, 1.5 inch bore and a 3.5 inch stroke, propelled the vehicle along at 12mph. The Baronet became famous because its very presence on the road broke almost every law in the act governing steam-driven vehicles and it was not long before Sir Thomas Parkyns was up

before the magistrates for exceeding the speed limit and without a person proceeding the vehicle with a red flag and so on. He was fined a total of five shillings and appealed to the High Court; the case was lost but it did draw some publicity to the inadequate laws.

Barrellier 1919 France
This company was well-known for its 3-wheelers built specially to cater for the war wounded. By 1919 they had improved their vehicles and built a sporty vehicle along similar lines with either a single or two seats. Power was from an air-cooled horizontal twin engine located under the armchair seat, with direct drive by shaft through a 2-speed gearbox and worm-drive to the live back axle.

A substantial pipe chassis with small bicycle-type forks for the single front wheel was controlled by a steering wheel with most controls only a finger tip away. The chassis was underslung at the rear and gave a low ground clearance of about 5 inches and all wheels were shod with low pressure balloon tyres to take care of bumps.

Barriere 1898-1900 France
A 'Sociable' tricycle built in Paris seating two side by side. Also built was a conventional trike with a 2hp motor running at 1,200rpm and a top speed of 30mph.

Barrows 1896-1899 USA
Charles H Barrows of Willimantic, Connecticut and New York, built a front wheel drive electric tricycle that was to become one of the early New York self-drive-hire fleets. Very few of these were sold to the public. Another oddity from this firm was a one wheel mechanical horse, which was put between the shaft of a gig replacing the horse.

Bartsch Cabin Cycle 1980s Australia
'A Trim Transport Trike' was the press heading for Dieter Bartsch's 3-wheeler when it was introduced to the Sydney public. Full of novel innovations, a basic vehicle that could be adapted for many uses. In prototype stage we have a simple ladder-type chassis made up of 2 inch diameter mild steel tubing that runs outside the bodywork and acts as roll-over and crash bars. The 3 wheels are all carried in trailing forks and suspended by coil spring/telescoping damper units with disc brakes and are interchangeable all round.

The engine is a Hirth 26bhp petroil pushing power through a Salsbury belt drive torque converter and a F.N.R. gearbox and final chain-drive to the single rear wheel. The cabin is a single skin fibreglass shell with a floorpan stepped to the rear to form a seat base to which is clipped vinyl cushioned seat and backrest. The cabin roof is attached at the rear to the roll over bar and the front to a Land Rover style vertical windscreen. Roll down side and rear curtains complete the weather protection. Over the engine at the rear is a parcel basket but there is plenty of space for a tray or van attachment.

Bureaucracy is believed to have stifled further development.

Basson's Star 1956 USA
Coming from the same stable as the Martin Stationette and built in 1954, the firm of Basson's Industries of New York offered a fibreglass bodied single cylinder 2-stroke engined 3-wheeled car for $999. Few units were built.

Baston Spyder   1971   **GB**
Another trike from the stables of Antique Automobiles Limited and named after the town of Baston, Lincolnshire where it was conceived. With a Mini Cooper engine and trimmings up front, the prototype went on obliterating the opposition on the race tracks in England. Another four with different versions of BMC/Leyland front wheel drive packages were built. One found its way to Australia and with less than 100 miles on the clock is still in mint condition. Australian laws frown on oddball machines, especially cars with only 3 wheels, so it will have to reach thirty years old before it is able to receive Restricted Car Club Registration.

Bat   1903-1909   **GB**
Coming from The Bat Motor Co, Penge, in the London area, the Bat, with variations also known as the Bat-Kar, was first built along bicycle lines with two widely spaced front wheels and space for a wicker passenger chair placed over the axle. Engines are single cylinder 3.25hp or 6hp vertical located low down in the centre of the sturdy frame. By 1904 the Bat had changed dramatically, the chassis had been lengthened, the passenger compartment had been enclosed with a waist high surround with a front opening door. The 2-cylinder 6hp Fafnir engine, placed transversely low down in the frame supplies 3 speeds through a friction clutch to an independently sprung rear wheel. The driver has not been forgotten, he now resides in a sprung padded armchair seat with a raked steering wheel and easily reached controls. Both water- and air-cooled engines were available on the many models of Bat 3-wheelers produced.

Battery Box   1974   **USA**
A very long and low single seat streamlined race car specially built to attack the speed records at Bonneville Salt Beds for electric-powered cars. Driven by Roger Hedlund it reached a record of 174.378mph on the 19th August 1974. Power came from 32 batteries powering a 25hp dc motor running at 8000rpm and driving a fully enclosed single rear wheel.

Batavus   1930-1962   **Netherlands**
Originally introduced as a 3-wheeled delivery bicycle by Batavus Rijweil-en Motorenfabriek, Oudeschoot. Ilo engines were added in 1934 ranging in power from 48cc to 250cc to move the variety of models offered. Over the years was a range with a single wheel in front, others had a single wheel at the back. Tiller, handlebar or steering wheels were offered. A fully enclosed cabin was later to be included in the larger vehicles.

    In 1960 they produced an 'Elec-Triffid' powered by a 4.5hp electric motor. 3-wheeled production ceased in 1962 and the company went back to the business of making bicycles.

Battled   1898-1899   **Switzerland**
Built at Steckborn, and shown at the 1899 National Show in London, this egg-shaped motor tricycle could not have been popular as only six are believed to have been made.

Bayliss Thomas   1920s   **GB**
Bayliss and Thomas were cycle makers in Coventry under the brand name of Excelsior. They moved to Tyseley in Birmingham and began to produce cars under the name Bayliss Thomas because the Excelsior name was already in use on a

Belgian car. The prototypes were 3-wheelers with air-cooled engines but they soon began to build 4-wheeled cars from proprietary parts. Production continued until 1929.

Beeston   1899-1900s   GB
Coming from the well-known Coventry cycle factory that also built motorcycles, the Beeston was a motor tricycle using a 3.5hp single cylinder engine located just behind the rear axle with direct drive through a small cog wheel on the driveshaft to a large cog wheel on the axle. A speed of 27mph was recorded. A special 2-seat cabin on 2 wheels was available as a trailer, complete with hood and doors and may have been one of the earliest forms of chauffeur-driven motor transport.
  A cargo carrier from the same firm was built on the bicycle frame, with two wheels in front but had the large wicker carrier mounted over the rear wheel. It was not long before the Beeston came out as a 4-wheeled 2-seat car.

BCB Ant   1950s   GB
Based on a Reliant chassis this was a tug built in Lancashire and until recently was still in use on the Isle of Man.

B E F   1907-1913   Germany

Bekamo   1926-1928   Germany
First built in 1926 by Bekamo Vertreibgesellschaft Donath & Co oGH, Berlin. This was a trivan following the usual pattern of two front wheels with a cargo box between and a single rear wheel driven from an engine under the driver's seat. An open tray body was also available as was a 4-wheeled version.

Belcar   1955   Switzerland
A 3-wheeled 197cc minicar produced in Switzerland in limited numbers.

Bell   1920   GB

Bella 125   1960s   Italy
Built by Tibicar srl, Vie de Peitralata, Rome. A 2-seater with a classy fibreglass body and comfortable side by side seating for two. A long sloping body that included the windscreen, covered the single front wheel and had twin headlights and trafficators. A removable roof panel gave the option of convertible or coupé. Side opening doors with slide-up windows gave perfect weather protection. The almost vertical rear treatment hid a 123cc twin cylinder 5.5hp engine that could zip along at a steady 70km/h.

Bell Motors Veloto   1976-1981   France

Benelli   1930-1970   Spain
The Fratelli Benelli Spa, Pesaro, motorcycle factory introduced a 3-wheeled light commercial into their range about 1930. Built on Italian lines it had an open motorcycle front end with power to the two rear wheels supplied by a driveshaft. A 500cc single cylinder 4-stroke engine was used but on the post war model a 5bhp 124cc 2-stroke with a 4-speed gearbox was featured.
  By 1960 vehicles were provided with an enclosed cabin and either tray or box cargo containers

Benz **1885-1895** **Germany**
The start of the famous Mercedes Benz motoring empire was a 3-wheeler, chain-driven from a gasoline engine under a single seat wide enough for three, using what was to become the standard design of two large rear wheels with a smaller front wheel steered from a very small control wheel on a vertical column. The first engines were running in 1884, the first 3-wheeled vehicles were on the road in 1885, with the first patent granted on the 29th January 1886. Speed was recorded as between 6mph and 9mph. Later models had an extra seat for two facing the driver. A 1.5hp engine was used in models from 1886-1887, upgraded to 2hp in 1888, and in 1893 a fourth wheel was added. More information under Roger-Benz.

Bergmann **1953** **Germany**
Built by Erwin Bergemann of Hanover. A heavy 2-seater, powered by a 200cc DKW motorcycle engine, weighed in at 750 kilos, was 3.35 metres long, 1.50 metres wide and able to cruise at 40-50 km/h. Appears not to have got past prototype stage.

Berkeley **1950 to date** **GB**
Built in Biggleswade, Bedfordshire, by the Berkeley Coachwork Ltd, caravan manufacturers and pioneers in the construction of fibreglass caravans. They were building a 4-wheeled sports car when convinced by Lawrie Bond, the prodigious microcar designer, that 3 wheels was the way to go. Modifying the rear end of the 4-wheeler to take a single wheel, well hidden under a squarish rear end, calling it the T20 or T60 and launching in August 1959. Power came from an Excelsior 328cc twin cylinder engine with front wheel drive through an Albion 4 speed and reverse gearbox and Albion multiplate clutch, it had a top speed of 60mph with consumption of 50 mpg. The car was an instant success.
   Following a slump in caravan sales, and strikes by the suppliers of driveshafts, the company went bust in 1960 but the Berkeley name has been kept alive by a faithful following of enthusiasts who, after obtaining the original moulds, have reintroduced the Berkeley under the name Bandini.

Berkeley Bandini **1994 to date** **GB**
Using the same fibreglass body shell as the original Berkeley but with the Mini as a donor car for the engine and suspension, this car looks the ugly duckling when compared to its ancestor.

Bernardi **1893-1901** **Italy**
Working with internal combustion engines since 1874, Professor Enrico Bernardi built his first petrol engine in 1884 which he promptly mounted on a single wheeled trailer to propel, or rather push, a bicycle round the streets of Verona. He later fitted this engine, a single-cylinder, water-cooled unit of 265cc, (called the Lauro after his son), to tricycles. He went on to produce more elaborate vehicles and by 1896 was producing a light car, seating two side by side. A single horizontal cylinder 624cc engine developing 4hp at 800rpm, platinum mesh ignition, spiral metal cable clutch, 3-speed gearbox and chain transmission to the single rear wheel. With an enormous pram hood on its buggy-type body progress into the wind must have been difficult.
   As Count Enrico Bernardi he is credited with advancing the motor car with impressive and far-seeing technical innovations that include a detachable cylinder head, overhead valves actuated by a camshaft and rockers, filters for petrol and air, automatic lubrication and much more.

Blackburn   **1878**   **GB**
A B Blackburn, a Tunbridge Wells engineer, built a 3-wheeled, belt-driven, steam dogcart that had many unique features. The single front wheel was steered by reins, its tiny water tube boiler was no bigger than a top hat, worked at 60 psi and was of a very advanced design. The amendments of the Locomotive Acts in 1878 brought forward many novel forms of road transport during this period.

Blackleigh   **1925**   **GB**
The LSD was sold under a number of different names, probably in deals with the sales outlets. More information under LSD.

Blenheim Electric   **1947**   **GB**
Now owned by the Imperial War Museum at Duxford in Cambridgeshire, is an electric 3-wheeler (almost, as two wheels are very close together) built from the nose section of a Blenheim Fighter aircraft that had taken part in the Battle of Britain. Constructed just after the war by Bristol Aeroplane Company employee Ralph Nelson, the vehicle was in constant use from 1947 to 1954.

BMA Amica, Brio, Nuova   **1971 to date**   **Italy**
The BMA Amica featured plastic bodywork with gullwing doors, its engines ranging from 47cc Sachs up to 223cc and a production run until 1980. The BMA Brio was introduced in 1979 as a surrealistic cyclecar nothing like its big brother, clothed in sculptured plastic, it was the minimum in transportation. The tiny 47cc Sachs engine puttered along at 25mph driving one of the two rear wheels. Production of the Brio lasted until 1986. The BMA Nuova was introduced in 1980 with more sedate bodywork and a choice of 50cc, 125cc and 250cc petrol engines and, unusual for microcars, a 359cc diesel engine. Still in production are two Nouva Amica models with either 125cc and 250cc engines.

BMW   **1928, 1939, 1955 to date**   **GB & Germany**
Between 1932 and 1934 the Bayerische Motoren-Werke A.G. produced a 3-wheeled van with a front platform and a single driven rear wheel. Engines used were 200cc and 400cc 4-stroke of their own design. From 1954 BMW built the Italian Isetta bubble car under licence. Later there was the BMW-Isetta using 298cc and later 582cc ohv flat twin engines of their own manufacture. The 3-wheeler was later built in England until 1964. Production from both countries ceased soon after the introduction of the Mini which seated four people in comfort on 4 wheels at a price equal to the then current bubble cars.

BMW C1   **1991**   **Germany**
A plastic bubble with wheels tacked on at either end. The two rear wheels were close together with a 1000cc air-cooled flat twin only inches away. The tear drop bubble had a hinged canopy that allowed entry into the car-like interior. Steering was by handlebars and the body tilted or leaned into the corners. The 68bhp engine produced 125mph through a five speed and reverse gearbox. A concept vehicle built by the Vehicle Department of the Pforzheim College of Design, it has been geared toward performance and speed. The vehicle came in either open or closed versions and in very limited numbers.

BMW Isetta   **1955-1962**   **Germany**
Information available in notes on BMW or Isetta.

Bollée   1873-1924   France

Bollée was a prominent name in the early history of motor vehicles. The steam carriage of d'Amédée Bollée, built between 1873 and 1881 (now in the Paris Technical Museum) was a 3-wheeled bus seating about ten passengers. The driver sat in front while the engineer was able to attend the boiler situated at the rear. In 1896 another member of the Bollée family, Leon, made a nippy trike with a petrol engine of conventional design that would be exported in quantity all over the world.

Bonallack   1951-1952   GB

See notes under Minnow.

Bond   1948-1976   GB

A very modern looking open sports car, the Bond started life as a basic 3-wheeler with a 122cc engine mounted over the single front wheel driven via a chain. This layout gave the vehicle an exceptionally small turning circle. Engines were gradually improved along with body style and progressed through the open sports category to a totally enclosed mini car seating four and the futuristic Bond Bug, a tangerine fibreglass wedge powered by a 700cc 4-cylinder engine from the Reliant factory who were now the owners of the Bond name.

Bond started life at Sharps Commercials Ltd, Preston, Lancs and later as Bond Cars Ltd of the same address. A series of commercial vans were also produced until Bond were taken over by the Reliant Cars and the Preston Bond factory was closed down.

Bond 875   1966   GB

Launched in 1966 to replace the old range of Bond 3-Wheelers, the 875 was a totally different car to the previous vehicles. Still with the single front wheel, the engine was now a rear mounted 875cc Hillman Imp; if you could stand the pace a top speed of 82mph was possible. It was available as an enclosed 4-seater car, a Ranger Van or an estate version, the latter produced as a prototype only but a total of 3,431 Bond 875s were built before the Reliant takeover.

Borgward   1926-1962   Germany

The first commercial vehicle from the Borgward factory was a 1-ton capacity 3-wheeler named the Goliath. In 1931 Goliath-Werk Borgward and Co GmbH merged with Hansa-Lloyd-Werke AG and a new company was formed as Hansa-Lloyd und Goliath-Werke Borgward und Tecklenburg who updated the Goliath with increased engine capacity. Goliath 3-wheelers continue in use mainly in the Indian continent.

Boselli   1933-1979   Italy

The Boselli Brothers built commercial 3-wheelers from 1933 until Italy entered the Second World War. At the end of hostilities they concentrated on 2-wheelers marketed under the name of FB-Mondial until 1952 when they again added commercial 3-wheelers to their range.

Both   1940-1943   Australia

Produced by Both Electrics Ltd, Adelaide, and later by J A Lawton and Sons in the same city, the Both was a 3-wheel electric vehicle intended for house to house bread and milk deliveries. Powered by a 90 volt 3hp motor mounted above the front wheel, power was transmitted by an enclosed chain and the whole unit turned by a large steering wheel. The driver could either stand or sit in the front cab with wide doors for easy access. Range was 45/50 miles for normal delivery work at a speed of 20/25mph. About 100 vehicles were made over a three year period.

Bottger Trike 1990s Switzerland
Inspired by the BMW C1, this was an Art Center of Switzerland project. The twin rear wheels were set wide apart and subject to more streamlining and wheel covers. This has not got past the prototype model stage.

Bouffort 1945-1960 France
Based on the Citroën Traction Avant, this was a large streamlined fully enclosed 3-wheeler with an extra long tail. Two front wheels were enclosed under a long rakish mudguards that swept way past the cabin door. Seating for two was side by side.

Boult 1898 France
A luxury 3-wheeler built on similar lines to the Bollée.

Boulton 1859 GB
Isaac Watt Boulton, of Ashton-under-Lyne, who became famous as a rail locomotive builder, went on to construct a number of small private road carriages, a total of six are recorded with one a 3-wheeler, fully sprung, with a coke burning fire tube boiler working at 60psi, and a 2 cylinder engine driving one of the two rear wheels by chain. A speed of 10mph was claimed and long journeys made without accident.
 Boulton also converted a 12 passenger rail car to a road going 3-wheeler with a top speed of 20mph.

Bowden 1927 GB
The Bowden Brake Company Ltd, Birmingham are better known as the makers of brake cables. In 1927 they produced a 3-wheeled light van of conventional design. Built for local delivery work, very few were made.

Bow-V-Car 1922-1923 GB
Built ahead of its time with a integral chassis/body the Bow-V-Car used the cyclecar theme with a 10hp V-twin Precision engine. A limited number were built.

Boydell 1855-1862 GB
The Boydell was a massive traction-type engine employing an early form of track laying wheel patented by James Boydell in 1846. The 3 wheels, one small steering at the front and two large powered wheels at the rear had attached interlocking iron shod timber slabs called swamp shoes allowing the heavy vehicle to travel over farm roads. Boydell & Glaisher, of London built the wheels while a number of firms manufactured the tractors. Richard Bach of Birmingham is believed to have built the first in 1855, the second by Garrett in 1856, while other firms appear to have been Burrell, Clayton & Shuttleworth, Lee & Tuxford. After the death of Boydell in 1862 no further vehicles were built.

Bozier 1901-1914 France
Bozier started making motor tricycles of their own make but by 1905 were producing the Austral under licence. The 4hp Aster water-cooled engine was carried in a cradle just aft of the well-padded passenger seat, which was equipped with a water-proofed weather protector. Drive was through a Bozier 2-speed gear,

shaft and final chain-drive to the single rear wheel. Various 4-wheelers were made until the 1914 war but production was never resumed.

Brack Burn 1928-1930s Japan
The name may have lost something in translation but this cargo trike was built by Yamashita and used the English Blackburn engine of 300cc and 500cc.

BRA CX3 1992 to date GB
From the manufacturers of the Cobra replica, came the CX3 launched in 1992, a trike of conventional lines using a Honda CX motor, a water-cooled 8 valve V-twin as the power supply. Production has been limited.

Bradbury 1900-1905 GB
Bradbury & Co Ltd of Oldham are known for both motorcycles and trikes. Their basic models were powered by a single cylinder air-cooled engine that drove the single rear wheel via a belt and later chains. The wicker work passenger seat was placed between the two front wheels, later versions had the governess body, a waist high wicker seat with a front opening door and space for a lady and two children.

Bramham 1924 GB
See Stanhope for more information.

Bramwell-Robinson 1898-1901 USA
Built by the Bramwell-Robinson Company of Hyde Park, Massachusetts, a firm generally known for their paper box machinery, this 3-wheeled sociable was noted in the motor magazines as 'natty'.

Brennabor/Brenna 1908-1934 Germany
As well as building prams, bicycles and cars, Brennabor of Brandenburg also built 3-wheeled vehicles for both private and commercial use. Using Fafnir 2- and 4-cylinder engines and later units of their own make, the vehicles were 'of good quality and advanced design'. Many were exported to England as the Brenna in both 3- and 4-wheeled versions.

Bremach 1971 to date Italy
In 1971 the commercial 3-wheeled division of AMF-Harley-Davidson Varese SpA, was taken over by Frantelli Brenna who continued to manufacture the Aermacchi 1.5-ton version under the name of Bremach. A 1-litre 23bhp 2-cylinder petrol engine, drove two rear wheels through a 4-speed gearbox with shaft-drive. A fully enclosed cab with steering wheel and hydraulic braking completed the improvements made by Brenna. A variety of drop-side trays and enclosed vans were available.

Brogan 1946-1948 USA
Built by the B&B Specialty Co in Rossmoyne, Ohio. This was a small 3-wheeler powered by a 10hp Onan air-cooled engine mounted in the rear and featuring clutchless gears. A speed of 50mph with a return of 65 mpg are claimed.

Brooke 135 1993 GB
The Brooke is a one-off and looks like a 1950s Formula racing car but with 3 wheels. The single rear wheel is hidden under a racing-type flaring and single seat.

Brooklands Swallow 1993 GB
Another dream that came to nothing, built from bits and pieces on a massive chassis with a power base from a Mini, this was a large 4-seater that was far too heavy to qualify for motorcycle registration. Designer and builder Ian Ayre was still trying to work out its future.

Brush (Pony) 1904-1968 GB
Brush Electrical went through a variety of name changes in its long history in the motor trade but settled into two major fields, that of vehicle body builders and manufacturers of electrical equipment. Soon after the end of the Second World War Brush began to build a range of battery electric vehicles including the Pony Electric Van which remained in production until 1963. A large box with a capacity of 18.5cwt the Pony had the usual single front wheel with electric drive and tiller steering all included in the one unit. A large range of 3-wheeled industrial trucks were produced and at one time 17 separate models were catalogued including a 4 ton 'Cob' towing tractor.

Brütsch 1951-1958 Germany
Designed by former motorcycle and racing car driver, Egon Brütsch, they were never to reach quantity production. The Brütsch Mopetta was a single seater that could have been mistaken for the sidecar of a modern motorcycle. A streamlined fibreglass body with two wheels at the rear and the single front totally enclosed under the nose cone. A motor, open to the elements but tucked within the body drove one of the rear wheels. From the same stable came the 200 Spatz (1954), Zwerg (1954), Avolette (1955), Rollera (1956-1958) and the Bussard (1956-1958).

Brütsch-Avolette 1955-60 Germany
One of the better vehicles to come from the Brütsch stable, the Avolette was based on a tubular backbone chassis, two front wheels and a boat-shaped fibreglass body of a open sporty design seating two. The long rounded tail hid a Ydral 175cc single cylinder engine with enclosed chain-drive to the single rear wheel through a 3-speed gearbox. Wraparound windscreen, large steering wheel and full car controls. A clip-on fabric hood was available for wet weather but would have made entry difficult. Further information of the French version under Avolette.

BSA 1929-1940 GB
BSA Cycles Ltd produced a front wheel drive sports car powered by a variety of V-twin air-cooled engines and 4-cylinder car-type units ranging to over 1000cc, with a single rear wheel. Both cars and vans were produced for a few years but conversion was made to the usual two rear wheels in 1932 while still retaining the front wheel drive. Production ceased with the change over of the parent company, Birmingham Small Arms Co Ltd, to military contracts at the start of the Second World War. Production of the 3-wheeled twin (1930-1936) was about 5,200 units and the 4 cylinder sports (1933-1936) near to 1,700. In 1946, BSA Cycles built a few delivery trikes using a motorcycle rear end and mated to a large tray between two wheels for the up front portion. Power came from a M20 engine through a Albion gearbox and shaft-drive to the single rear wheel.

BSA Ladybird 1960 GB
A one only prototype still exists. A compact open 2-seater with a Triumph Tigress 250cc engine driving the single rear wheel through an enclosed chain via a 4 speed

gearbox. The hand-built body was the work of BSA craftsman, Ben Johnson, and in a brilliant red finish it was a show stopper. A second prototype with a slab sided body was scrapped. Production was never approved owing to the expected high cost of production.

Bubu Cabin Scooter 1982 Japan

Buckeye Gas Buggy 1890-1904 USA
J W Lambert of Anderson, Indiana, who built the Buckeye Gas Buggy, is also considered to be one of the early inventors of the automobile, and some even contend that he was the first in the Americas with his fragile high-wheeled copy of a Surrey with the fringe on top. With the engine under the seat, the single front wheel was steered by a series of levers, its very high clearance was needed for the rough roads of the day.

Buckland B3 1985 to date GB
Powered by a Ford 1300cc engine of 95bhp and built in the Morgan style of the 1940s this vehicle has a possible top speed of 130mph. A handcrafted Zintec steel backbone chassis and GRP bodywork to a high standard of finish made this a desirable vehicle. Available in kit form.

Budweiser Bullet 1979 USA
Built for one thing only, to break the sound barrier, this was a needle nosed rocket powered car, with a single front wheel. The two rear wheels were located on outriggers aft of the engine. With a total length of 12 metres, mostly rocket engine with a booster of a sidewinder missile, the car was designed by Bill Frederick and driven by Stan Barrett who achieved a speed of 1,178.78km/h.

Bulley 1910-1917 USA
For more information see listing under Mercury.

Bully 1933 Germany

Bunger 1947-1949 Denmark

Burgess 1899-1900s GB
WHM Burgess of Farringdon Road, London, displayed a number of de Dion-type tricycles with many improvements over the original de Dion machine at a Motor Cycle and Car show in London in 1899.

Burrell/Boydell 1855-1862 GB
In the 1850s, James Boydell, a Worcestershire ironmaster, adapted a 1770s invention of Richard Lovell Edgworth for an endless track device attached to the wheels of a vehicle to spread the weight over a larger area: a forerunner of the caterpillar track of later years.

About 20 vehicles, both 3- and 4-wheeled were built by Charles Burble, who had the factory capacity. The vehicles were equipped with fire tube boilers powering a twin cylinder engine giving 2 forward speeds. Vehicles weighed from 7 to 11 tons and were said to be able to haul loads of 34 tons. All 3-wheelers used a single front wheel for steering.

Burrow-Strutt　　　　　　　　　1900　　　　　　　　　　　　GB
Supposedly built in both England and Germany, this was a 3-wheeled motor carriage with such innovations as seat adjustment both back and front for the comfort of either passenger or driver.

Bushbury Electric　　　　　　　1897　　　　　　　　　　　　GB
Built at the Star Cycle factory in Wolverhampton for the Electric Construction Company of the same address, these were vehicles still in the transition from the horse and buggy stage. Powered by electric motors placed under the two place bench seat with direct drive through a differential to sprockets and Reynolds pitched chains to the back axle. Batteries were slung under the body just in front of the rear axle. The larger single front wheel was controlled by reins. Switches were placed near the driver's seat and a foot/hand brake close by. Three speeds were provided through a hand control.

Bussard　　　　　　　　　　　1956-1958　　　　　　　　　Germany
For more information look under Brütsch

The Busy Bee　　　　　　　　　1920　　　　　　　　　　　　GB
Joseph Mills was an engineer who had a garage at Larch Farm Crossroads near Mansfield, Notts. In 1920 he built a cyclecar for his own use and drove it without trouble for the next 27 years. He used a tubular steel frame with sliding pillar front suspension and the single rear wheel mounted in forks suspended on quarter elliptic springs, damped by Hartford shock absorbers. The original power came from a 763cc side valve Stag engine of 1914 vintage, but still unused, and was to be replaced in 1928 by a AJC 6hp sidevalve V-twin that had already seen service in a motorcycle combination.

The aluminium and plywood body was made in three sections and required the removal of 10 bolts to strip down to bare chassis. The engine was set longitudinally in the frame up front and drove the rear wheel through the original Sturmey-Archer motorcycle-type clutch and gearbox, then through a central transmission tunnel. Car-type seating and steering wheel with foot pedals placed either side of the tunnel completed the open cockpit. After Mr Mills death the vehicle passed through a number of hands and is now believed to have found a home with a Birmingham collector.

Butler Petrol Cycle　　　　　　　1883-1888　　　　　　　　　GB
One of the first genuine self-propelled vehicles with power to a single rear wheel. In 1884, drawings were exhibited at the Stanley Cycle Show and it is believed that Butler applied for a provisional patent in that year, a year before Daimler's 'Einspur' was shown to the public.

Edward Butler was a brilliant pioneer in the automotive industry. After a number of improvements he registered his patent in 1887 and built his first trike in 1888 using a 2.25 x 8in bore and stroke, water-cooled petrol engine, which had two horizontal cylinders – one each side of the driven rear wheel. The driver sat in front of the engine in a seat made for one. Scrapping the 2-stroke principal, converting to 4 and reducing the stroke to 6in, he added a radiator for water cooling and called the vehicle a Petro-Cycle, only to fall foul of the Locomotive Act restricting its speed to 2mph.

The engine was produced for motor boats and the patent rights were sold to H J Lawson in 1896.

Caffort   1920-1922   **France**

This was a 4-wheel car trying to look like a 3-wheeler. It had an unusual front wheel drive set-up of a 1-litre flat twin air-cooled engine, mounted above two closely aligned wheels which were driven through bevel gears and allowed the wheels to turn while the engine stayed firmly attached to the pressed metal chassis. The driver sat behind a vertical windscreen in an open-top cabin while the rear was built as a closed half-ton van body, or a closed passenger compartment or a taxi, both with side opening doors.

Californian Commuter   1985   **USA**

Aero Visions Inc. from Irvine, California, built a single seat commuter round a 85cc Honda power train. Shaped like a surf-board with bumps, the trike had a futuristic appearance, a plastic bubble-style body with tail fins and enclosed wheels. The body was claimed to be aerodynamically efficient to allow the little Honda motor to push the vehicle to 82mph with an average 155 mpg. Believed to have only reached the prototype stage.

Cambro   1920   **GB**

The Cambro was a tiny 3-wheeler with a 192cc air-cooled Economic single cylinder engine mounted over the driving and exposed single rear wheel. Production was by the Central Aircraft Co, at Northholt, Middlesex. It had a single seat with a wraparound metal body. The billycart central pivot steering was controlled by a large steering wheel. The vehicle was priced in 1920 at £83.

Canadian Motor Syndicate   1895-1900   **Canada**

Canada's first commercially built truck was a battery powered 3-wheeled delivery tricycle with a single front wheel and a tall compartment behind the driver for parcels. Also known as the CMS the vehicle used a special lightweight battery produced by the W J Still Battery Manufacturing Co of Toronto.

In 1899 W J Still took over CMS and renamed it the Still Motor Co Ltd only to be taken over himself in 1900 when the company was renamed the Canadian Motors Ltd and under British control. 3- and 4-wheeled vehicles continued in production for the next few months and included a fleet of Taxi Cabs and a 15 seat bus.

Capdevila   1960-1965   **Spain**

Tallares Mechanicas Capdevila, Barcelona, were manufacturers of motorcycles and motor scooters who also made a small delivery tricycle with engines of either 175cc or 197cc capacity.

Carpeviam   1902-1905   **GB/Germany**

This was a 3-wheeled 2-seater, using a 2.25hp engine driving the single rear wheel through a 2-speed friction drive and chain. Constructed by Hamburg engineer, Victor Gottwald, the name Carpeviam was derived from a quotation from Virgil roughly meaning 'Life is short, enjoy it while you can'. The engine was placed low in the centre of the frame under a bench seat with tiller steering on the right hand side of the open vehicle.

Capucine   1970s   **Italy**

More information under Mathis

Carrett (1)   1861-1866   **GB**

W. O. Carrett of Carrett, Marshall & Company, built what today would have been called a small bus for 10 to 20 passengers plus driver and stoker. This was a 3-wheeler with the usual single front wheel, a fire tube boiler with a 2-cylinder engine of 6 inch bore and 8 inch stroke and 2 forward speeds. Claims of up to 20mph with a full load were noted. Range was 10/12 miles between water stops.

Carette CMC (2)   1912   GB
See Crouch for more information.

Carette (3)   1925-1927   GB
The Carette Trade Carrier Co Ltd of London made a parcels carrier with the usual box between the two front wheels. Powered by a single cylinder air-cooled engine situated under the driver's seat and with a 2-speed gearbox and chain-drive to the single rear wheel. The driver sat in a reasonably comfortable seat with handlebar steering. An unusual feature was that the rear wheel was fitted with a Ducasble semi-pneumatic tyre said to be unpuncturable, and was smaller than the ordinary Dunlop shod front wheels.

Carter   1950s   GB
Built from the 1940s by J & A Carter, this 3-wheeler was used primarily as a carriage for the disabled on public roads. It looked like a pre-war baby Austin with its nose cut off and the engine bay replaced by a small single front wheel that was tiller steered from within the pram hood covered cabin. One single side opening door on the driver's side, battery power and able to climb the steepest hills. This was the only vehicle allowed by the Dame of Sark on her Island. Other cars built for the same reason and of similar configuration are the Argson, Dingwall De Lux, Larmar, Invacar, Nelco and Padwin.

Casalin   1957 to date   Italy
Manufacturers of both 2-wheeled motorcycles and 3-wheeled commercials using 50cc and 125cc engines.

Casalini Sulky   1957 to date   Italy
Manufacturers of both 2-wheeled motorcycles and 3-wheeled commercials using 50cc and 125cc engines. The Piacenza-based company built a passenger version called the Sulky that stormed into the microcar world in 1975 with production as high as 1,000 cars a year in its original 3-wheeled guise and later 4-wheeled versions.

Castle-Three   1919-1922   GB
The Castle Motor Co was set up in Kidderminster before the First World War. At the end of the war the company was faced with what to do with their surplus engineering capacity so the founder, Stanley Goodwin, decided to manufacture a small car. He set his sights on 'Rolls-Royce-ing' the Morgan 3-wheeler. The Morgan of that era was still a light 3-wheeler with an air-cooled V-twin and changing the rear wheel was a major and dirty job.

    The car used a channel section V-shaped frame, a 4-cylinder water-cooled engine and a simple push-out axle on the single rear wheel. With a sporty body and full weather equipment, the car's popularity at the London Motor Show was its undoing as they received 3,000 orders with deposits of £20 but were unable to manufacture enough nor raise the capital in time to complete the advance orders.

    An unusual extra was the 'mother-in-law' dicky seat that opened out behind the rear wheel but left the single passenger out in all the weather. However, when closed it had ample luggage capacity, unusual in 3-wheelers of the day. A variety of engines were used, the first batch of 12 had the Dorman-type 4KL engine fitted but most of the 330 vehicles that followed used the Belgian Peters of 1,207cc, the largest engine used in any 3-wheeler.

Catley and Ayes   1868-1871   GB
In 1869, Catley and Ayes built a neat steam wagonette in York. This 3-wheeler was 8ft 6ins long weighing 19cwt. A fire tube vertical boiler with superheating worked at 120psi, capable of propelling this 4 passenger and driver vehicle at 20mph along Yorkshire roads. It ran with very little complications for four or more years.

Cavac   1910-1911   USA
Made by the Small Motor Co of Plymouth, Michigan. This was a small delivery vehicle of extra light weight and a low centre of gravity.

Cedre   1974-1987   France
The Cedre was only available as a battery powered shopping commuter, with a top speed of 30mph and a range of 35 miles, with space for the driver and the groceries. It had a single front wheel and a fully enclosed cabin with clear perspex doors. It was designed by Toulouse-based engineer, Francious Guebert.

Celeripede   1900-1901   GB
Built in High Barnet, this was a motor tricycle of limited numbers. Designer and builder was a John Thomas

Century (1)   1899-1901   Germany
A tricar built in Germany.

Century (2)   1899-1906   GB
Century was a popular name for 3-wheelers. The Century Engineering & Motor Company built the Century Tandem in 1899 but soon sold out to a London firm who continued production under name of Century Tandem. The first machines had a 2.25hp single cylinder engine with the usual layout of the passenger in front of the driver. Continually improved, the 1901 vehicle had the choice of a 4hp, 5.5hp or 6.5hp Aster motors. By 1902 a more robust vehicle was produced under the name of Century Tandem Forecar using a 6.5hp engine and transmitting power to the single rear wheel by a Hans Reynolds silent chain. A tubular frame, wire spoked wheels and a steering wheel were among the improvements. Also included was a luxury padded seat suspended on springs, with the driver able to direct the exhaust through the passenger's footplate to act as a foot warmer on a cold morning. Commercial vehicles were also offered with a delivery box replacing the passenger seat.
   Production lasted until 1906. More information listed under Eagle.

Century (3)   1928   GB
Century Cars Ltd proposed a car with a 750cc 2-stroke engine that was going to sell for £100. It is believed a prototype was made.

Century Tandem   1903-1905   GB
For more information see Eagle.

Ceres   1983   USA
Using a Cd efficient body (all slopes and curves), this was a side by side 2-seater in a fully enclosed cabin with power from a Daihatsu Charade rear-mounted engine fitted between the two rear wheels. Costs were high and production numbers low.

Certain   1907   France
Using a tubular A-frame chassis powered by a Lurquin-Courdert single cylinder engine, set low down at the driver's feet and driving the single rear wheel via a belt. The Certain was a robust vehicle with the passenger compartment placed between the two front wheels which could be changed to a delivery box if required. The driver's seat was unusual as it was well padded with a high back rest. A steering wheel with hand controls was standard equipment.

Cezeta   1961-1963   Czechoslovakia
Information listed under CZ.

Chantecler   1957   France
Information listed under Valle-Chantecler.

Chase   1900s   GB
A tricar with the two wheels in front with the usual passenger's seat in between. The driver sat over the single cylinder air-cooled engine with chain-drive to the single back wheel.

Cheeta   1992 to date   Switzerland.

Chenard & Walcker   1901-1946   France
Chenard & Walcker of Asnieres were one of the great motor firms in France who made their start in the industry by building motorised tricycles in 1901. Cyclecars followed and the firm stayed with 4-wheels until taken over by Peugeot in 1946.

Chevy Minis   1972   USA
Information noted under G M Minis.

China   1947 to date   China
China has built a basic 3-wheeled cargo carrier based on the Japanese vehicles left behind after the war. Motorcycle front with a chassis extended to take a cargo body, usually a tray with hoops for a canvas cover. Mostly chain-driven to a live rear axle. Local name for the vehicles is the Three Legged Chicken. For more information see Dong Feng.

Chinnock   1899-1900   GB
The Chinnock-Davis Manufacturing Co of Penge were well-known as bicycle makers who had a brief fling at producing 3-wheeled vehicles. They built a number of 3.5hp air-cooled single cylinder engined 3-wheelers with a 2-seater dog cart body as well as a standard tricycle with a 2.75hp motor.

Church's Steam Coach   1833   GB
Dr Church's Steam Omnibus was puffing back and forth on its 3 wheels between Birmingham and London almost seventy years before the Gasoline car appeared on the scene. It ran on solid tyres, advertised '22 inside and 22 outside seats'. It was

running a regular schedule at 14 miles per hour until English law set a three miles per hour speed limit, in an endeavour to stop competition with the steam trains that were emerging as the most common form of transport.

Cicostar 1960 ?
With a fibreglass enclosed cabin, side opening doors, a single front wheel, this was a 2-seater shopping commuter powered by a 49.9cc rear-mounted engine with electric starter and Variomatic drive, a steering wheel and car type controls. It was a very compact vehicle and just 2.09 metres long.

Cimatti 1949-1966 Italy
From the motorcycle factory of Cimatti Enrico SpA in Bologna, came conventional 3-cwt 3-wheeler vans with 50cc 2-stroke engines, 3 forward speeds and with brakes on all wheels. Early models were open saddle types with chain-drive to the twin rear wheels but were later improved to have a fully enclosed cabin with a shaft-drive. The company still makes mopeds.

Cimem Girino 1951 Italy
The Cimen Company of Rome introduced a number of open tricycle-type wagons powered by a 125cc single cylinder Piaggio motor. The Motospyder (1955) was improved with an aluminium body and detachable roof. All had the single front wheel with power to the two rear wheels configuration.

Cingolani 1952 Italy
Based on parts from the Vespa scooter, engineer Ezio Cingolani built a very natty enclosed coupé 2.6 metres long with side-opening doors, sliding windows, a bench seat for two, and disc brakes on the two front wheels. The 125cc 3hp Piaggio motor drove a single back wheel via an enclosed chain. Claimed top speed was 60 km/h.

Citadine 1970-1983 France
Built in France by Teilhol Voiture Electrique as an electric all-purpose vehicle that could be equally at home as a delivery vehicle with a 1 cubic metre rear opening van body, as a .5 metre side opening container, or as a shopping vehicle with a large automobile style luggage trunk, each with a 250kg capacity. A bank of eight 12 volt batteries power the single rear wheel through a reduction motor, capable of reaching a top speed of 50km/h in 10 seconds with 40 to 60km between charging.

The spacious cabin will seat two adults in comfort with full weather protection, a large steering wheel, a foot controlled accelerator, amp-meter and the usual on/off switches comprise the instrumentation. Other versions available: the Citacome with a 420kg capacity and the Messagette with a range of 80/100km.

Citeria 1958 Holland
Another Brütsch original. Built in Holland, powered by a 600cc BMW 2-cylinder engine to a single rear wheel, this was an open 2-seater that sold for more than an equivalent 4-wheeler. As usual with Brütsch inspired vehicles few were built.

Citroën 2CV Special 1970s to date GB
The Citroën 2CV has been used as a base for so many specials that it now has its own Citroën Specials Club in England. The vehicle lends itself from simple rear end adaptations to total rebuilds, and very seldom do two vehicles look alike unless they have come from a kit supplier and even then it is doubtful.

City-Com/Cite-El   **1987 to date**   **Denmark**
Beginning life as the Mini-El (Rover objected to the name), the City-Com and City-El were meant as a means of low cost transport for one person, averaging about 30 miles per charge. Reasonable purchase cost and reliability have kept this natty little 3-wheeler in production. With its 2-piece fibreglass body, the canopy hinges up to allow entry for the driver and space for groceries or a child size passenger. Intended to replace the bicycle it has been exported to England and a batch was used at the Barcelona Olympic Games. More information under Mini-El

Clarke   **1897-1911**   **USA**
When Louis S Clarke built his first trike in 1897, an exact copy of the de Dion of that era, he was to start an empire that still exists today. Until he started to experiment with a commercial forward control heavy truck in 1907, his output had been trikes and small cars. In 1908 he started the Autocar Co, Ardmore, Pa., and went on to concentrate on commercial vehicles. The production of cars and trikes ceased in 1911. In 1954, Autocar became a division of the White Motor Company.

Classic Images MSR 3   **1992**   **GB**

Clau   1956-1960   Spain
As well as making light 4-wheeled trucks and light cars the Construcciones Mecanicas Clua, SL, of Barcelona, made delivery tricycles with 125cc and 175cc engines.

Clement-Gerrard   **1911**   **GB**
More information listed under Gerrard.

Cloumobil   **1906-1908**   **Germany**

Club   **1930s**   **Japan**
A 500cc engined cargo trike listed as in production in 1937.

Clyde   **1899-1930**   **GB**
G H Wait was a cycle and motorcycle maker who built cars and commercials in small quantities for the local market. He produced a line of 3-wheeler 'Tricarettes' in his Leicester factory that were modern in design and driven by 6hp twin cylinder water-cooled engines. Both passenger and driver had their own bucket-type armchairs, and a steering wheel with both foot and hand controls was fitted to a stressed frame pipe chassis. Internal expanding brakes were fitted to all wheels.

CMC Carette   **1912**   **GB**
See Crouch for more information.

CMS   **1895-1900**   **Canada**
Information noted under Canadian Motor Syndicate.

Cob   **1931**   **GB**
Information under Karrier

Cock   **1958-1974**   **Netherlands**
Established in 1958, Cock N.V. at Asen built the Little Tyrant, a small 3-wheeled

commercial vehicle with the unusual feature of the 2.1hp Ilo single cylinder 2-stroke engine driving the single front wheel directly through a 26:1 ratio reduction box to the axle, without the need of chains. With capacities of 600kg and 1000kg these were slow vehicles with a top speed of 14km/h. They also imported the Italian MV Tevere 3-wheeled truck chassis and fitted their own custom bodies.

Colliday 1960 GB

Collier 1964-1965 GB
Bob Collier had been a development engineer with Norton and Feridax but with the demise of the AMC empire he went it alone to produce experimental machines of the 2- and 3-wheeled variety. His economy car was a blunt-nosed single front wheel open 2-seater with a vertical windscreen and a 50cc Suzuki engine that powered it along at a top speed of 22mph. The prototype is believed to still exist.

Colombe 1920-1925 France
This was a very unusual 3-wheeled light 2-seater car with the single front wheel coupled directly to the 345cc single cylinder engine. The long metal boat-tail body was fitted with a pram hood, full car-type controls with outside brake leaver. A single seat version set world speed records for its class in Arpajon in 1923. For more information look under Villard.

Colombo 1922-1924 Italy
As well as producing a light 4-wheeled car the Officine Mecchaniche Colombo, Milan, made a light 3-wheeled delivery van.

Colt 1931 GB
Information under Karrier.

Comet 1947-1948 USA
Built by The General Developing Co, Ridgewood, NY. and advertised as 'the World's handiest run-around-in-car' it had a fibreglass body on a tubular frame powered by a 4.5hp engine driving the single rear wheel.

Comiot 1899-1904 France
Importing the frames and transmission of the Eadie Tricycle from the Redditch (England) firm of motorcycle makers. The firm of Comiot of Paris added their own bodies and 2.25hp de Dion engines to create the Comiot Tricycle.

Computer Commuter 1968 GB
The CC car was designed by Mr R G Collier of Sutton Coldfield. The prototype was a 2-seater with a plastic snub-nose body, a two place bench seat (with a small petrol engine located underneath) with direct drive to a live axle for the two rear wheels. Handlebar steering was to the single front wheel, hidden behind a plastic grin that doubled for an access door. A flat, almost vertical windscreen completed the open bodywork. With a turning circle of seven feet, the car was proposed to sell at £300, with hood and side curtains as options. Production figures unknown but believed to have been small.

Complete 1970 GB
Built by the Complete Automobilist Ltd of 39 Main street, Baston, Peterborough,

this 3-wheeler was built in the Morgan style, had seating for two, aero screens, and an extra long boat-tail and mudguards reminiscent at the turn of the century. The body was made of fibreglass.

Components 1899-1900 GB
Built in Birmingham, these motor tricycles had a name change when the firm was taken over by Ariel in 1900. More information listed under Ariel

Compton Flyer 1980 GB
We can put this vehicle under the heading of 'potty machinery'. Start with a standard 3-wheeled bicycle, add a lawn mower motor over the back axle driving a propeller from an air-conditioning fan and for David Baston he had his own transport round the village and the Royal Naval Air Station at Yeovil. It had been 'clocked' at 28mph.

Comtesse 1950s France
From the premises of Acoma SA, in the Rue de Champfleur, came a variety of 3-wheelers, the Mini Comtesse was a single seater with a 49cc Motobecane engine and when parked three abreast took up the space of a VW. It had an upward folding driver's door to the cabin. The Comtesse, with two doors and a wedge-shaped body, had seating for two. Also available was a fully enclosed coupé, a soft top and a sports version, all with the same automatic engine, infinitely variable transmission with reverse.

Condor 1907-1914 GB
Built 2-wheeled motorcycles as well as trikes and commercials.

Convenient Machines Cub 1982-1983 USA

Contal 1905-1908 France
Better known as an entry in the 1907 Peking-Paris Race, it was able to get as far as the Gobi Desert before being abandoned. Built by Contal et Cie in Paris, the Contal was the typical tricar with a 4hp single cylinder water-cooled engine powering the single rear wheel by a chain. Available in both passenger and commercial versions with a capacity of 3cwt it was also known as the Mototri-Contal.

Cony 1946-1966 Japan
Made by the Aircraft manufacturer, Aichi Kokuki KK, of Nagoya, as a light commercial 3-wheeler along classic lines of a single front wheel with rear wheel drive. These vehicles went through the usual changes from an open motorcycle-type to an enclosed cabin with a steering wheel. Engines varied from a 359cc horizontally-opposed forced-air-cooled 2-cylinder engine which bore a close resemblance to the Volkswagen motor. A 2-ton truck was offered with a 1.5-litre water-cooled 4-cylinder engine.

The Aichi firm was absorbed into the Nissan group in 1965 and the production of 3-wheelers halted soon after.

Cope-Bohemian 1905-1906 GB
Built in Manchester these were a better class of tricars with a choice of 3.5hp air-cooled or 4.5hp water-cooled single cylinder engines. A 6hp water-cooled twin was also available.

Copeland   1881-1891   USA

Lucius D Copeland of Phoenix, Arizona, began work on steam engines in 1881 which were first used to power a Columbia bicycle that was credited a speed of 15mph. He was to find a backer and went on to build the Copeland tricycle, with automatic water level and an automatic oil-fired vertical boiler, mounted just in front of the small single rear wheel which was also used for steering. Power was transmitted to the two large front wheels. The Northrup Manufacturing Company was formed about 1884 to build these vehicles, and for publicity Copeland and a director, Dr Starkey, took the tricycle on a 120 mile round trip to Atlantic City. One of the vehicles is on display in the Smithsonian Institute.

Corat Lupetta   1946   Italy

A fully-enclosed coupé, with side opening doors, and a 5.5hp rear mounted motor driving the single rear wheel.

Cornubia   1862   GB

Richard Tangye was a Cornish engineer and the manufacturer of hydraulic machinery in his Birmingham factory when he saw the need for a road steamer to feed the up and coming railways. He built a 3-wheeler that weighed only 27cwt and could carry 12 passengers, plus the driver and stoker at a speed of 20mph. Using a fire tube boiler, power was transmitted to the rear wheels by outside cranks similar to the drive used on steam trains. What was projected to be a booming business was squashed by the Locomotive Act of 1865.

Coronet   1957-1960   GB

Built by Coronet Cars Ltd of Denham, Bucks, and based with some body modifications on the Powerdrive (1956-1958), this was a very sporty convertible 2-seater of very modern lines, fitted with an all-aluminium body and powered by a 328cc 2-stroke, 2-cylinder Anzani engine which drove the single rear wheel by chains. With big car looks and a top speed of 57mph, production ceased after 250 vehicles had been built. Other information under Powerdrive.

Courage of Australia   1972   Australia

The brain child of American Bill Fredericks, but built and produced in Australia, this needle-nosed monster is built around a rocket engine and is 44ft long. The single front wheel is tucked well back under the long sloping nose with the driver well to the rear but in front of the rocket motor. The rear wheels are on spindly outriggers, well clear of the body, and a vertical fin extends some 5ft above the ground. The original prototype, built in America, reached 311mph without the driver's canopy fitted in the first test runs.

Coventry Eagle   1898-1909   GB

Built by Humber, the Coventry Eagle was of the standard 3-wheel design of the day. The motor in this case was on an outrigger frame behind the rear wheel, driven via an open chain. The driver sat on a standard bicycle saddle and by peddling madly was able to start the machine. Peddle power was required to assist the engine whenever a hill was approached. Machines were improved with engines of up to 15hp (now placed under the driver on a very robust frame). A steering wheel replaced the tiller and luxury models such as the Humberett and the Olympia were introduced. The factory went on to produce 4 wheeled vehicles until 1976.

Coventry Premier 1919-1923 GB
Built in Coventry, the Coventry Premier had some unusual features. The front of the car was normal car shape with a 1,055cc Premier water-cooled V-twin engine under the bonnet, a driveshaft to a 3-speed and reverse gearbox placed just in front of the single rear wheel with final drive by chain. With a sports body it came equipped with electric lights, pram hood and spare wheel.

The company was taken over by Singer in 1920 and acquired a fourth wheel and a Singer engine soon after.

Coventry-Victor 1926-1938 GB
The Coventry name has been used on many cars over the years. The Coventry Victor built from 1926 to 1938 was chain-driven to the single back wheel by a variety of the company's own proprietary engines, ranging over the years from a flat side-valve twin of 688cc up to a 1100cc version. Commercials with 60 miles per gallon guaranteed from a 950cc engine in the 3-wheeled 5.4cwt delivery vans, built in the style of the 4-wheeled van of the 1930s, the single rear wheel was placed well within the centre of the loading floor with the engine up front in normal car style under a long bonnet.

For 1936 the company concentrated on a sports 3-wheeler using a 998cc side-valve water-cooled flat twin with drive through a single plate clutch, a 3-speed and reverse gearbox, a short shaft to a bevel box and final drive by chain. A very attractive two-tone body had a sports V-pattern windscreen, bench seating with adequate leg room for two, a large steering wheel and the usual instruments. Both cars and vans were produced up until 1938. A small flat twin diesel engine was available from 1932.

Coventry Motette 1896-1897 GB
The Coventry Motette produced in England was an Anglicised version of the Bollée.

Craig-Dorwald 1904-1906 GB
The Putney Motor Co built a limited number of commercial vehicles prior to the introduction of a 3-wheeled mechanical horse in 1904. Using independent coil suspension on the two front wheels, they also had the added advantage of being able to adjust the track for use as an agricultural tractor. It had a 2-speed gearbox with final drive by a chain to a large single rear wheel.

Cremsa 1953-1962 Spain
Cresma Motovehicules, was a motorcycle firm in Barcelona that made a variety of delivery tricycles. The Rata had a power unit of 125cc while the Toro was rated at 175cc. With fully enclosed cabins and drop-side bodies, the Toro had a load capacity of 500kg. Other models powered by the Hispano-Villiers engine were the Trailer, designed as a tug and able to haul a 500 bag trailer, and the Pato 200, using the same 197cc engine as the Trailer but with a shaft-drive to the two rear wheels instead of the normal chain-drive of the other vehicles.

Crescent 1958-1961 Spain
Built by Nymanbolagan AB, Uppsala, as an ultra-light moped-based 3-wheeled delivery vehicle with a choice of either 50cc or 100cc Sachs 2-stroke engines with 3-speeds and a chain-drive to the single rear wheel. The 50cc model had pedals for assistance in starting and in going up hills while the more sophisticated 100cc model had a kick starter. Both had a load capacity of 2cwt.

Creusen 1960 to date Netherlands
From the factory of Creusen Electro-Mechanische Industrie N.V. Roermond, manufacturers of electric trucks and delivery vehicles including mobile shops came the Creusen 1 ton 3-wheeled Van with a single front wheel. The main feature is the drive of the rear wheels with a separate electric engine for each wheel. The standard engine had a power output of 5hp.

Croft 1932-1936 GB
Croft Commercial Cars Ltd, Bradford, Yorks, made tri-vans with carrying capacities of 5cwt and 10cwt fitted with single cylinder engines of 300cc and 475cc. 600cc was offered after 1934. With the revision of the favourable tax laws in 1936 that had previously been offered in the registration of 3-wheelers, Croft ceased production, as did so many other manufacturers.

Crouch 1911-1928 GB
Built at John Crouch Motors of Bishops Street, Coventry, their first 3-wheeler was known as the Crouch Carette, a squat vehicle with a 740cc 'V' twin cylinder water-cooled engine of their own design, located behind the driver and just in front of the single rear wheel. Later on Coventry-Simplex engines were used. The wide 2-seater body had side doors and a pram hood.

A 4-wheeled car was added to the production line in 1913, and after the First World War the company moved to the Tower Gate Works and no further 3-wheelers were produced.

The factory closed in 1928 after 200 cars were sent to Australia and the payment cheques bounced.

Crown 1903 GB
Built by the Crown Car Company, the Crown was a light 3-wheeler with the engine mounted over and driving the single front wheel. The 2-cylinder V-twin air-cooled motor was rated at 5hp with power transmitted through a friction clutch and chain-drive. It was said that because of its lightweight body it could be expected to handle the steepest hills without a gearchange. A 2-seat bench seat and tiller steering with wire spoke wheels completed the picture. The vehicle was sold by a Holborn firm and is believed to have had a short life.

Crystal Sachs Trice 1992 to date GB
Starting life as a recumbent tricycle built by Cornish bicycle manufacturer, Crystal Engineering. In 1992, a Sachs 22cc engine was added to the rear wheel while still retaining pedal power. Steering was by a form of tiller. Most vehicles are exported to Europe where they can be driven without a licence or registration.

Csonka 1896 Hungary
This company built a few 3-wheelers for private car use alongside their commercial vehicle production around 1906. A Ganz-Csonka produced in 1897 is on show at the Haris Testverek Motor Museum in Budapest.

Cudell 1890s Germany
Max Cudell, an engineer from Aachen had the licences from France to build de Dion-Bouton engines in 1897 and Tricycles from 1898. Finding he had inadequate production capacity, he got the Adler factory build a batch for him. It is believed that these were sold under the various names of Boulton, Adler or Cudell.

Cugnot 1763-1771 France
Believed to be the amongst the first successful attempts at creating a powered vehicle. The Cugnot military tractor was built by a Captain Nicholas Joseph Cugnot of the French army in the belief that it would be able to haul a cannon into battle. After numerous experiments, documents maintain that he had built a four passenger vehicle in 1765 followed by a crude tractor a year or so later. His last effort was constructed in 1771 and tested on the 2nd of July. Built with enormous timber beams for the chassis, wooden wheels almost 1.75 metres in diameter, this heavy vehicle had a spherical boiler, carried ahead of the smaller single front wheel which supplied power by way of a rod pushing against a cog on the axle. As the double-walled boiler turned with the wheel it tended to make the vehicle very unstable. A speed of 4km/h was obtained during tests but the vehicle proved to be unmanageable on the cobbled stone streets and during driving tests demolished a stone fence, thus recording the first automobile accident and possibly the first fine for dangerous driving.

This vehicle was put into storage in a military barracks in Paris where it rested for over one hundred years. It now sits in a place of honour, complete with the dints of its accident, next to an 1873 steam bus built by Amédée Bollée, in the Conservatoire National des Arts et Metiers in Paris. Cugnot died unknown in Brussels in 1804.

Currie 1912-1913 GB
R S Currie & Co of West Kilburn, London were the builders of this 3-wheeled cargo carrier. Sold under the name of Currie and C & R, it had a load capacity of 5cwt and was powered by a 9hp vertical twin air-cooled engine under the seat and driving the single rear wheel through a friction transmission and worm drive. Tiller steering was used in the 1912 model but 1913 saw a considerably modified version with steering wheel and a 7hp water-cooled engine.

Cursor 1985-1987 GB
Allan Hatswell's Replicar Cursor was described as a GT hatchback convertible. It had a wedge-shaped single seat body that was pushed along by a mid-mounted 49cc Suzuki CS 50 moped engine, driving the single rear wheel. Top speed was 30mph for 90mpg. A 2-seater version followed the first 50 off the assembly line, with a larger engine and gullwing doors replacing the canvas hood arrangement of the first vehicle. Most of the Cursors were exported to Austria and the project sold to a firm in Belgium where the odd car is still believed to be in production.

Cushman 1936 to date USA
From a business started by the Cushman brothers in 1901 in Lincoln, Nebraska, making 2-stroke engines for fishing boats came the Cushman Motor Works in 1936 to manufacture a lightweight 3-wheeled cargo carrier of motorcycle design with two wheels in front with a 4hp 2-speed engine driving a single rear wheel, load capacity was up to 415 lbs. These were soon followed by passenger carrying golf carts with a choice of either electric or gasoline engines. Vehicles have become bigger over the years and now have horizontally opposed twin engines of 18hp and load capacities of 2000 lbs.

Although used widely as a people mover in factories, parks, airports and shopping centre, 65% of the production is golf carts. Road-going Cushman 3-wheelers include the well-known police model with a fully enclosed cab, single front wheel and a cargo box behind the driver. A speed of 35mph was obtainable.

Custer Electric Car 1930 USA
The Custer Specialty Company of Dayton, Ohio, built their first experimental electric car in 1898 and went on to build gasoline, electric, handicapped and amusement park cars well into the 1960s and possibly even later. They built a 3-wheeled vehicle during the 1930s.

CWS 1922 GB
From Tyseley in Birmingham, a JAP V-twin 8hp air-cooled engine drove the single rear wheel through a 3-speed and reverse gearbox and Reynolds chain final drive, all housed in a neat car type body with cycle wings and a pram hood.

Cycleauto 1919-1923 France
Built by the Compagnie Francaise du Cyclauto, this small 3-wheeled cyclecar with side by side seating for two used a tubular cycle style frame with a water-cooled 2-stroke side by side vertical cylinder Sicam 497cc engine mounted up front and driving the two rear wheels. Transmission is by chain to an epicyclic gear on the counter shaft, and two long belts running over large front pulleys to provide the final drive. For later models power was upgraded by the use of Ruby 4-cylinder engines of 903cc and 950cc. Vehicles had a comfortable body with pram hood and screens, a large steering wheel and car type controls.

Cykelaid 1924 GB
An odd vehicle built by the Seppec Motor Company of York. This was a peddle-powered 3-wheeled bicycle with a single cylinder engine mounted beside the fork of the single front wheel, balanced by the gearbox fixed to the other side. A round petrol tank was fitted above the mudguard and below the handlebars. A large carry basket could be mounted between the rear wheels.

Cyklon or Cyklonette 1902-1929 Germany
This Berlin pioneer motorcycle manufacturer was also a leading producer of 3-wheelers, with the Cyklonette in production until 1922. Coming in a variety of models for both passenger and cargo it had the unique engine layout that remained unaltered throughout its long life. Starting in 1902 with a single cylinder 450cc engine this was developed to a 1,290cc 2-cylinder power unit by the early 1920s. The engine was mounted directly above the single front wheel and driven via a chain, the whole unit turned as one by a tiller.
  The Cyklon was produced from 1902-1904, and the Cyklonette from 1904-1922. Then 4-wheelers dominated while 3-wheelers could continue only by using up surplus chassis and spare parts

CZ 1961-1963 Czechoslovakia
From Ceske Zavody Motocyklove n.p., better known as the CZ motorcycle factory, came a light 3-wheeled commercial using the front part of the successful Cezeta scooter with a single-cylinder 171cc engine and 4 speed gearbox attached to a tubular frame with independent suspension of the two rear wheels. Available with either a tray, dropside or van body. Load capacity was 200kg.

DA Mongoose 1994 to date GB
Using a spaceframe chassis that can be hitched to a water-cooled motorcycle engine, this will be a single or tandem seating, plastic bodied, futuristic 3-wheeler with a single wheel powered rear end. Believed still to be at the prototype stage.

Daihatsu   1930 to date   Japan

The Hatsudoki Siezo Co was founded in 1907 to manufacture internal combustion engines. The first motorcycle-type 3-wheeler was not made until 1930 and had the usual single front wheel, motorcycle style, with handlebar steering and a cargo space between the two rear wheels. Production volume in 1937 was 5,793 units but it was not until the end of the Pacific war that production of 3-wheelers really got started in Japan, retaining the pre-war style of handlebar steering, a saddle for the driver and no weather protection. Cargo space was a deep open box that sometimes had seats added for passengers but was usually seen loaded to twice its height with baskets of produce.

In 1956 the Daihatsu range included payloads up to 2 tons, engine sizes from 750cc single cylinder air-cooled units developing 17hp, and ranging up to 1.5-litre water-cooled V-twins, enclosed cabs, steering wheels, and body styles which included station wagons, taxis, vans, dropsides, dump trucks, fire engines, and garbage trucks. The first venture into passenger cars was the 'Bee' in 1951, a modern-looking vehicle with a single front wheel, two doors and seating four passengers – a 540cc air-cooled twin cylinder engine with overhead valves and producing 13.5hp was situated in the rear.

In 1966 the company was acquired by the Toyota Motor Company and the production of 3-wheeled vehicles finished in 1976. As with many Japanese firms the dies were moved to Third World countries and were to form part of their infant motor industries. In the following years Daihatsu made the odd venture back to 3 wheelers. The Daihatsu BC-6 of 1989 was short in length, tall in height, a 3-wheeled electric moped with a roof, a single seat, steering by handlebars, space for shopping but had no doors. The BL-7 of 1990 was simply a 3-wheeled motor scooter with a fibreglass body of a very modern design, with a roof but again no doors, although these would have been an option had it gone into production. Both had the usual single front wheel, lights and windscreen.

Dalifol & Thomas   1898-1899   France

Built in the Dulac Factory, Montreuil-sous-Bois, a de Dion powered motor tricycle with a 'dust proofed' 2-speed constant mesh gearbox.

Dallison   1913   GB

Dandey   1920-1925   GB

With a body that looked similar to a motorcycle sidecar, the single front wheel was positioned out in front on motorcycle forks with elliptical springing. The 8hp JAP air-cooled side valve twin of 988cc was slung in a metal pipe chassis under the body and drove the rear wheels via belts. Steering wheel, car controls, folding hood and side opening doors completed the vehicle.

Dandley   1910   GB

Dansk   1901-1903   Denmark

The first Dansk was built by the Dansk Fabrikat Christiansen in 1899 by Mr H C Christiansen, the owner of a cycle repair shop. The company was founded in Copenhagen in 1901 and went on to build mostly 4-wheeled cars and commercials.

Darmont   1920-1939   France

The French Morgan. Built by the ex-Morgan racing driver and French agent for the

Morgan cars, M Darmont. These were replicas of the English Morgan using either air- or water-cooled JAP or Blackburne 1084cc V-twin engines. Like Morgan he went on to produce 4-wheeled cars, but only until the outbreak of war in 1940.

Darracq 1896-1900s France
Former bicycle maker, Alexandre Darracq, turned to light cars after selling his French company. The new factory made motorcycles, tricars and quadricycles, all with a strong cycle influence. The trike had tiller steering to the single front wheel, a curved pipe chassis with the engine, located under the single armchair seat, driving the live rear axle underslung on elliptical springs.

Dasse 1894-1928 Belgium
Like most car manufacturers the Dasse started life as a belt-driven 3-wheeler using a single cylinder engine. The first car of Gerard Dasse had a single front wheel. His most successful 3-wheeler followed, but now the single wheel was at the rear with its Benz engine low down between the wheels, a wide bench seat perched way above everything, and a pram hood and tiller steering. The company went on to produce commercial and passenger cars although concentrated on military vehicles from 1924 until it went out of business during the depression in 1928.

Daulton 1950 France

David (1) 1905 France
Shown at the Paris motor Show in 1905, the David was noted as a Tri-voiturette with a single rear wheel powered by a 3.5hp Buchet engine, with transmission through a Bozier 2-speed gear, via belts. The driver had a amply padded bucket seat in the well sprung vehicle.

David (2) 1950-1957 Spain
The Fabrica Nacional de Cyclecars David, formed by Jose Maria Armangue and his brothers in 1914, had a chequered history, first building 4-wheeled cyclecars and later becoming a large operator of taxis and hire cars. From 1950 to 1957 they produced a 3-wheeled car using a single-cylinder 345cc 2-stroke engine driving the single front wheel. The fibreglass body had a long rounded front, side opening doors and a fabric hood while standard car controls were used. Production numbers were limited.

Davis (1) 1910 GB
Joining the 'Sociable' line up with Scott, Seal and AJS, the Davis was another motorcycle and sidecar-type combination where the driver sits in the 2 seat, side by side cabin and in this case controls the steering with a lever, forward to go left, back to go right. A JAP vertical twin engine powers the driver's side rear wheel by chain. Windscreen and a pram hood completes the weather protection along with side curtains. Entry is by a door on the passenger's side only.

Davis (2) 1947-1949 USA
One of the largest 3-wheeled cars ever built. The brainchild of Glenn Gordon Davis, and built by the Davis Motor Car Company of Van Nuys, California, it was powered by a 60hp Hercules engine at the front, driving the two rear wheels through a conventional gearbox and driveshaft. The single front wheel was supposed to allow the car to turn in a smaller circle than a standard car of the same length and at a

faster speed. Top speed was claimed to be 116mph but probably fell far short of this mark. Body styles included a car that seated four abreast, a utility jeep and a station wagon. Only 17 prototypes were made before Davis was convicted of fraud.

DD 1949-1950 Vietnam & Morocco

De Boisse 1900-1904 France

Dechamps 1900s France
A copy of the de Dion Bouton built in Paris.

Decolon 1957 France

Decsa Lisa 1982-1987 San Marino
The one and only microcar to come from San Marino, the Decsa Lisa was available in 3- and 4-wheeled versions powered by 50cc or 123cc single cylinder and 250cc twin engines. Good sales were recorded in France. It had a 2-seater fibreglass body.

De Dion-Bouton Automobile 1883-1901 France
Albert Comte De Dion, scion of one of France's most noble families, backed the mechanic, Georges Bouton (formally a penniless toy maker), and his partner Trépardoux in the production of steam carriages during the 1880s and early 1890s. The first steam powered tricycle was built in 1887. Trépardoux resigned in 1894 when the firm started to dabble in petrol engines which were to prove so reliable that they were sold to manufacturers the world over, becoming the power plants of many of the early automobiles.

In 1895 the De Dion factory was to build a 3-wheeled trike of their own design using a 137cc vertical single cylinder air-cooled engine. By 1902 with many special engines of up to 8hp, the trikes set many of the speed and reliability records of the day. It was noted that drivers were having difficulty in keeping the front wheel on the ground during these trials. These 3-wheeled vehicles were to remain in production well into the 1900s and many survive to this day and are still used at rallies.

Another invention of that period was the de Dion axle which is still used in many sports cars to this day. 4-wheeled cars were produced from 1900-1932 and commercials into the first years of the Second World War.

Delamarre-Deboutteville 1883 France
Edourad Delamarre-Deboutteville in collaboration with a Mr Maladin built a steam powered tricycle which was to blow up on its trial run. They had no better luck in their venture into 4-wheeled vehicles.

Delaugere Et Clayette 1900-1926 France
Using a 2hp Romain engine the Delaugere et Clayette factory at Orleans produced a powered tricycle until switching to 4 wheels in 1902.

Delfin 1954-1960 Spain
Built by the Fabrica Espanola de Motocicletas y Triciclos Delfin, at Barcelona, was a range of small 3-wheeled goods carriers using a 197cc Hispano-Villiers engine with an enclosed 2-seat cabin and a variety of trays or van bodies.

Delta Cargo Tricycle   1968   Greece
The Delta was an ultra-light tricycle built by Vioplastic S.A, Moschaton, Athens, with a austere fibreglass cabin for two, car type controls, a 50cc Sachs engine powered the two rear wheels via a chain. Night driving was assisted by a single headlight. More information listed under Attica.

Deltamobil   1954-1955   Germany
Built by the 'Deltawerkes Linder GmbH' in Munchen, this was a good looking open coupé with the usual 3-wheeled configuration of two in front and one at the back, all enclosed under a sleek fibreglass body with side opening doors and a folding pram hood. A comfortable bench seat for two, a vertical screen and a very short stubby nose. Power came from a Ilo 200cc single cylinder motor with a top speed of 75 km/h. It is believed around 50 vehicles were built.

Demm   1954-1962   Italy
Officine Meccaniche Daldo e Matteucci of Milan built motorcycles but also included a 3-wheeled cargo carrier, using their own 172cc single cylinder 2-stroke engine and a 4-speed gearbox, transmitting power by shaft to the two rear wheels. It had the usual motorcycle front with a tray or van body behind the driver.

Denison   1895-1899   US
For more information see listing under Tinkham.

Dennis   1898 to date   GB
In the transition of the Dennis Brothers from cycle makers to the construction of modern double decker buses, they flirted briefly with 3-wheelers. John and Raymond Dennis built bicycles in their Guildford, Surrey, factory until 1898 when they made their first motor vehicle, a rear engined tricycle powered by a 3.5hp motor.
  Within a year they were into 4 wheels and cars, then eventually to its thriving commercial vehicles.

Derbi   1952-1962   Spain
Beginning as a bicycle repair shop that turned to the actual manufacture of bicycles, the Nacional Motor, SA, in Barcelona, followed by adding small engines to its bicycles and then to the manufacture of motorcycles. By using the rear portion of their motorcycle, with a box van placed between two front wheels, the Derby delivery tricycle was introduced in 1952. In this the driver sat behind the van or tray and was able to carry up to 300kg. Drive was by chain to the single rear wheel.
  A larger version reversed the procedure and used the front half of the motorcycle with shaft-drive to the two rear wheels and a van or tray able to carry 500kg. The driver sat exposed to the weather in both models.

Derby   1937-1938   GB
Country Commercial Cars Ltd, of Fleets, Hants, were doing conversions to Ford Trucks that included the Devon, a cargo version of Ford or Fordson Tug. The Derby was a small 3-wheeled fire engine made to Home Office requirements and powered by a Ford 8 or Ford 10 engine with either a 200 or a 350 gallon water tank. The auxiliary pumps were powered by an Austin Seven engine. Equipment included a 30ft extendible ladder and accommodation for a crew of four.

Derlan　　　　　　　　　　**1953-1960**　　　　　　　　　　**Spain**
Telleres Basor, Zarauz, Guipuzcoa. Built a conventional motorcycle-based delivery tricycle powered by a 125cc engine and with a tray capacity of 300kg.

Devon　　　　　　　　　　**1937-1938**　　　　　　　　　　**GB**
Built by Country Commercial Cars Ltd, Fleets, Hants, as a load carrying version of the Ford Tug, this was a 3-wheeled van powered by the Ford 10 engine and able to carry 15cwt. The single front wheel, tucked in under the radiator, was shod with an 18ins tyre while the rear wheels wore a larger 23ins tyre. It used parts compatible from the Model-Y and the BB truck of that year.

DG Phoenix　　　　　　　　**1982 to date**　　　　　　　　　**GB**
Motorcycle devotees have been mating a VW engine assembly to a motorcycle front end for years and coming up with some weird and wonderful monsters. The DG Phoenix is no exception, it comes in kit form and was available in 2-, 3-, and 4-seater configurations.

Diable　　　　　　　　　　**1919-1924**　　　　　　　　　　**France**
Built in Paris, a 3-wheeled cyclecar with a 1096cc vertical twin 'V' cylinder engine, located just behind the front axle and transmitting power by shaft from a 2-speed and reverse gearbox with final drive by chain to the fully exposed single rear wheel. A metal boat-tail car body with vertical windscreen, steering wheel and pram hood with car type controls completes the picture.

Diabolo　　　　　　　　　　**1922-1927**　　　　　　　　　　**Germany**
From Diabolo Kleinauto GmbH, Stuttgart. A small 3-wheeler with a 1.1-litre Motosacoche engine.

Dick　　　　　　　　　　　**1929-1933**　　　　　　　　　　**Germany**
Built by Carl Dick, Frankfurt/Main-Hausen. This was a trivan built on the style of the Cyklonette from Berlin, using a DKW engine mounted above and driving the single front wheel. Later versions had the engine fully enclosed.

Dickinson Morette　　　　　**1903-1905**　　　　　　　　　　**GB**
Made by B E Dickinson & Co, Birmingham. A 3-wheeler with a single wicker bath chair-style passenger seat, with the choice of 2.5hp single or a 4hp twin cylinder engines mounted over the front wheel in a unit with final drive by chain. Tiller steering was used and the motor was started with a cord fitting into a groove in the flywheel. Shades of the 1950's lawn mowers!

Diehlmobile　　　　　　　　**1962-1964**　　　　　　　　　　**USA**

Dietz　　　　　　　　　　　**1832-1834**　　　　　　　　　　**France**
Jean Christian Dietz was born in Darmstadt in 1788 and settled in Emmerich where he made a name for himself as an inventor and manufacturer of heavy machinery for digging canals. Dietz was versatile and also made musical instruments, mechanical saws, turbines, steam boilers, and so on. In 1818 he moved to Brussels and started to design steam-driven machines. Joined by his son, Charles, together they worked on many projects taking out a patent for a 3-wheeled steam driven road tractor in 1832. His second tractor, patented in 1834, was still of the 3-wheeled design but for ease of steering he had placed two wheels on either side

of a vertical axle only a few inches apart. This vehicle ran a regular schedule between Brussels and Antwerp drawing a train of carriages, a forerunner of the European trams. He was to produce further vehicles but was so far ahead of his time and with his available capital drying up, he was obliged to return to the manufacture of the more profitable pumps, turbines and presses in his Paris factory in the Rue Marbeuf.

Dingwall De Lux   1950s   **GB**
A vehicle built mainly built for invalids that was able to be used on the roads. Similar to the Carter.

DK-2   1950s-1960s   **Japan**
Showing a strong resemblance to the Italian Vespa Piaggio, the Daihatsu-built passenger taxi had bench seating each side of the canvas covered rear opening cargo bay. A 249cc engine pushed a full load along at a good pace. A cargo version with a tray back or utility back was also available. These were known as the DK-A

DKW   1927   **Germany**
Nicknamed the Das Klein Wunder and built by J S Rassmussen at the old D-Rad motorcycle works. This single front wheel drive 584cc twin cylinder 2-stroke engine and wheel were mounted as one, with chain-drive and handlebar steering at the front of a enclosed van-style body. The driver sat on a bench seat in the open fronted cabin. More information under D-Rad.

DKW   1928-1929   **Japan**
Built in Japan from parts supplied from Germany. Engines used were 206cc and 293cc. They did not have the carrying capacity of the German product and were of the standard Japanese configuration of two rear wheels driven from an engine under the driver's seat up front. Handlebar steering was used.

DMC   1913-1914   **GB**

Doddsmobile   1947   **Canada**

Doherty   1895   **Canada**
One of the oddities that actually worked. Tom Doherty, of Sarina, Ontario, built a 3-wheeled prototype car powered by a giant clock spring!

Dolphin Vortex   1990   **USA**
Another DIY from America. A set of plans and a building manual was available from Dolphin Vehicles of California. Power to the single rear wheel was from a motorcycle engine of your own choosing, Kawasaki 750cc units were most recommended. The front end was supported by Triumph Spitfire double wishbone with coil springs and disc brakes. A tear shaped body was built up from fibreglass covered plywood panels over metal subframes. A battery version was also offered and it is reported that a number of both types of vehicles have been built.

Dong-Feng   1946 to date   **China**
China has come a long way in the production of 3-wheeled trucks. Starting with what appears to be a copy of a Japanese vehicle probably left there after the war they now produce vehicles which are exported to neighbouring countries. Powered

by 2-stroke, single cylinder air-cooled engines of 248.5cc and developing 12hp. Situated under the seat of the enclosed cabin, the engine drives the rear wheels via a chain with a maximum speed of 65km/h obtainable. Bodies are usually a dropside tray with a canvas hood supported by a pipe frame. Drop down seats along the sides allow passengers to be carried while easily converting to cargo when required.

Doniselli   1953-1957   Italy
Offering a range of 3-wheeled delivery trucks, the factory of Fratelli Doniselli SA, of Milan produced a number of vehicles with backbone frames, 125cc and 175cc 2-stroke engines with shaft-drive to the two rear wheels with differential axles. Bodies were the standard continental with tray, drop-side and vans with enclosed cabins. A Metropoli-powered delivery tricycle, with power to a single rear wheel by chain with 2 forward gears only was the baby of the family.

Dorigny   1898   France
The Dorigny was another of the odd tricycles to usher in the motoring age, using a rear engine with power to the two rear wheels, the two occupants sat side by side on saddles, each with their own handlebars and brakes.

Dorran   1991   USA

Dot   1947-1956   GB
Dot Cycle and Motor Manufacturing Co Ltd, of Manchester, built a light delivery vehicle with a front mounted box and motorcycle rear, powered by a 197cc 2-stroke Villiers engine driving the single rear wheel by a chain. Top speed was 30mph. Versions included ice cream vans and for export, a motorised rickshaw.

Douglas   1946-1952   GB
Long time motorcycle manufacturer, Douglas Ltd, of Bristol began to make a range of battery electric delivery vans just after the end of the Second World War. Its venture into 3-wheelers was short and noisy when the first Handy Van milk floats were put on the market in 1948. Using a 596cc flat-twin engine mounted over and driving the front wheel, and governed to a speed of 8mph, they were far too noisy for early morning delivery work and the engine filled the cabin with oil fumes. Only 8 of the 100 to be built were sold.

Dragonfly   1994 to date   GB
A creative copy of the F-type Morgan using a 'Z' section steel ladder chassis available in kit form from the designer, Bernard Beirue. Using parts from a variety of vehicles, the body would be your own creation.

D Rad or D Wagen   1927-1931   Germany
Built by Deutsche Kraftfahrzeugwerke AG, Berlin. A range of 3-wheeled wagons using the pattern of two front wheels with the single rear wheel driven by their own 4-stroke motorcycle engine of 500cc, with an output of 10hp.

D-Rad Riksha   1951   Austria
Built by Franz Weisinger using a 496cc motorcycle with a rating of 12hp, this 2 passenger 65km/h vehicle had a rear facing bench seat between two rear wheels with minimum protection from a slab-sided body and Plexiglass over the driver only.

Dreiad SGS 1983 Germany
Incredible styling in a trapezoid-shaped fibreglass body stole the show at the International Automobile Exhibition in 1983. This is a one seater 3-wheeler using a single cylinder 80cc Honda engine to propel it along at 35mph through its single rear wheel.

Dreirad 1924 Germany
Basically a motorcycle and wide sidecar with side by side seating for two. However, the motorcycle has been stripped of seats, handlebars etc and the sidecar has now acquired a steering wheel, car type controls, a windscreen and a folding hood.
   A similar lookalike to the Scott.

DRK 1994 to date GB
The DRK is a kit car with a difference. Built in the style of the 1930s, it has a ladder-frame chassis with plywood and aluminium panels over hardwood frames. The car is very taut and built by craftsmen in the good old fashioned way with attention to detail. With a practical and neat hood and side curtains, it is ideal for touring. All the buyer has to do is add the engine and suspension from a donor Renault 5. With a full order book more than 50 examples have been built.

DS Malterre 1922-1958 France
Better known for their 2-wheelers, a quality motorcycle using a 500cc single cylinder JAP engine until the start of the Second World War. After the war, commercials were added to the line using Ydral or AMC side-valve engines.
   In 1955 an enclosed coupé with a car-type front end with a 125cc 2-cylinder Ydral motor (tucked into a long sloping tail), driving the single rear wheel was produced but only a few prototypes were built before the project was dropped.

Dual E Turconi 1899-1901 Italy

Ducson 1958-1960 Spain
Founded by Don V Sola, Industria Ciclista SA, in Barcelona, builders of bicycles and motor scooters. He made a brief entry into the commercial field with a delivery tricycle powered by a 125cc engine.

Dumas 1889-1903 France
Experimenting with car production, this Paris-based firm of M.A. Dumas made a number of 3-wheelers using a 4.5hp engine under the bonnet, driving the single front wheel via a series of chains and couplings that allowed the wheel to steer. It had a side by side 2-seater body, a steering wheel and ample luggage space under the bench seat.

Dunjo 1954-1960 Spain
Normally the builders of motorcycle and motor scooter chassis and frames, Talleres Mecanicos de A. Dunjo, of Barcelona, made a number of delivery tricycles.

Dunkley 1913-1915 GB
A pram maker that built scooters, mopeds and trikes using their own manufactured 65cc engines.

Duo Delta   1974   USA

Designed by Walter Korff and created by Unisport of California, another mating of a motorcycle to a 2-seater cabin built round a steel frame with roll-over bars. The fibreglass cabin has side opening doors, a sunroof, cycle guards, large steering wheel and standard car controls. Mated to a 750cc motorcycle with infinitely variable automatic transmission, the Delta boasts 98mph with an average of 56 mpg.

Available in kit form or plans, it was designed so that the power source can be quickly removed to revert back to a motorcycle.

Duryea   1891-1916   USA

The very first cars that Charles Duryea built had two rear wheels, while the single front was steerable. The body was unusual as each side was formed to resemble a mermaid. This rather odd looking little car had a control stick at the driver's left hand. The car was supposed to do something with every movement of this stick, forward, backwards, turn left or right as one wished. Usually a movement provided the unexpected!

Charles Duryea once drove this odd little car to the top of Mount Penn, not far from his factory in Reading, Pennsylvania – an ascent full of steep grades and hairpin turns, and all in high gear. He went on to build a normal 3-wheeler with a 3-cylinder horizontal motor located under the bench seat. It had tiller steering and a pram hood for weather protection. The 1900 model had novel springing for the single front wheel, the spring formed part of the axle and the wheel was arranged to pivot on the spring. Despite this fine performance he very soon added a second front wheel and went on to manufacture top quality 4-wheeled vehicles for many years.

The birth of the American Motor Industry and the brothers Charles and Frank Duryea go together. Experimenting with powered wagons in 1893 it was not until 1895 that Frank began making 3-wheeled vehicles in his factory in Springfield, Illinios, similar to the Benz then in production in Germany. Thirteen cars were built in 1896 and two of these were sent to England to participate in the London-Brighton Emancipation Day run. Powered by a 8hp ohv 3-cylinder engine mounted transversely at the rear and driving the rear wheels by a chain. The 2-speed and reverse epicyclic gearbox was operated by a single lever control, with throttle and brakes controlled from the tiller steering arm. Used as passenger and commercial vehicles, the 3-wheeler had a chequered career but was not forgotten as it was soon to be modified and to be built in England under licence from 1904 to 1907; in Belgium until 1908.

The Duryea Gem, an improved 3-wheeled friction drive cyclecar, was built by Cresson-Morris of Philadelphia up to 1916, alongside the 4-wheeler buggies from the same firm.

1914 saw a Duryea Parcel car with a single rear wheel and enclosed box for cargo in front of the driver.

Dutemple   1905   France

Shown at the Paris Motor Show in 1905, the Dutemple was noted as a 3.5hp single engined tricar with mechanically-operated valves.

Dymaxion   1933   USA

Buckminister Fuller was both an eccentric and a genius who was famous for his way out designs, an architect, an artist and an engineer and amongst his many projects had designed was a flying car, though this did not get off the ground(!) it was to form the basic idea for the Dymaxion: a standard Ford V8 chassis with the front wheels removed, a large V-shaped subframe to hold a single steerable wheel, then turn the lot around so that we have a front wheel driven, single rear wheel steerable vehicle, to which is added a aluminium tear-drop body nearly 20ft long that overhangs the now front axle by 6ft. The driver and passenger sat in this glass house area while another 9 passenger seats were proposed in the vehicle's vast body. Three, some reports say four, vehicles were built in the Buckminster factory at Bridgeport, Connecticut, and were said to be capable of 120mph and over 40 mpg. The prototype was sent on a tour and was involved in an accident where all the occupants were killed. The adverse national news coverage ended the project.

Of the vehicles built, one was destroyed in a fire, of the others at least one vehicle is still in existence – it surfaced in Arizona and was purchased by five graduate students of the Arizona State University with the hope that it could be restored and go on display.

D'Yrsan   1923-1930   France
These were luxury Morgan-style, well-built, long boat-tail sports cars. They used a tubular spaceframe, dual transverse front springs in lieu of front axle, and all wheels were detachable. The water-cooled 7.5hp 4 cylinder Ruby engine drove the single rear wheel through a 3-speed and reverse gearbox with final drive by chain. A top speed of 80mph was recorded. Another luxury was brakes on all wheels. Vehicles were built in Asnieres by the Marquise, Siran de Cavanac.

Eadie   1898-1900   GB
A motor tricycle with a 2.25hp De Dion engine and built by the Eadie Manufacturing Company of Redditch. Using a ridged-type pipe frame, the company also built 2- and 4-wheeled machines.

Eagle   1885-1913   GB
From Altrincham in Cheshire, a Mr Ralph Jackson started building Ralpho bicycles in 1885. In 1899 he founded the Century Engineering and Motor Company to build his own design of 3-wheeled car, powered by a 2.25hp single cylinder engine. Jackson sold the company and the car, called the Century Tandem, to a Mr Begbie who changed the name to Eagle and continued to manufacture the vehicle using 8hp and 10hp De Dion engines in 1902. By 1904 the Eagle Runabout had become a sporty open single seater with a 5hp water-cooled engine placed low behind the front axle, with shaft-drive to a multi-speed gearbox and then by Reynolds silent chain to the single rear wheel. Begbie appeared to have some arrangement with Mr Jackson because the Century Tandem still appeared from a factory in Willesden, and the two actually had adjoining stands at the 1904 Crystal Palace Auto Show.

In 1907 the original Century Engineering and Motor Company was wound up by Mr Begbie. Mr Jackson continued to assemble the vehicle under the name of New Eagle until 1910. A commercial tricar was also built, powered by a single cylinder engine of 4.5hp. Both vehicles had the driver at the rear sitting over the engine which drove the single rear wheel. Passenger seat or cargo box was placed in front of the driver. In 1910 Mr Jackson opened a garage and continued to build a cyclecar which he also called the Eagle Runabout. A long low vehicle with a 16hp 4-cylinder engine along the lines of the original runabout of 1904. A vehicle that was very popular with motorcycle clubs and the sports-minded drivers of the time.

Eaglet 1948 GB
Silent Transport Pty of Dorking, Surrey, built a little tricycle-car with Electro-Drive. It had a top speed of 45km/h with a range of about 50 kilometres per charge. Production ceased after six or so vehicles were built.

Eastman Electro Cycle 1899-1902 USA
America's first all-steel car was the 'Electro Cycle' built by H F Eastman, of Cleveland, Ohio. This was a 3-wheeler powered by an electric motor but with the drawback that its batteries took up most of the available space and accounted for three quarters of the vehicles weight.

EBS 1924-1927 Germany
Ernst Bauermeister & Sohne, Berlin-Baumschulenweg, built a trivan with the front half along motorcycle lines and the rear box placed between the two rear wheels. The driver sat on a saddle over the engine (with a choice of 200cc, 250cc or 350cc air-cooled single cylinder motors), transmission was by chain to a gearbox and shaft to the rear axle. Handlebar steering and the usual motorcycle controls were used.

A 2-seater car body was available with pram hood for use as a taxi or a private vehicle but the driver was still exposed to all weathers.

Echasa 1956-1958 Spain
The Echasa, Arizmendi y Cia S.A, Eibar, Guipuzcoa, manufactured motorcycles, scooters and a range of delivery tricycles using engines of 125cc and 175cc.

Eclipse 1906 GB
Built by the XL-All Motorcycle Co, this was a tricar with a coachbuilt body and powered by a 5.5hp V-twin engine

Econom 1950-1953 Germany
As well as equipping trucks with steam engines during the Second World War, Econom-Werk Hellmuth Butenuth, Berlin, built 5 ton commercial trucks and articulated tractors from 1950. Amongst their range was a 3-wheeled street sweeper using a single cylinder diesel engine.

Economic (1) 1899-1902 USA
Believed to be a steam powered tricycle built by Economic Manufacturing Company of Orange, New Jersey.

Economic (2) 1921-1922 GB
This was a spindly cyclecar with the single steering wheel in front, the rear mounted 200cc twin horizontal cylinder engine drove the offside rear wheel by a chain, it had very basic basket-weave seating for two and absolutely no weather protection. Built by Economic Motors, Wells Street, London on an Ash frame, it cost £60 with £4 for tax.

Ecrin 1950s France
A luxury version of the Isetta, the basic version was called the Velam, built in France. A total of more than 7,000 cars were produced.
More information under Isetta.

Edith   1953   **Australia**

Built by Grey & Harper Pty Ltd of East Oakleigh, Victoria. A fibreglass 3-wheeled open 2-seater with a sloping front and back of equal dimensions. Double quarter-elliptic springs were used on each wheel, a Villiers 2-stroke engine drove the single rear wheel by chain. Top speed was 40mph with petrol consumption of 60 mpg.

Few were ever made.

EEC   1952-1954   **GB**

The EEC came from a factory that built boats during the war at the small Devonshire town of Totnes on the banks of the River Dart. Six prototypes were planned, using a steel framework panelled in an aluminium body with a 250cc Excelsior twin cylinder 2-stroke engine driving the single rear wheel. Production was abandoned after one vehicle, a hard top saloon with accommodation for up to three people on a single bench seat had been built. It was used as a factory runabout then sold to a Somerset antique dealer when the project was wound up.

The remaining parts of the other prototypes were destroyed in a factory fire. The vehicle was advertised as the Workers Playtime Model.

EFAG   1920   **Czechoslovakia**

See Tribelhorn for more information.

Egan   1952   **GB**

Egg   1893-1919   **Switzerland**

Rudolf Egg built his first car in 1893 but it was not until 1896 that the 'Egg & Elgi' appeared, this was a tricar using a single cylinder De Dion engine achieving 3 forward speeds through a 2-speed belt drive. In 1898 he switched to 4 wheels and the tricar was withdrawn.

Eibach   1921-1925   **Germany**

A trivan with the delivery box situated between the two front wheels was built by Eichler & Bachmann GmbH, Berlin. The rear followed usual motorcycle lines with a 200cc DKW engine powering the single rear wheel.

A passenger model was available with a body that looked like a motorcycle sidecar complete with split windscreen and built for two. The driver sat over the engine in a contoured seat and used handlebars for steering.

Ekamobil   1913-1914   **Germany**

Elactra   1911-1915   **USA**

Battery powered, both 2- and 3-wheeled models, these were manufactured in small numbers.

Electra-King   1961 to date   **USA**

B & Z Electric Car Company, Long Beach, California, built both 3- and 4-wheeled cars powered by a 1hp DC Electric motor and five 6 volt batteries. Vehicles have a range of 45 miles at a speed of 18mph.

1972 saw a change of owner, now Robert E McCoy, who introduced a choice of four motors and a top speed of 36mph. Vehicles are used in airports and factories as well as on golf courses and they are available in a variety of passenger or cargo bodies.

Electricar-Scammell   1936-1939   GB
Built and designed by Electricar Ltd, Birmingham. This was a 3-wheeled battery-electric 'mechanical horse'. A special tractor with a 302.5cm wheelbase using Scammell steering gear to the single front wheel, it had automatic coupling and a fully enclosed cabin with all accessories for highway use. Rated as a 6-tonner, it actually grossed over 11 tons when coupled to an Eagle Compressmore refuse trailer. Many were used by councils for garbage collection.

Electric-Shopper   1956-1962   USA
Built by the Electric Shopper Company, Long Beach, California. A 3-wheeled shoppers' cart built for use in the larger shopping malls.

Electricar   1920-1921   France
M. Couaillet of Paris built a 3-wheeled single seater urban car with a single front wheel. Driven by a .5hp electric motor it had a limited range. Not many were sold.

Elec-Triffid   1960   Netherlands
For more information see under Batavus.

Elactrodrive   1950 to date   Australia
Electrodrive Pty Ltd of Victoria produce a range of electric transporters for efficient transport of goods and personnel in factories, airports, golf clubs and resorts and with speeds of up to 30km/h. All have motorcycle-type front wheel steering with the electric motors and batteries stored over the rear wheels.

Electron   1956   GB
Another Fairthorpe mistaken in some accounts to be a 3-wheeler. Definitely not. All Electrons had 4 wheels. For more information see Fairthorpe.

Electrotrike Super 48   1980s   Sweden
Developed by the Swedish Telecommunications Administration (Televerket) for their telephone installation personnel in urban areas. This is a single front wheel panel van built of reinforced fibreglass on modern lines. Driver's cabin has a steering wheel and normal car type controls with a single entry door on the right hand side. Batteries and motors are under the floor and drive the rear wheels. Range is about 50 miles, recharging time 8 hours and the vehicle is fitted with a heater and defroster for winter work.

Electruk   1937-1961   GB
T E Lewis were established in 1854 specialising in dairy vehicles. They became part of the Express Dairy Co Ltd. In 1937 the first 3-wheeled milk float powered from a 12-volt battery was produced, it carried 6/7cwt of bottled milk but left the driver to walk behind. Power and capacity was increased over the years and by 1949 was carting 12cwt. This was soon replaced by a 4-wheeled version with a 1 ton capacity and a walk through cabin for the driver.

Elieson   1898   GB
This was an almost 3-wheeler. An electric vehicle with different bodies for a passenger car, a taxi cab or a delivery van, all built by John Warrick & Co Ltd for Elieson Lamina Accumulator Syndicate Ltd, battery manufacturers. The two front wheels were very close together while power was carried to the rear wheels by a

chain-drive. John Warrick went on to later build his own 3-wheeled parcel van, details of which are listed under Warrick.

Elite   1955-1958   **Spain**
Elementos de Transporte, Barcelona, built a small number of delivery tricycles using the 197cc Hispano-Villiers engine powering the single rear wheel, with a tray or dropside cargo platform in front of the driver.

Empolini   1930 to date   **Italy**
Empolini Milano di Silvestri Aldo, of Milan are specialists in the construction of ultra light 3-wheeled delivery vehicles with payloads about 300kg. Amongst the engines used are the 48cc single cylinder Minarelli, with shaft-drive to the two rear wheels through a 3-speed gearbox, handle bar steering and a variety of bodies including a miniature tipper and a refuse collector. They also have the usual tray, dropside and van bodies.

EM3   1950 to date   **GB**
See Electron for more information.

E.M.W.   1927-1930   **Germany**
Built by the Motor-Transportwagenwerk- H. Schivelbusch, Leipzig, a tri-van with a large cargo box between the two front wheels and the single rear wheel driven by a choice of engines including a 200cc D.K.W. or a 340cc Villiers.

Energie   1899-1902   **France**
Known as the Renaux, a motor tricycle made by Society L'Energie of Paris, who began building a light car in 1902 powered by a 8.5hp vertical twin Buchet engine.

Enfield   1899-1900s   **GB**
From the Redditch factory of the Enfield Cycle Company, their first trike was a copy of the Bollée, adapting the De Dion engine and making improvements to the frame. Later versions were on the usual configuration of two wheels and the passenger seat, or cargo box, out in front of the driver who sat over the single cylinder air-cooled engine, placed just in front and driving the single rear wheel. It would appear that they also supplied parts to the Eadie Manufacturing Co who also built trikes in the same town.

Enfield Autoette   1918   **GB**
From the long standing Enfield Motorcycle Works, another version of mating a current motorcycle to a delivery box.

Entrop   1909   **Netherlands**

Entwurf   1929-1935   **Germany**
More information to be found under Neimann

Ercole   1945 to date   **Italy**
Information under Moto-Guzzi

Ercolino   1956   **Italy**
Information listed under Moto-Guzzi.

Eric   1911-1914   GB
A solid snub nosed cyclecar with using a 6hp water-cooled flat twin engine, a 3-speed gearbox with chain-drive to a single powered rear wheel. Body was equipped with a vertical windscreen, a steering wheel and standard car type controls with a pram hood for weather protection. From 1913 a Salmons 4-cylinder engine and a closed coupé body was offered.

Erla-Bond   1950-1952   Germany
The Erla Automobile Company in Linzenz was to build the German Wendax under licence. However, this project failed and the company looked to England and the Bond as a replacement.

A number of prototypes were built but the program ended when the market failed to materialise.

Etna   1902   GB
Built by the Brixton Motor Works, Brixton, South London. Weighing in at 7cwt and nominally rated at 14hp, this tandem tricycle had an enormous water-cooled V-twin motor with overhead inlet and side exhaust valves and had many De Dion features. This was a special built by/for Herbert F Harding, an engineer at the Brixton Motor Works.

The trike gained the name of *The Portsmouth Ghost* for regularly evading the low speed limits enforced at that time. It was 1913 before the police were able to book our Mr Harding. When almost 50 years old, the Etna was clocked at an honest 70mph on the M25 but was most happy cruising at a sedate 45mph. Brixton also made a 9hp single cylinder motor to be fitted to the Lagonda post office trikes.

Euricar   1930   GB
This was a 'supposed-to-be' that did not get past the prototype stage. To be built in Manchester by J V & E G Eurich, using a rear mounted air-cooled engine driving the single rear wheel, and clothed in an all-metal body with a retractable metal hood. The Yanks classed the retractable metal hood as something new in the 1980s.

Europeene   1899-1903   France

Excelsior (1)   1902-1905   GB
Bayliss & Thomas of Coventry built a tricar powered by a 4.5hp engine. They moved on to other manufacturing until 1922 when a light car under the same name was produced. Both ventures seem to have had little success.

However, it is noted that an Excelsior 'Fore-car' was imported into Australia in 1903 and reputed to be the first of its kind to ever have been seen in Victoria. It had a long stroke single cylinder air-cooled engine with belt drive to the single back wheel housed in a sturdy bicycle frame. The passenger seat was a wicker basket weave which was located over the front axle between the two front wheels. Known locally as a motorised bicycle with pedal power for starting and assistance up the hills.

Excelsior (2)   1907   France
From the Bourgogne area in France, a tricar built by the Excelsior Motor Cycle factory. They appear to have no connection with any of the other Excelsior brands on the market at that time.

Fada   1955-1958   Spain

Fada, Vallodolid, built a 3-wheeled truck for the Spanish market with a 1500kg capacity, using a tubular steel frame, 5-speed transmission and shaft-drive to the rear axle. A 673cc single cylinder petrol motor rated at 20bhp was used.

Fairthorpe   1953-1976   GB

Fairthorpe Ltd, founded and run by Air Vice-Marshal Don Bennett, had a successful history as producers of unusual fibreglass cars and sports cars of the 4-wheeled variety. Fairthorpe has been acknowledged (mistakenly) by some as having built 3-wheelers. Perhaps this is not surprising if you look at the usual culprit, the Atom, which looks decidedly 3-wheeled from its side-on view. Take a glance at the recently published book *Fairthorpe Cars* and you will see all 4-wheels (of Triumph TR origin) on the Atom – and 4 wheels on all the other interesting cars made by this company.

The Fairthorpe name was resurrected again in 1986 by an enthusiastic company hoping to begin production once again of the sports cars. It did not last.

Fairy   1907   GB

Most motorcycle companies produced a 3-wheeler at some time; with the Fairy we have a tricar from the firm that became the Douglas Motor Cycle Company. Using the usual format of a single front wheel with a 6/8hp flat twin engine at the back.

Faka   1951-1957   Germany

This was an unusual 3-wheeled van built along the lines of the standard motor scooter delivery vehicles of the day. The 118cc Ilo 2-stroke engine was mounted above and drove the single front wheel, while the driver sat in the usual scooter fashion with his back against the large lockable van body.

Falcon   1986 to date   GB

After playing around with a 4-wheeled kit car, Peter Bird of Falcon Design, launched a Lotus look-alike based on the Citroën 2CV floorpan. After a number of updates the Falcon LX3 was by now not unlike a Lomax, and available as a set of plans or as a kit. More than 200 have been built.

FAM   1948-1950   Italy

Sarl FAM Pesaro built conventional 3-wheeled delivery trucks in motorcycle style.

FAR   1919 to date   France

SA des Trains Chenard-Walcker-FAR, Gennevilliers, Seine. This company produced under licence the Scammell 'mechanical horse' using Walcker or Citroën petrol and diesel engines, a range introduced about 1937. After the Second World War a smaller version for loads up to 2.75 tons was introduced using an air-cooled flat twin Dyna-Panhard petrol engine. As well as its use as a tractor unit this chassis was the basis for a range of street sweepers and water trucks used in street cleaning. From 1952 these 3-wheelers were powered by Renault gasoline or Perkins diesel engines and were increased in size to include a 6 ton articulated truck. With the advent of a 4-wheeled articulated tractor in 1970, the company stopped manufacturing its 3-wheelers.

Fascination   1971   USA

From the builder of the Lewis Airmobile of 1937, at 17ft, this was possibly the longest passenger carrying 3-wheeler to be conceived. The five-seater Fascination had a teardrop body attached to a wide flat pod that housed a 70hp Renault 16 engine and its two rear wheels. It featured air bag suspension and spring loaded bumpers, but never got past the prototype stage.

Le Favori 1921-1923 France
Built in Paris, a tiny 3-wheeled cyclecar using a 987cc twin cylinder engine.

Favorit 1908-1909 Germany
Believed to have built a number of trikes in this period. The same name was used in 1933-1938 for the manufacturer of motorcycles and sidecars with a small number of commercial 3-wheelers. JAP V-twins were used and later Sachs 2-stroke engines were built under licence.

Felber Autoroller 1952-1954 Austria
A collector's item as only a handful of the 400 made still survive. It had a Rotax 398cc rear mounted engine developing 15 bhp and driving the single rear wheel. A motor car style front with a 2-seater cabin, side opening doors and a sunroof with a canvas rear window gave this neat little vehicle a open coupé appearance.

Fend Flitzer 1948-1953 Germany
Designed by Fritz Fend at the end of the Second World War, the Fend Flitzer was to become the prototype for the Messerschmitts. First produced with bicycle wheels and pedal power, this was soon followed by one of the smallest engines ever fitted to a vehicle, a 38cc single cylinder Victoria. A top speed of 19mph and 235 mpg was achieved. Upgrading to the now available motor scooter wheels and fitting a 98cc Fichtel & Sachs engine, speed was increased but so was fuel consumption. By 1950 came the much improved Kabinroller with a 98cc Reidel engine. It was about this time, January 1952, that Fend started to collaborate with Professor Willy Messerschmitt. First vehicle from this venture was the Fend FK 150.

Fend FK 150 1953 Germany
This was the Kabinroller with a 148cc Fichtel & Sachs 6.5hp engine. More mph but less mpg. For more information see Messerschmitt.

Feora 1982 USA
With a body like a fighter plane, stubby wings projecting each side on the nose to hold the two front wheels clad in their own streamlining, the flaring and wheels turn as one unit. This was a one-off built by a Los Angeles mechanic named Chuck Ophorst.
 The all fibreglass bodywork covered a complicated spaceframe chassis with entry to the tandem seating via a lift-up canopy. Power came from a 22 bhp 175cc Honda twin cylinder engine with a top speed claimed as 92mph. Production costs made any copies prohibitive.

Frere/Ferro 1935 Italy
Probably other names used by Frera. More information listed under that name.

FIAT/Miniauto 1970s-1980s Italy
Fabric Inaliana Auto Moto called it a Miniauto with the name of 'Johnny Panther'. A fibreglass body closely resembling a Reliant Robin up to the seat backs; from

there it was a two door coupé with a hatchback finish. Powered by a 125cc engine, single front wheel and normal car type controls.

Fiberfab Scarab   1957-1959   USA
Fiberfab of Bridgeville, Pennsylvania probably started the craze of mating a motorcycle to a simple chassis and creating a sports car destined to turn heads. Using a twin rail front end supported by VW suspension and trim, a Kawasaki 900 motorcycle, minus front wheel and forks, mated only at the rear end and covered by a teardrop fibreglass body. The front hinged canopy tilted upwards to allow entry to the comfortable 2-seater cabin. Production was few as the concept was too way out for Americans of the '70s but has been taken on with glee in the 1990s.

Fioretti F 50   1978-1981   Italy
Based on the Piaggio delivery truck chassis and using a 50cc Piaggio engine, this was an attempt to make an economical passenger vehicle that still looked sadly like a small utility truck with cutaway doors. The square sided fibreglass body was the usual single front wheel, motorcycle style, and power to the two rear wheels was usual Piaggio. A removable canvas hood and doors convert from an open coupé to a closed but draughty vehicle. Extra seats could be put in the load area. Production was not a commercial success and sales were limited.

Fire Aero   1980   SA

Fleet   1932-1936   GB
Fleet Motors Ltd, Selly Oak, Birmingham, built a 3-wheeled commercial using Ariel components: a single cylinder 557cc side-valve engine with turbo-fan cooling and a 3-speed gearbox transferring power to the single rear wheel in the usual motorcycle layout. The cargo box had a capacity of 10cwt and was placed in front of the driver. About 900 vehicles were built over a four year period.

FN   1900s   GB
A standard 3-wheeler of the 1900s with the passenger sitting in a wicker seat in front of the driver. The single cylinder air-cooled engine was located just in front of the single rear wheel and under the padded seat of the driver.

FN AS 24   1980s   Belgium
Designed by Nicholas Straussler for the Belgian Army, the FN AS 24 is an all-purpose vehicle able to carry a driver and three men, or up to 250kg of cargo into battle after being dropped by parachute. Built by Fabrique Nationale, 24 units were put into service.

Ford (Dearborn)   1980s-1990s   USA.
On show at the Ford Museum at Dearborn is a sleek Star Wars created 3-wheeler. with a tear drop body. Two rear wheels are located in teardrop spats on the end of stubby wings that extend from the roof line, aft of a 2-seater cabin enclosed in a clear wraparound plastic windscreen that reaches past the seat backs. It rates among other automotive stylist dreams which never got past the mock up stage.

Ford Ghia Cockpit   1981   USA/Italy
Designed and developed by the Ghia Operations in Turin, Ford's International Design Think Tank. A tandem seated 3-wheeler with a vague resemblance to the

Messerschmitt. Code-named the Cockpit, with advanced aerodynamic design and a rigid triangular chassis clothed in a sleek fibreglass body with a front hinged canopy exposing contoured seating, a steering wheel and car type controls. The two front wheels are covered by mudguards that form part of a nose cone featuring headlights to the front and recessed mirrors to the rear (a spare wheel and small parcel compartment is also located within this compartment). A 12hp 200cc Piaggio petrol engine drives the single rear wheel by enclosed chain. Fuel consumption is rated at 95 mpg.

This is a dream car slated to emerge in times of petrol crisis or as a battery powered commuter.

Ford Tug 1934-1937 GB
Production of the Ford Tug started on the 16th of September 1935 and ended two years later after 121 vehicles had been built. Using the modified chassis of a BB light truck, a single castor style front wheel replaced the normal front assembly, the engine was a 8hp Y, and the all-steel cab and bonnet were standard Ford. Available in a long wheelbase Panel Van or as a short wheelbase Fordson Tug to be used as a tractor or a prime mover. Two or three units still survive. For other derivatives see information under Devon.

Ford Volante 1961 USA
Another American designer's dream, a 3-wheeler that was to become a hovercraft, never got past the model stage.

Forecar (1) 1896 GB
Information under Humber.

Forecar (2) 1900-1907 GB
See Singer for more information.

Forward 1911 Denmark
Paul Christensen, a cycle dealer of Copenhagen announced the availability of the Forward 3-wheeled cyclecar to be in his shop from December 1911. Powered by an 8hp water-cooled V-twin with a 2-speed planetary transmission with reverse and a fully enclosed chain-drive to the single rear wheel. Twin radiators were fitted on either side of the 2-seater body next to the low mounted engine. It is believed the vehicle was imported in pieces and put together in his own workshop. It was later announced that a 4-wheeled version would be available.

Forsyth Velocipede 1870 USA
On 19 April 1870 a patent was granted to F J Forsyth of Bay City, Michigan, for the invention of a spring-powered Velocipede. Design showed a tiller steered single front wheel, sprung bench seating for two, with reverse gear. It is not known if this vehicle ever got past its design stage, but it was reported that a similar vehicle was demonstrated in Richmond, Virginia and Manchester, Vermont, during that decade.

FR 1927-1928 France

Fram King Fulda 1960s Sweden
The Fuldamobil built under licence.

Framo-Piccolo 1927-1940 Germany

From 1927 the light DKW van construction was transferred to Metallwerke Frankenberg GmbH, Frankenberg, and renamed the Framo. The trivan had a van body with a 300cc engine driving the single front wheel. In 1930 a much improved LT200 was introduced, with a 200cc engine producing more power than the old 300cc unit, a fully enclosed cabin with steering wheel and full car controls.

In 1933 the name was changed to Framo Werke GmbH, and moved to Hainichen. The 3-wheeler was built along side 4-wheeled commercials. Model names included the Piccolo and the Stromer. Design was by Abram Neiman. Production of the 3-wheelers ceased with the start of the Second World War.

For more information see under Neiman.

Frankl Autoroller 1949 Germany

Built in Austria by Erich Frankl, this was a wide 3-wheeler sitting three abreast on a bench seat, with normal car controls. A metal body was hand-formed over a metal tube frame, tapering to a long tail enclosing the chain driven single rear wheel powered by a 250cc motorcycle engine. Believed to have been a one-off.

Frera 1930-1939 Italy

Better known for its motorcycles, the Srl. Leonardo Frera, Tradate factory built 3-wheeled delivery vehicles in the early 1930s. Drive was to the two rear wheels from a 500cc single cylinder engine.

Free-Way 1977 to ? USA

After years of development H M Vehicles Inc., of Burnsville, Minnesota, started building the Free-Way in 1980. This was a single seat cabin cruiser with a unique wraparound square steel pipe chassis, clothed in a sleek fibreglass body. Using standard automotive controls it was available as either an electric powered vehicle or as a 340cc or 540cc petrol engine variation. The luggage area could be used as a temporary tandem seat. In petrol engine form the vehicle was claimed to reach 65mph and return 100 mpg. Available in completed form only.

Frisky 1959-1964 GB

The Frisky was designed by Captain Raymond Flowers and started as a small 4-wheeler, redesigned by Michelotti, the Italian stylist, as the 4-wheeled Frisky-Sport complete with American style fins. In 1958 Captain Flowers again redesigned the vehicle as the Frisky Family Three, a 3-wheeler with a 197cc engine uprated in 1959 to a 2 cylinder 246cc.

In 1960 came a larger version called the Frisky Prince with either 324cc or 328cc engines, and with either a coupé or a convertible body added. Production came to a halt in 1964 when the design was taken to Australia where it then became the Zeta.

Fuji Cabin 1957-1958 Japan

The egg-shaped body was a departure from the usual motorcycle 3-wheeler that clogged the roads of Japan after the Second World War. A very attractive two (side by side) seater in small car style with a single headlight moulded into the curved fibreglass body. A 125cc Fuji 5.5hp air-cooled engine drove the single rear wheel giving a top speed of 37mph. The cabin was totally enclosed with the doors hinged on the front bulkhead, opening forward and upwards. A total of 85 units are said to have been built.

Fulda N2   **1950**   **Germany**
A rare vehicle built by the Elektromaschinenbau Fulda and probably the ancestor of the Fuldamobil.

Fuldamobil   **1950-1960**   **Germany**
Built under licence in England (1959-61) as the Nobel, and in Greece in 1970 as the Alta. It was also produced in Chile as the Bambi, and in India as the Hans Vahaar. The Fuldamobil was intended as a 2-seater coupé or roadster on car lines with the engine mounted beside and driving the single rear wheel. Early models were nicknamed 'the sticking plaster bomber' as the bodies were built in plywood covered with imitation leather. Later versions were clothed in aluminium while the final body style was done in fibreglass. A variety of engines were used that include the 200cc Ilo and the 360cc Sachs. More information noted under Noble and Alta.

Fusi   **1949-1957**   **Italy.**
Another motorcycle factory that offered a 3-wheeled delivery vehicle to its clients after the Second World War. A. Fusi & C SpA, Milan built a light truck with a 250cc engine driving the two rear wheels.

Gaita   **1950**   **Spain**

Galbusera   **1950-1955**   **Italy**
A motorcycle company that made a cargo carrier of 300kg capacity. Moto Galbusera & C. Brescia used a 125cc Sachs engine in the standard single rear wheel drive vehicle.

Galland   **1927-1934**   **France**
Using the standard rear portion of a motorcycle the Ets Galland company of Paris built a parcels van powered by a JAP 500cc engine driving the rear wheel through a Burman 3-speed gearbox. Utilising handlebar steering the factory improved the models and by 1930 had added 350cc and 600cc JAP engines to the range. A further improved model with a car-type panel van body was offered with a single front wheel and a choice of 500cc Train or 600cc JAP engines.

Gamage   **1900-1915**   **GB**
The well-known London department store Gamages sold cars and tricycles under their own name – most were continental imports.

Garrard   **1904**   **GB**
Built by the makers of the Clement-Garrard motorcycle. Advertised as the 'Suspended Tri-car', this was a well-built machine with the usual layout of the passenger sitting in front while the driver sat in armchair comfort over, but slightly in front of, the single rear wheel, which was chain-driven from an engine located between the driver's feet. Handlebar steering was used.

Garrard-Speke   **1911**   **GB**
Possibly related to the Clement-Garrard this was an advanced open-bodied trike with a twin cylinder air-cooled engine placed between the front wheels with a shaft-drive to the single rear wheel. Armchair seating was for two with the steering wheel and car controls on the right hand side. All wheels had cycle guards and there was no cover over the engine.

Gashopper	**1980**	**USA**

Gasi	**1921**	**Germany**

Gasi Motorradwagen GmbH, Berlin, produced this cyclecar with a body something akin to an aeroplane of the day. The two seats were in tandem in their own cockpit. One climbed over the side and slid down into the seat, each cockpit had separate aero screens and like an aeroplane the rear seat housed the driver. An air-cooled 2-cylinder engine was located at the front, just behind the single front wheel. Power was conveyed by chain to an intermediate shaft close to the engine, and then by exposed belts from a V pulley at each end of the shaft to each of the rear wheels.

Gasmobile	**1900**	**USA**

Gavonis	**1952-1966**	**Italy**

Built by the Motom SpA. Milan motorcycle works, the Gavonis was an ultra-light 3-wheeled commercial using a 48cc 4-stroke engine driving the two rear wheels and using a motorcycle front end. Payload was 3cwt. The name was changed to Motom early in the production run. More information under that name.

GB	**1922-1924**	**GB**

From a cramped factory in Wilton Mews, Grosvenor Place, London, George Baetz built a small number of cyclecars with a unitary body/chassis. A 668cc Coventry Victor side-valve engine drove the rear wheels via a Sturmey-Archer 3-speed gearbox and a Chater Lea worm axle. Normal car type controls with a large steering wheel linked to the single front wheel. A 2-seater body with pram hood completed the vehicle.

Geest	**1938**	**GB**

The Geest was a 3-wheeled electric platform trolley with a petrol or electric motor mounted as a unit with the single front steering wheel. It was used as a load carrier on railway platforms or in factories.

Geha	**1910-1923**	**Germany**

A 3-wheeled electric van from Elitewerke AG, Zweigniederlassung, Berlin. The electric motor was mounted with the single front wheel and the batteries were carried under the floor. It was also available as a four passenger Phaeton. In 1917 the company was taken over by the Elite group

General Motors Astro 111	**1969**	**USA**

A product of the GM Dream Car Division, this dynamic futuristic-shaped single seater had the two rear wheels totally enclosed in outriggers while the single front wheel was lost under yards of nose cone.

General Motors Lean Machine	**1982**	**USA**

A single seat torpedo-shaped fibreglass body, powered by a 30hp 185cc Honda motorcycle engine made this a potential machine. The 2-wheeled rear engine and drive compartment stayed square on the road while the passenger pod, complete with single front wheel, tilted into the curves. It came as no surprise that its first public appearance was at Disneyland – it has remained in the 'dream only' category.

Gerosa 1953 to date Italy
Starting in 1953 with lightweight motorcycles, Moto Gerosa, Brescia, started building a delivery 2 wheeler with baskets front and rear. A 3-wheeler was then introduced with a van body and drive to its two rear wheels. This improved and by 1964 became the company's main product. By 1975 further improvements had the driver enclosed in a cabin with a variety of bodies available. The early vehicles had a tubular frame with a F. B. Minarelli 48cc 2-stroke engine powering the rear wheels through a 3-speed gearbox. Payload was 3cwt.

Ghia Cockpit 1981 Italy
Futuristic 3-wheeler similar to a Messerschmitt with tandem seating for three at a pinch. Piaggio 12hp 200cc engine drove the single rear wheel. The plexiglass hood hinged at the front lifted up to allow entry. Performance did not match the looks. This was a motor show car and only a few were built for study and publicity.

Giant 1930-1966 Japan
Production for this maker began in the 1930s with a commercial motorcycle-based trike. Engine was a choice of either 650cc or 750cc units and the cargo box was between the two rear wheels. Some 636 units were built in 1937. The company went on after the war to build some of the larger trucks still using a 3-wheel configuration in Japan. The Giant was one of the largest 3-wheeled trucks built by Aichi Machine Products, (Aichi Kokuki K K. of Nagoya). A length of 5.185 metres with a wide cabin and a single front wheel. Engine was a 4 cylinder water-cooled 1,488cc with shaft-drive to the rear wheels. Another vehicle along the same lines was the Giant Tug, an articulated vehicle using the same engine but in a chassis only 3.810 metres long. Further information is listed under Cony.

Gilcot 1972 GB
Based on a Reliant Regal chassis, this was a fibreglass slab-sided body with gull-wing doors that made even the old Reliant look exotic. Production was in kit form and in low numbers.

Gildax 1968-1976 France
See Vitrex Riboud for more information.

Gilera 1939-1960 Italy
In addition to a range of motorcycles Moto Gilera SpA, Arcore, Milan built commercial vehicles using the front half of a motorcycle wedded to a tubular box frame chassis, ending in two sprung rear wheels attached to a chain-driven axle. Power came from a 250cc side valve engine with 3 forward speeds. A variety of bodies were available. The larger 30cwt trucks had the option of 500cc or 600cc ohv engines with 4-speed gearboxes and semi-enclosed cabins. Later versions after 1945 had shaft-drive and hydraulic brakes. In 1956 a smaller truck was offered with a cargo capacity of 6cwt using a 150cc ohv engine and a 4-speed gearbox. After 1960 the production of 3-wheelers was dropped in favour of motorcycles which they still manufacture as a subsidiary of Piaggio.

Giles Runabout 1948 GB
The Giles first appeared to be a very well built one-off using an underpowered Douglas Industrial type engine located under a long bonnet and close to the front wheels. Drive was through a propshaft to an Austin Seven differential and by final

chain from a BSA gearbox to a single rear wheel. The neat body had a two place bench seat and a car type windscreen. About 1973, some photos showed a frontal update, new headlights, mudguards and a bonnet air scoop with a new exhaust system indicating a larger engine update.

Gilgen   **1880-1890**   **Australia**
This vehicle first came to public notice after a Royal Tour of South Australia in 1890. In 1904, a Mr C A Blake who accompanied the Royal Party wrote of a visit to the property of a Mr Gilgen, a Swiss-born engineer, where they were invited to witness a demonstration of a 3-wheeled steam car with seating for nine people. It was claimed by Mr Blake that the vehicle had a 5hp steam engine with a 3-speed gearbox and was able to travel at 32km/h. A date somewhere in the 1880s was claimed as the date of manufacture. South Australia was at the forefront of steam vehicle manufacture as the Shearer Steam Carriage had been developed during that same period – the Shearer was first announced in 1885.

Girling   **1912-1914**   **GB**
Girling Motors Ltd of Woolwich built a 3-wheeled delivery van where the single rear wheel was driven through a friction disc or epicyclic transmission, depending on the model of van you required. Driver and his helper sat in the front of the van with no protection from the elements – a choice of either a 4hp or a 6hp air-cooled engine was located under the seat. Payloads were 5cwt or 7cwt, depending on the engine installed. Tiller steering was used. This unit was built in considerable numbers and exported to many countries: the majority to New Zealand and Ceylon.

Glory   **1928-1930s**   **Japan.**
Built by Maruto, a cargo carrier using the English Blackburn engine of 350cc.

GM 511   **1960**   **USA**
Featuring a large opening canopy, a wrap-round windscreen, seating for two and fitted with a 1100cc Opel 4-cylinder engine, this early concept car was only 40 inches high and was reported to be able to achieve 80mph. It had a vague resemblance to a Bond Bug with curves.

GM Lean Machine   **1980**   **USA**
Information listed under Lean Machine.

GM Minis   **1972**   **USA**
Better known as General Motors, this firm took time out from building their block long Detroit Tanks to dabble in some mini cars. The Chevy Mini was a smooth fibreglass creation with a very low profile, seating two on a bench seat it had car controls and a wrap-round windscreen just like its big brothers. A number of 4-wheeled vehicles were produced in the same exercise.

GMT Riverlain   **1981-1983**   **France**
Produced by Generale de Mecanique et Thermique in 1981 as a 4-wheeler with a Fichtel & Sachs 47cc engine – a 3-wheeler was contemplated and it is believed a few prototypes were produced.

G.N.   **1910-1928**   **GB**
H. R. Godfrey and Archie Frazer-Nash started building cycle-cars in 1910, they added a commercial traveller's car using the cyclecar chassis and a cargo box. This

was followed by a 3-wheeled light van version using a single cylinder engine – these came on to the market in 1928 and were the last vehicles built by the firm until they went out of car production in 1929.

Gnom 1950 Germany
Starting in 1921 as the Gnom 63cc clip-on engine for bicycles and built by Columbus, a firm later to be absorbed by Horax Motorcycles. 3-wheeled commercials were built at odd times and marketed under the name of Gnom, as was a neat little convertible with single front wheel and rear mounted motor.

Go-Byk 1964 USA
Built in Rothsay, Minnesota, by Go-Byk Industries, a 3-wheeled bicycle with a 3hp engine mounted over and driving the live rear axle. A 'modern' 1900's De-Dion

Godet 1919 France
The Godet Triauto was built by a M Godet, a 2-seater 3-wheeler powered by a 8/10hp engine. With the idea of future production the tricar was shown at the Paris Salon where, because of the lack of orders, no further vehicles were built.

Golem 1930s Germany
Eichler & Co of Berlin advertised the Golem as "Armchair motoring for the business man." The driver sat in armchair comfort over the engine that drove one of the two rear wheels by belt. The tiller steered single front wheel incorporated footrests with enclosed mudguards. A 2-wheeled scooter-like version was offered.

Goliath 1924-1963 Germany
The 1924 version of the Goliath Delivery Car was a very crude vehicle compared to the streamlined record breaking passenger and commercial vehicles of a few years later. It looked like a bathtub with two wheels stuck either side at the plug end. Its single front wheel was steered by an arrangements of cables and pulleys to the driver's compartment at the rear. The engine was under the tub close to the road and supplied power to the left side rear wheel via a V-belt.
   In 1931 Borgward merged with Hansa-Lloyd-Werke AG to form the Hansa-Lloyd und Goliath-Werke Borgward und Tecklenburg and proceeded to update the range of 3-wheeler commercial vehicles. Increasing engine and load capacities the new layout incorporated a single front wheel, 2-seater cab ahead of the body and shaft-drive to the rear wheels. The company had name changes in 1937, '38 and '49. Over the years improved engines included 2-cylinder 465cc, 586cc and by 1953 a 2-cylinder 700cc fuel-injected under seat unit, increasing in 1957 to a 1.09 litre 4-cylinder 4-stroke petrol engine which lasted until production changed to 4-wheeled vehicles. Body styles included van, truck, kombi and mini-bus. See Borgward.

Goliath Pioneer 1929-1935 Germany
Information under Goliath and Neimann

Goliath Rekordwagen 1951 Germany
Built for one reason only, to break records. This Goliath had a ladder chassis, underslung at the rear where the 2-cylinder Zeiakt mid-engine drove the two rear wheels via a short driveshaft; the single front wheel had semi-elliptical springing while the back wheels had full elliptical springs. The teardrop body was very low. In 1951 the Goliath broke 19 world speed records for 3-wheelers (mostly held by Morgan) with a top speed of 161km/h.

Gommel   1947   Germany
The Gommel Vehicle Construction Works of Honenheim produced a number of tricycle-based vehicles before embarking on a totally enclosed single seater coupé. Using the engine and back wheel of a 147cc single cylinder 2-stroke motorcycle it had a two piece aluminium body, of which the top half, including the windscreen, lifted up to allow entry and access to engine and luggage compartment. The front wheels, outside the bodyline, had their own mudguards that turned with the wheels. Production numbers are not known but believed to be low.

Goodchild Carrier   1907-1920   GB
Information under Autocarrier.

Goodman   1869   GB
G H Goodman, an engineer from Southwark, built a 3-wheeled dogcart that was only 8ft 6ins long and powered by a diminutive 2hp 2 cylinder steam engine capable of 8mph, final drive was by chains to the two rear wheels.

Gordon (1)   1931-1933   GB
Built by Metropolitian-Vickers Ltd of Trafford Park, Manchester. A battery/electric delivery vehicle with three small wheels shod with solid tyres. It was intended for delivery and factory work and had a top speed of 12mph. With tiller steering, single front wheel drive, the operator could work either on or off the vehicle.

Gordon (2)   1954-1958   GB
The builders advertised the Gordon as the finest 3-wheeled family car in Britain. Side by side seating for two, the single front wheel hidden under a long bonnet, the eccentrically positioned 197cc Villiers 2-stroke engine was outside the body beside the driver and covered by a blister. Drive was to one of the rear wheels only. A pram hood and the usual car type controls completed the picture. Vehicle was built in Cheshire by a division of Vernon Pools. See Vi-Car for additional information.

Gorham   1920-1922   Japan
An 8hp air-cooled twin cylinder engine powered this light 3-wheeler designed by American, William R Gorham, who resided in Japan from 1918 to oversee the construction of aircraft engines. The Jitsuyo Jidosha Automobile Company was established to market the car with its front wheel exposed motorcycle style, handlebar steering, a tandem seating body with a hood, windscreen and a single light. The underfloor engine drove the right hand rear wheel. A 4-wheel version using the same engine was also built, both were listed until 1923 and probably marketed under the name of 'Lilla'.

Goricke   1903-1959   Germany
A well-known motorcycle manufacturer who produced a 3-wheeled passenger carrier in its early years and a number of 3-wheeled commercials in later years.

Gorke   1921   Germany

Gottschalk   1900-1901   Germany
Berliner Motorwagen-Fabrik Gottschalk & Co, Berlin. As well as building a number of passenger cars using a 3hp engine they also built a 3-wheeled parcel van adapted from a motorcycle using De Dion engines.

Gova   1973   Netherlands
A light 3-wheeled delivery truck built by Gova Trucks BV, of Wormerveer. The single front wheel, combined with the engine and steering, powered these vehicles.

Grandex   1930   GB
A cargo carrier of the 1930s with the usual two front wheels and a chain-driven single rear wheel, motorcycle style.

Graiseley   1937-1939   GB
Diamond Motors Ltd Wolverhampton, built conventional battery electric delivery vans for a couple of years before concentrating on 3-wheeled pedestrian controlled cargo vehicles for factory use.

Grenville   1875   GB
The Grenville was a steam carriage employing a rear mounted vertical boiler driving the two solid tyre, steel disc rear wheels. The fireman stood on a platform at the rear while passengers were accommodated over the single small front wheel in two sets of forward facing benches, able to seat three abreast. Designed by George Jackson Churchward and Robert Neville Glenville, both star pupils in the South Devon Railways Newton Abbot workshops. This vehicle was capable of 18mph and is still running and occasionally seen at rallies today. It is possibly the only British survivor of the nostalgic days of steam passenger vehicles and is maintained by Bristol City Museum. On 28 April 1994 the Grenville repeated a famous journey of one hundred years ago, the steamer was able to maintain a steady 17mph on a journey from Butleigh Court to Glastonbury and then on to Wells.

Greyhound   1904-1905   GB
From Ashford, Middlesex came the Greyhound, a 3-speed tricar with a choice of either a 3.5hp Antoine or a 3hp Fafnir engine.

Grewe and Schutte   1904-1905   GB

Grice   1927   GB
Built by GWK of Maidenhead this was a prototype with a rear mounted 680cc air-cooled JAP V-twin engine driving the rear wheels. With coil springs all round, the 2-seater metal body had a long bonnet (enclosing the single front wheel), a vertical windscreen and a pram hood. It never went into serious production though a few were believed to have been built.

Griffon   1900s   France
A passenger trike with the wicker seat between the two front wheels and the driver sitting over the single rear wheel. Built by Courbrvoie, Seine, cycle and motor tricar manufacturers.

Grinall Scorpion   1994   GB
Futuristically designed with a lightweight fibreglass body fitted over a spaceframe chassis, this 2-seater sports car is powered by the back end of a K series BMW motorcycle grafted to the chassis. Also available in kit form this vehicle is capable of 125mph plus and comes with a price tag to match. With examples already sold to Australia and Japan it is expected that future production will head for Europe from the manufacturing plant in rural Bewdley, Worcestershire.

Grosse-Boubault 1899 France
Exhibited at the Automobile Exposition, this French tricycle was praised for its advanced design. A very small motor developing $2^1/2$ hp delivered power to the two rear wheels through an automatic friction clutch. Used as a pacer for bicycle races, this machine won many races against more powerful 4-wheel cars of the day.

Guazzoni 1949-1964 Italy
Officine Meccaniche Guazzoni, Milan, was a motorcycle factory which, from 1949, included a simple 3-wheeled light delivery vehicle, that utilised standard motorcycle components. This was a cargo carrier with a motorcycle front end, a 163cc 2-stroke engine, 4 forward gears and chain-drive to its two rear wheels.

Gurney 1820s-1840s GB
Goldsworthy Gurney was amongst the early pioneers in applying steam power to road coaches with the purpose of the carriage of freight and passengers. Gurney was a Cornishman who had trained as a surgeon, physician and a chemist. As an inventor he was credited for the introduction of limelight (a fusion of lime and magnesium) and the oxy-hydrogen blowpipe, the forerunner of the modern welding equipment. He built his first full scale steam carriage in 1825. According to Gurney's own publicity he was supposed to have built a number of carriages over the years that ranged in size and may have included the odd 3-wheeler but was better known for a mammoth 4 wheel vehicle over 20ft in length that used an extra pair of wheels on a pole in front of the coach as an aid to steering.

Guymar 1935 GB
A delivery van with a 3-wheeled layout utilising a tubular frame with a single front wheel. The engine was a single cylinder 598cc Phelon & Moore mounted at the extreme rear of the vehicle and drove the rear axle via a spur gear. The van had a capacity of 10cwt. Further press reports show a substantial and well thought out chassis with a 598cc Model 100 Red Wing Panther engine, possibly an additional prototype. A 2-seat passenger coupé and a short wheelbase tug with a 2-wheeled articulated trailer were on the drawing board. It is believed that only a few prototypes of the van were ever produced.

GWK 1930 GB
Arthur Grice, J T Wood and C M Kellor formed GWK Ltd at Maidenhead, Berks in 1910 and built a friction drive 4-wheeled car. A rear engined light delivery van was added in 1914 but it was not until 1927 that they attempted a 3-wheeler. This was an industrial truck with friction drive that appeared in their catalogue for one season only. A long nosed 3-wheeled car appeared at the same time with friction drive to the rear wheels, bench seating for two and a pram hood. The GWK faded away in favour of Imperias, a Belgian car built under licence.

Haargaard 1950 Denmark

Hamilton/Holdon 1950s Australia
Keith Hamilton built this special 3-wheeler using the rear end of a Norton 16H 500cc single (later to be replaced by a BSA 500cc twin) mated to a special built car type front end. Small front wheels were suspended from Morgan-type pillars and a modern column gearchange was fitted. The bench seat was a snug fit for three. The car is believed to still exist in South Australia.

Hammonia   1901   Germany

A standard type of tricycle with space for one passenger facing backwards on a padded seat complete with armrests. The engine was directly under the passenger seat and between the two rear wheels.

Hancock   1827-1830   GB

Walter Hancock was a professional engineer who in 1827 patented his own design for a steam engine that he proposed was light and safe. In 1829/30 he mounted it on a four passenger road vehicle with a single front wheel driven by a crank similar to the Cugnot gun carriage of 1769. Reports show he used the carriage as a test bed for the boiler and made many journeys totalling many hundreds of miles.

Hanomag   1905-1970   Germany

The Hanomag firm was started under the name of Hannoversche Maschinenbau AG, at Linden near Hanover, building steam trucks. There were many name changes until 1963 when they took over Tempo Vehicles and maintained the Tempo range of 3-wheeled light trucks. Much improved and now with rear wheel drive but still using the same cabin and body styles. In 1970 the name and body dies were sold to Bajaj Motors in India where the 3-wheeled vehicles are still manufactured under the Bajaj name and exported to many countries bordering the Indian continent. More information under Tempo and Neimann.

Hans Vahaar   1960s   India

The Fuldamobil built under licence from Germany. For more see Fuldamobil.

Hansa   1925-1935   Germany

Information noted under Neimann.

Hantsch, Johann   1649   Germany

In 1649 Johann Hantsch of Nuremberg built a novel carriage. Two large wheels with a single armchair fitted directly above the axle, a single rear wheel on a castor and steering achieved by applying a brake to one of the main wheels. Power came from a clockwork spring arrangement. Reports indicate it had a great reputation throughout Germany and was later sold to Prince Charles Agustus of Sweden.

Harbilt   1947 to date   GB

Harborough Construction Co Ltd, Market Harborough, Leics, started producing pedestrian controlled factory 1 ton capacity battery electric trucks, with a variety of body styles using a 4-wheel configuration. In 1960 the vehicles were improved and ride-on driver-controlled 3-wheelers were added with a 1.5 ton capacity. Since 1973 the company has concentrated on both 3- and 4-wheeled battery-electric personnel-carriers sold under the name of Harbilt-Melex.

Hardy   1905-1906   GB

Possibly the first 'kit car', the Hardy tricar was supplied as a chassis with a 6hp water-cooled twin cylinder Stevens engine and a kit of parts to be completed by the customer. Most buyers were enthusiasts who built specials for racing and hill climbing – much the same as the specials of today.

Harley-Davidson   1901 to date   USA

Better known for their chrome covered 2-wheelers, William 'Bill' Harley and Arthur

Davidson built their first engine in 1901. Originally it was destined for a boat but instead was put into a bicycle frame. Further developed, the first motorcycle was produced in 1903, clocking up over 100,000 miles over the next ten years. In 1916 a V-twin delivery vehicle was built utilising the 1000cc engine in the standard configuration of a box between the two front wheels and the driver behind the load. In 1932 the ServiCar entered the market as a police bike with the two wheels at the rear and a seat over the box. For civilian use this box was designed to suit and many variations were seen. This form continues today with the majority of these 3-wheeled vehicles used for police work. In 1908 the Northover/Harley-Davidson machine-gun carrier was built as an experimental vehicle by Sergeant Northover of the Canadian Militia, using a sidecar frame to mount a heavy Maxim machine gun. An idea quickly taken up by other armies and widely used in all wars since then.

Harley Davidson   1928-1930   Japan.
A number of commercial trikes were built in Japan using engines imported from America.

Harper   1921-1926   GB
Designed by R O Harper and built by the A V Roe and Co Ltd, this was an early cross between a motor scooter and a small cyclecar. With an enclosing slab-sided metal body/chassis, the single front wheel was under a long overhang and steered by handlebars. The 269cc Villiers air-cooled single cylinder 2-stroke engine with three forward speeds with a cone clutch and chain-drive to the rear wheels was located under the back-to-back seating. Brakes were an early forerunner of the modern discs. Some 500 vehicles were built.

Harper Runabout   1921-1926   GB
Using aircraft construction techniques the Harper Runabout was built at the Avro (A V Roe) aircraft factory at Manchester as a single seat 3-wheeled runabout with a 269cc Villiers engine driving the rear wheels. Using integral body-chassis construction, this nippy vehicle was able to do 80/100 miles per gallon of fuel with a top speed of 40mph. It came equipped with a 3-speed gearbox and disc brakes, and accommodation for a pillion passenger. The rear seat was placed on the body with foot-rests forming part of the rear mudguards – no place for the girlfriend in the long a dresses of the '20s. Another version had the passenger facing the rear with a common backrest shared with the driver.

Hawkins-Xenia   1914   USA
For more information see Xenia.

Hayball   1864   GB
Charles T Hayball of Lymington, Hampshire built a 3-wheeled steam carriage weighing less than two tons and able to carry 10 passengers at up to speeds of 20mph. Power came from a 2-cylinder engine with drive to the two rear wheels.

HD   1930s   Japan.
A very solid cargo trike using a pressed metal frame and a 498cc engine of their own make.

Heathfield Slingshot   1993 to date   GB
Another Morgan lookalike with the engine between the two front wheels and the

single rear wheel clothed in a long boat tail with the spare fitting neatly into the stern. Using a robust spaceframe tube chassis with power from a Honda Cx V-twin 500cc or 650cc engine. Built by Highfield Automotive of Chesterfield as a kit car.

Heinkel   1955-1958   **Germany.**
The Heinkel Kabin was similar to the Isetta and the BMW600 with a front opening door, using a 175cc (later 198cc) 4-stroke air-cooled engine with a fuel economy of 100mpg and a top speed of 56mph. The rear driving wheels were a few inches apart on examples built in Germany, while those built in Ireland and the UK a single rear wheel only was used. Seating was for two side by side with a parcels compartment, or a child's bench seat, over the engine in the rear of the cabin. A number of convertibles were built by sealing up the front door and removing the cabin down to waist height. To enter you simply stepped over the side and slipped into your seat.
  Heinkel production in Ireland was over 8,000 vehicles. In Argentina production was about 2,000. In England the Heinkel became the Trojan in 1958. Overall more than 30,000 units were built.
More information under Trojan.

Heinle & Wegelin   1899-1900s   **Germany**
A firm located at Augsburg in Germany who constructed motorised trikes along Bollée lines and exported to France and England. The Patent Trading Syndicate Motor Company of Chiswell Street in London, were the British importers.

Helicak, Helitruck, Helipickup   1970 to date   **Indonesia**
See Italindo for more information.

Helo   1923-1925   **Germany**
Built both 2- and 3-wheeled motorcycles and cargo carriers using 149cc 2-stroke Bekamo engines.

Henriod   1888-1899   **Switzerland**
The first vehicle built by Fritz Henriod of Bienne in Switzerland was a steam tricycle in 1888. He built a single cylinder 4-wheeled car in 1893 followed by a rear engined vehicle that went into production in 1896 and ended in 1899.

Hercules   1932-1933   **Germany**
One of the early cars that combined motorcycle techniques for propulsion, not unusual as the Nurnberger Hercules Werke AG, Nuremberg had produced motorcycles since 1904. A metal car body in hard top coupé configuration, semi streamlined, car controls and a boat tail rear that hid a 200cc Schnellgong or Ilo engine and single rear wheel hooked up motorcycle style. Design was by Abram Neimann. More information under that name.

Hero   1934   **Germany**

Heros (1)   1921-1929   **Germany**
A Saxony-based firm that built a few commercial trikes. Known formally as H & R.

Heros (2)   1923-1924   **Germany**
A commercial 3-wheeler built in Berlin using a 142cc DKW engine.

Highway   **1918-1919**   **USA**
The Highway Tractor Company of Indianapolis built a 3-ton, 3-wheeled tractor with a Martin fifth wheel coupling for warehouse use. It had an unusual feature that the single front wheel was used not only for steering but had the engine and the driver's seat all combined into the one unit.

Highland   **1894-1900s**   **Australia**
C. Highland, 93 Market Street, Sydney, were possibly one of the first to build motorised transport in Australia. Charles Highland and his son Charles Jnr, built their first motor tricycle in 1894 using a Daimler engine and hot tube ignition. A number of trikes were built, followed in 1897 by a 4-wheeled car using a De Dion engine, together with motorcycles, powered lawnmowers and electric lighting.

Hille   **1898**   **Germany**
A German adaptation of the De Dion tricycle using a 1.25hp air-cooled engine. Only a few were produced.

Hillman Sociable   **1880s**   **France**
It was noted in the press that the Frenchman Raffard had converted a Hillman Sociable Tricycle to electric power in 1881 and later that same year built the first electric car of note. Alas it was a 4-wheeler.

Hino   **1961 to date**   **Japan**
Starting as an off-shoot of the Tokyo Gasu Denki in 1917, Hino Motors went through several name changes until assuming its present name in 1959. Better known for their heavy trucks and buses they took over the marketing of the Humbee range of 3-wheeled light vans and trucks from 1961 until the 3-wheeled vehicle faded from the Japanese scene in the '70s. More information see Humbee.

Hirano   **1936-1940**   **Japan**
Hirano Siezakusho Ltd, Nagoya, were loom makers when they ventured into the manufacture of a 3-wheeled delivery truck built with the front half of a motorcycle mated to a delivery box rear end. Steering was by the single front wheel and chain-drive to the two rear wheels. Engines were Hirano 675cc units. Production began in 1936 with 105 units in the first year and carried on until the start of the Pacific War. They entered the transport field again with a range of motor scooters built between 1952 and 1960.

H M Freeway   **1979-1983**   **USA**
Starting life as a battery powered shopping commuter, this was a fully enclosed tandem seating fibreglass hatchback, with entry through a single side door into the cabin. Shopping was deposited through a small rear hatch. A petrol version soon followed with a claimed top speed of 55mph.
  Originally built by H M Freeway of Minnesota, the project changed owners in 1982 then faded from view.

Hobart-Bird   **1905-1907**   **GB**
Built by Hobart-Bird & Co, Coventry, as a cargo carrier with the carrier box placed in front of the driver. Power was from a 4.5hp water-cooled White & Poppe engine transferred to the single rear wheel by a chain. Production was dropped around 1907 in favour of motorcycles which continued to be built until 1923.

Holley 1897-1904 USA
George H M Holley began building tiller steered 3-wheelers in 1899 before moving to 4-wheelers with steering wheels and seating for two. All vehicles were dropped from the catalogues in 1904. His factory was in Bradford, Pennsylvania.

Holmes 1895 USA
A trike of ungainly design, with direct drive to a live rear axle housed in a box resembling an upright piano was the report in the *Horseless Age*, an American automobile magazine in the 1890s.

Honda Dream Car 1990s Japan
Specially built for the annual Solar Powered Race from Darwin, Australia, this 3-wheeled single-seater has been 'clocked' at 130km/h. The single rear wheel has an electric motor in the hub, a style first pioneered in the 1890s. Power is from a roof of solar panels. In 1993 it did 3,013km in just over 4 days, averaging 84km/h.

Honda Trike 1990s Australia
A special converted in Australia, using a Honda motor scooter as the donor vehicle. A fibreglass tub over a metal frame with a flat floor able to hold a wheelchair. The front end accommodates the complete front of the scooter to provide for the steering, lights, etc. The motor, complete with enclosed chain and wheel, is mounted exposed on the right hand corner under a wide skirt with a matching wheel on the opposite corner, while a ramp forms the back of the vehicle. This allows the freedom of wind in the hair for the wheelchair-bound, in a sporty little vehicle that can hold its own in city traffic.

Hope Star 1952-1962 Japan
Hope Jidosha Co, Tokyo, built a 3-wheeled truck with a 7cwt load capacity. The power came from an unusual 350cc twin-piston 2-stroke engine driving the two rear wheels. A range of bodies were available. A 4-wheeled 5cwt truck was introduced in 1960 as well as an ultralight 4x4. No more vehicles listed after 1962.

Horex 1923-1960 Germany
For more information see Gnom.

Hornet 1994 to date Australia
Using a donor motorcycle this trike is customised to the owner's specifications using an 'A'-frame swing arm in aluminium box section, mated to a Harley differential to the widely spaced rear wheels. The conversion is covered in aluminium sheet and high gloss painted. Baggage carriers can be added. Conversion is designed to be easily reverted back to two wheels.

Horrocks 1918 GB

Hostaco Bambino 1952-1957 Netherlands
Built by the Dutch company Hostaco Mobiel, these 3-wheeled cars followed the style of the Fuldamobil with a leather covering over a wooden frame. Seating two they were powered by a 197cc Ilo single cylinder 2-stroke motor developing 9.5 hp.

Howard 1906-1907 GB
A sociable tricar with side by side padded seating. A Fafnir twin cylinder water-

cooled engine was enclosed under a front bonnet and carried on a tubular chassis that featured semi elliptical springs on all three wheels. Power was transmitted to the single rear wheel through a 3-speed gearbox with final drive by chain. Steering wheel and normal car controls were used.

Howecette　　　　　　　　　　**1980s**　　　　　　　　　　　　**GB**
After a lifetime of motorcycle riding and a wish to get something safer, Mr Howe decided to build his own machine. The front axle wheels and steering were fabricated from a 1930s Y Ford. The driving train came from his trusty water-cooled Velocette, all clothed in an aluminium body with contoured seating for one. Mr Howe and his creation were regular visitors to microcar rallies.

Hoxon　　　　　　　　　　　**1930s**　　　　　　　　　　　**Japan**
A cargo trike using a home produced 650cc engine or an imported JAP 670cc unit.

H.P.　　　　　　　　　　　**1926-1928**　　　　　　　　　　　**GB**
Hilton Peacey Motors from Woking, Surrey, built about 40 very fast cyclecars. A 500cc JAP single cylinder engine drove the lone rear wheel through a Sturmey-Archer gearbox with final chain-drive.

HSM　　　　　　　　　　　　**1913-1915**　　　　　　　　　　　**GB**

Hubbard　　　　　　　　　　**1904-1905**　　　　　　　　　　　**GB**
Built in Coventry, this advanced tricar had a coachbuilt body and front wheel brakes – the 4.5hp engine drove the single rear wheel.

Hudson Free Spirit　　　　　**1989 to date**　　　　　　　　　　**GB**
Built in 1989 by Roy Webb for his own enjoyment, the Hudson was for the loner. It had luxury seating for the driver under a classy fibreglass body with donor parts from a Renault 5 housed in a straight forward twin rail chassis. The long body with widely spaced front wheels under cycle guards made this an impressive vehicle. So much so that orders started rolling in. Improvements followed after requests for more room so a tandem 2-seater was produced and marketed under the name of Kindred Spirit. More than 140 examples have been built with vehicles exported to America, Germany, New Zealand and South Africa.

Humbee-Surrey　　　　　　　**1947-1962**　　　　　　　　　　**Japan**
Mitsui Precision Machinery Co, had its origin in Okegawa about the time of the First World War. When manufacturing restarted in 1947 they began producing 3-wheeled vehicles, including light vans and trucks with a 285cc single cylinder engine transmitting power to the two rear wheels via a chain. Later products were given fibreglass cabins and a range of bodies including vans, trucks and Surrey with a detachable top and space for three passengers. The company sub-contracted for Hino in 1961 who marketed the Humbee range as Hino from 1962.

Humber　　　　　　　　　　**1896-1976**　　　　　　　　　　　**GB**
Nottingham born Thomas Humber established a bicycle business there in 1868 and with the advent of the internal combustion engine it was not long before he was experimenting with powered tricycles. His first vehicle the Forecar was offered for sale in 1896 from a factory in Coventry where after a number of moves he had settled in Humbertown, a self contained community. The first tricycle was actually

a bicycle, with a 2.5hp single cylinder engine running at 750rpm, attached to a tubular frame for two front wheels which had a cane chair slung between for the passenger. While improving the 3-wheeled vehicles, Humber was also experimenting with 4-wheeled vehicles. By 1904, the Humber Olympia tricar had advanced to a comfortable wrap-around padded seat for the driver, a raked steering wheel, a fully enclosed 5hp single cylinder engine driving the rear wheel, and a comfortable metal framed padded chair for the passenger. The only weather protection supplied was a waterproof sheet for the passenger's compartment.

As the 4-wheeled cars gained popularity so the 3-wheelers were gradually withdrawn.

Humberett 1905-1909 GB
Information under Coventry Eagle.

Hunslet 1957-1965 GB
Information under Scootacar.

Huracan 1955-1960 Spain
Huracan Motors SA, Barcelona, built a range of 3-wheeled vehicles alongside 4-wheelers during their 5 years of production. The 3-wheeled cargo carriers were powered by 25cc or 197cc single cylinder Hispano-Villiers engines.

Husqvarna 1943 Sweden
Bicycle and arms firm making motorcycles. A 3-wheeler commercial listed in 1934.

Hyogo HMC 1930s Japan
The HMC commercial trike used the usual configuration of a single front wheel with the cargo box between the two rear wheels. Power came from a 2 cylinder 750cc HMC engine. Production for the year 1937 was 611 units.

Imperia 1927 Germany
Following the continental lines of the parcels box in front of the driver, Imperia-Werk A.G. of Bad Godesberg, built a trivan with power to the single rear wheel from an engine made in their own factory.

Inder 1898 GB
Built by Henry I Inder of Dartmouth, this is believed to have been the first car ever seen in this seaside town. Loosely following the Bollée layout of a single rear wheel, this vehicle was designed by Inder with a two passenger bench-type seat in front of the driver but behind the front axle. The carburettor was of his own creation and almost as big as the single cylinder engine. Power was transmitted to the rear wheel through a series of chains and shafts from the engine located under the passenger seat while the driver sat in a padded armchair over the rear wheel.

Indian (1) 1901-1970s USA
George Hendee and Oscar Hedstrom founded the Hendee Manufacturing Co in Springfield, Massachusetts in 1900 to build the popular moto-cycle, basically a bicycle with a add on engine. Early production models established the firm's reputation for quality. They soon added a trike with a padded seat between the two front wheels. This was listed as the Indian Chair Cycle and became popular as a motorised rickshaw in Cuba and other outlying tourist Islands. Replacing the chair

with a box we had a popular goods vehicle, built in quantity between 1905-1910.

Indian (2)   1928-1930   Japan
A number of commercial trikes were built in Japan using Indian motorcycle engines and parts imported from the American factory.

Induhag   1922   Germany

Inter   1953-1956   France
The French equivalent of the Messerschmitt but with innovations: the two front wheels were capable of folding upwards under the car allowing easy entry through a doorway to enable parking in the hallway! Power came from a single cylinder 2-stroke Ydral 175cc engine, with a 50mph top speed.

Internationale   1942   Netherlands

Intramotor-Gloria   1972 to date   Italy
Intramotor-Gloria SpA, Arcole, Verona are builders of 3-wheeled cargo carriers – ultra-light delivery vehicles using a 49cc F. B. Mimarelli engine with uncoupled 3-wheel brakes and leaf spring rear suspension. A range of bodies include vans and dropside trays and also a miniature refrigerated van. The Titano, introduced in 1978, could carry 250kg.

Invacar   1947-1975   GB
Originally designed as motorised transport for the disabled, the Invacar progressed from an open box where the driver could enter by a rear ramp and control the vehicle from his wheel chair. A side-mounted 1.25hp motor drove one of the two rear wheels while the motorcycle front wheel was tiller steered. By 1952 the vehicle had advanced to a soft top with a vertical windscreen, side curtains and a rear luggage compartment. More advancement saw a top speed of 55mph, fully enclosed fibreglass car-type bodies, controls to suit the driver, independent suspension and larger engines. By 1974, changes in the law and the use of the ordinary car with adapted controls saw the end of vehicles built specially for the disabled.

Iresa   1956-1959   Spain
Industrias Reunidas Espanolas S.A. of Madrid, motorcycle manufacturers who built 3-wheeled cargo vans from 1956 to 1959. With a fully enclosed one man cabin using the standard motorcycle front wheel and handlebar steering, these vehicles came in a variety of van and truck bodies. Power came from a 200cc engine with final drive by shaft to the rear axle.

Isetta   1953-1955   Italy
A 3-wheeled bubble car with a front opening door and cramped seating for two. Built by Revolta Iso SpA, of Milan. Not very successful it was sold to BMW in Germany who improved the vehicle and found it to be a gold mine.

Isetta-BMW   1955-1962   Germany
The German BMW company obtained a licence from Revolta Iso SpA and soon improved it by using their own 247cc engine. Body styles and engines were improved, the single rear wheel soon became two very close together but still it was classed as a 3-wheeler. 162,000 were built in Germany and even more under

licence in England and Ireland. Amongst its many nicknames it became known as the 'rolling egg'. Body variations include saloon, convertible, panel van and pickup.
In the late 1950s the RAC used a modified fleet of 6 for traffic duty in London.

Iso   1950-1960   **Italy/Spain**

Iso SpA, Bresso, Milan, were building motor scooters when they introduced a commercial 3-wheeler with a payload of 300kg and a 125cc engine with shaft-drive to the back axle. By 1963 vehicles had a fully enclosed two man cabin, a variety of enclosed van bodies and a larger payload. Built in Spain under licence by Borgward Iso Ecpanola SA they were sold as the Isocarro, an improved version with a payload of 400kg, a larger engine featuring a 4-speed and reverse gearbox. Other cars built were the Isetta bubble car with a double piston 2-stroke 236cc engine. After the bubble car market 'burst' in the early 1960s the Iso Milan factory built big luxury cars using Ghia and Bertone bodywork and big Chevrolet V-8 engines.

Isocarro   1950-1966   **Spain**
Information under Iso.

ISSI   1953-1954   **Italy**

Italindo   1970 to date   **Indonesia**
P.T. Italindo, Jakarta, assembled the range of Lambretta 3-wheelers and using the same chassis with a 148cc single cylinder 2-stroke engine produced a taxi called the Helicak with tiller steering to the single front wheel. In the 1970s they imported the British Reliant chassis and built the Super Helicak passenger range of vehicles with a modern slab-sided fibreglass body, side opening doors and full car type controls, it was built to carry three passengers and the driver. The Super Helicak comes in a standard or deluxe trim and is built in large numbers to fulfil the vast transportation needs of Indonesia. Using the same Reliant chassis we also have the Helitruck and a pickup to satisfy the commercial needs of the country. Many are exported to other Asian countries.

Itar   1928-1929   **Czechoslovakia**
Itar Tovarna Motocyklu, Prague-Radlice, was established as a motorcycle manufacturer about 1920. A number of delivery tricycles were built in 1928 powered by 350cc engines and with a load capacity of 100kg. After selling a few machines to neighbouring countries, production reverted back to the 2-wheeled cycles in 1929.

Ivy Karryall   1929-1930   **GB**
A 3-wheeled pick-up truck that in 1930 became the Raleigh. See under that name.

Ivry   1905-1907   **France & GB**
A tricar with a 5.6hp engine and 2-speed gears built by an electric company.

Iwasaki   1932-1942   **Japan**
Asahi Nainenki K.K. started building commercial delivery vehicles in the standard Japanese style in 1932. With a motorcycle front end and the two rear wheels driven from an engine situated under the driver, the large cargo box was situated between the rear wheels.
One version was used by the Japanese army as a troop carrier during the Second World War.

Jackson 1899-1914 GB

Reynold Jackson & Co Ltd of Altrincham built his first doctors' carriage in 1899, a 3-wheeled 2-seater using a 3.5hp De Dion engine. He built a variety of vehicles over the years using Lacost & Battmann chassis and De Dion engines until introducing in 1913 a JAP 12hp V-twin engined 3-wheeler, with chain drive to a single rear wheel. It had a substantial channel steel frame chassis with a modern appearance for its day. Using the car chassis, a parcel van was offered with limited space in a box in front of the driver. The advent of the First World War ended production.

Jackson and Kimmys 1900-1906 GB

By 1904 this machine had many advanced features, including a raked steering wheel, a tubular chassis frame, a 8hp MMC single cylinder water-cooled engine, with a block-type radiator (mounted at the front of the vehicle in modern car style) which drove the single rear wheel by means of chains and a gearbox. The single seat was enclosed in a form of cabin: it was much ahead of its time.

James 1929-1939 GB

James Cycle Co Ltd of Birmingham, were better known as motorcycle manufacturers when they introduced their 3-wheeled Handyman in 1929, using their motorcycle front end and chain driven rear live axle. A box body was installed between the rear wheels and had a capacity of 5cwt. Early machines had a 247cc 2-stroke Villiers engine. Updated in 1931 the engine was a 500cc side-valve twin of their own manufacture and the body had a basic cab for driver protection added.

1933 saw the introduction of a new vehicle: the Samson, boasting a welded steel frame, steering wheel, 3 speed gears and a spiral bevel final-drive from a 1096cc engine. By 1935 its load capacity had been increased to 12cwt and the cabin improved to allow room for a passenger but still without doors. Production ceased in 1939 with the onset of the Second World War. More information under Samson.

Janssen 1934-1940 Netherlands

Building a number of 3-wheeled commercial vehicles, the firm of W A Janssens & Zoon, of Rotterdam started with a light duty model increasing in size and style until 1935 with the introduction of 5G model with a capacity of 1000kg using a 2-cylinder Ilo 2-stroke engine transmitting power to the rear wheels. The single front wheel was used for steering. By 1938 the range had been increased to a load capacity of 1250kg powered by a 400cc 2-cylinder air-cooled Ilo 2-stroke engine. The company never recovered after the Second World War.

JAP Dual Car 1905-1906 GB

The JAP Dual Car was built by the firm of J A Preswich and Co, better known for their motorcycle engines that were to power so many other vehicles for many generations. Designed by a Mr A E Bower-Lowe, the Dual Car had two very substantial side by side armchair style padded seats, a steering wheel, lamps mounted on the two front mudguards and power from one of their own 3-cylinder 8hp engines driving the single rear wheel from a location just behind the front axle giving a low centre of gravity and stability not so well known in so many of the early 3-wheelers. Over the two years that the Dual Cars were in production a limited number only were built.

Jawa 1950-1952 Czechoslovakia

Established builder of motorcycles, Zbrojovka Brno n.p. of Prague-Nusle built a small number of delivery tricycles from Jawa 250 type 11 components. Using stock front forks, fuel tank and saddle, the Jawa 250cc 2-stroke engine drove, by chain, the two rear wheels. A variety of bodies were offered with a 200kg cargo capacity.

JBF Boxer 1992 GB
John Fernley had plans for this do-it-yourself trike, built along traditional lines using a 2CV as the donor for engine and parts. Similar in shape to a 1950's Morgan, the only vehicle produced was stylish and looked good on the road.

JB Minor 1949 Australia
Manufactured for the Automotive Company of Australia by the Jeffres Brothers, Northgate, Brisbane, the JB Minor was supposed to satisfy the war-starved Australians for a car, any sort of car. Featuring hydraulic transmission, front wheel drive, 3-wheel independent coil springing, hydro-balanced rear wheel steering (single wheel), all metal construction and low price. A 2-seater hardtop, step-over-the-side entry and removable side curtains. A number of prototypes were built.

Jephcott Micro 1983 GB
Engineer Dr Jephcott was a pioneer in the use of technology that allowed the body of a 3-wheeler to lean into a corner and act like a motorcycle. The Jephcott Micro was a totally enclosed single or tandem seater with a side opening door in a smart and functional fibreglass body. The project did not get past the prototype stage.

Jet 1955 Spain

JMB 1933-1936 GB
Produced in Ringwood as a 2-seater sports car or a 3-seater sports saloon, this natty 3-wheeler was powered by a 497cc JAP single cylinder 21bhp ohv engine, with a 3-speed box driving the fully enclosed single rear wheel. A motorcycle style kick start was used to fire up the engine, which proved to be under powered. The bodies of the 1934 models were fabric covered while 1935 saw metal panelling. The long front bonnet was for luggage while the engine was tucked in beside the rear wheel. Designed by G H Jones, the car was named after the initials of the partners, R W Mason and Cecil Barlow. The company went out of business in 1936 after about 250 vehicles had been built.

Junior 1954-1961 Spain
S.L. Barcelona built a line of tubular framed delivery tricycles with a single rear wheel, chain-driven from a 197cc Hispano-Villiers single cylinder engine fitted motorcycle style under the driver. The wooden cargo tray or metal box was in front of the driver who used motorcycle handlebars to steer the two front wheels. Body variations included a tipper tray.

JZR 1994 to date GB
Created by John Zembia Restorations, this is a trike with a motorcycle engine driving the single rear wheel. It looks like a very close relation to the pre-war Morgan. As a kit car it comes with a multi-tube chassis and a steel panelled body with the hood and rear in fibreglass. Donor engines can be Honda CX500 or Moto-Guzzi V-twins. Continual updates have created a choice of bodies, a barrel back or a boat tail, and engines have included a 1100cc Honda or a 1340cc Harley Davidson for increased performance. Production has exceeded 250 units to date.

Kaiser   **1935**   **Germany**
Kaiser Fahrzeugbau, Aschersleben, built a 3-wheeled car with a way-out aerodynamic Zeppelin-shaped body, widely spaced front wheels in totally enclosed spats, a single rear wheel and a 200cc (or up to 600cc) NSU or Columbus-Horex single cylinder motorcycle engine, enclosed in the body with a large air scoop above the body line. It had a single seat, large steering wheel, full car controls and a half door and windscreen resembling an aircraft cockpit. Speeds above 75mph were claimed.

Kapi   **1950-1958**   **Spain**
Army Captain turned vehicle manufacturer, Federico Saldana Ramos, built 3-wheelers at Gefisa, Barcelona, using 2cv single cylinder 2-stroke engines.

Karivan (1)   **1930**   **GB**
For information see Vanette.

Karivan (2)   **1955**   **USA**
Tri-Car Inc. Wheatland, Pa., built a 3-wheeled passenger car and, using the same chassis, produced a forward controlled van powered by a 30hp Lycoming vertical twin engine with Westinghouse-Schneider torque converter and drive to its single rear wheel. Goodrich torsilastic rubber suspension on all three wheels gave the van a 700lbs capacity.

Karrier   **1908-1970**   **GB**
Karrier Motors Ltd, Huddersfield, Yorks started life as Clayton & Co (Huddersfield) Ltd, builders of heavy commercial trucks. In 1931 they built the 3-wheeled Colt, a 2-ton mechanical horse powered by a 7hp Jowett flat twin engine. An improved model was called the Cob and powered by a 4-cylinder Humber engine with shaft-drive to the rear wheels (dual tyred for added traction). The fully enclosed roomy cabin had space for the driver and mate. Standard automotive controls completed the workplace with a very large steering wheel coupled to the single front wheel that allowed the vehicle to almost turn in its own length. The Karrier Cob had a variety of bodies including an interchangeable dropside tray body that could be replaced by a articulated trailer.
    Regulations made building the 3-wheeled heavy-duty vehicles impossible so production changed to 4-wheelers in the late '60s.

Keinath   **1949**   **Germany**
A totally enclosed single seater. The entire front cabin along with the steering wheel lifted to allow entry. A motorcycle rear end enclosed under a sloping tail supplied power. Two small front wheels had mudguards that turned with the wheels.

Keller-Dagenhardt   **1890s**   **USA**
Powered by an electric motor, two 3-wheeled carts were built for the 1890 American Exposition. With the driver sitting on an extended seat behind the rear axle, without the two passengers in the seat just in front of the two rear wheels, the vehicle would have been very unstable. The small single front wheel was directed by a tiller from the rear.

Kelsey (1)   **Early 1900s**   **GB**
A tricycle built in Kent.

Kelsey (2)   1898-1924   USA

American motoring pioneer C W Kelsey built his first car, the Auto-Tri, in 1898. His subsequent offerings were 4-wheelers called Pilgrim and Spartan. He spent some time as sales manager for Maxwell, then formed his own Kelsey motor car company in 1921. He is probably better known for the Motorette (more under that name).

Kelsey Motorette (3)   1910-1912   USA

The Kelsey Motorette was built by the C W Kelsey Manufacturing Company at Hartford, Connecticut. More information under Motorette.

Kent's Pacemaker   1900   USA

This was another oddity in the early motoring world. Built by the Colonial Company of Boston it had the usual single front steering wheel but at the other end we had three wheels, the centre one powered by a steam engine while the other two acted as outriggers and could be raised to allow the vehicle to behave like a motorcycle. It is believed only one or two were made.

Kerry (1)   1905-1907   GB

Tony Huber & Thams Cars built a tricar with the usual basket forecarriage. Using an A-type tubular frame, the V-twin engine was slung low down and supplied power to the rear wheel via a belt. They also built 10/12hp 4-wheeled cars.

Kerry (2)   1965-1968   GB

Kerrys Ltd London had a 3-wheeled ultra-light parcels carrier built for them in Italy, utilising a 50cc 2-stroke F B Minarelli engine with a 3-speed gearbox and uncoupled 3-wheeled brakes. It was not popular and few were sold.

Kettenkrad   1940-1945   Germany

This was an all-terrain vehicle built by NSU using a standard motorcycle front end mated to a tracked cargo box. It resembled a miniature Bren gun carriage, able to tow multiple trailers and was used extensively by the German Army in Africa.

Kikos   1980-1983   France

Kindred Spirit   1990 to date   GB

See Hudson Free Spirit for more information.

King   1904   GB

Using what was a standard format, a 5hp water-cooled engine drove the single rear wheel, and the driver sat in a well-padded seat over the engine while the passenger or cargo box was situated between the two front wheels, ahead of the driver.

Kiwiwagon   Mid 1960   New Zealand

Developed by the Government's Department of Scientific and Industrial Research, the Kiwiwagon was a 3-wheeler, chain-driven single rear wheel via a Ford 3-speed gearbox and a Ford 100E engine. The idea is believed to have gone past prototype stage in developing New Zealand's own low cost car. The known example is said to handle well and demonstrates care and workmanship in its concept.

Klaus   1894-1899   France

A trike with a belt-driven single rear wheel built in Lyon. Unusual was the dead man's handle – if you took your hand off the tiller then the vehicle came to a halt.

Knap　　　　　　　　　　　　**1898-1904**　　　　　**Belgium & France**
Frenchman George Knapp built his first production car in Belgium in 1898, a 3-wheeled voiturette-type vehicle with a 4hp engine. In 1904 he returned to France to build 4-wheelers.

Knight (1)　　　　　　　　　　**1860-1896**　　　　　　　　　　　　**GB**
John Henry Knight of Surrey had built steam cars during the late 1860s and by 1893 he had produced a 3-wheeled single bench seat, petrol driven car. It was a tiller steered single front wheeler with the petroleum engine located just in front of the rear axle and under the seat that would accommodate two. It was so far advanced, coil springs to all wheels, that it went into limited production in 1894.

It seems another version was built in 1895 because the remains of a 1895 Knight car is in the National Motor Museum at Beaulieu – a photo and caption shows a V-shaped chassis with the two front wheels at the top of the V, a single cylinder engine under the seat (about the centre of the vehicle) driving, via a belt, the single rear wheel at the point of the V. John Henry Knight was convicted for speeding near Farnham, Surrey in 1896 - his speed was 9mph.

Knight (2)　　　　　　　　　　**1955**　　　　　　　　　　　　　**Spain**

Knollner　　　　　　　　　　　**1924**　　　　　　　　　　　**Germany**

Knox　　　　　　　　　　　　**1895-1924**　　　　　　　　　　　　**USA**
Starting as the Knox Automobile Co Springfield, Massachusetts, with many name changes during its history, the first Knox was actually built by H A Knox at the old Waltham Watch Tool factory in 1895 but production did not start until 1899 by the Overman Cycle Company. These were 3-wheelers with an air-cooled 'porcupine' engine, using pegs instead of fins on the cylinder head. The formation of the Knox Automobile Co in 1901 saw production of a delivery van version of the car with a 4hp single cylinder air-cooled engine (like all Knoxs until 1908). These were basic vehicles with 2 forward gears, no reverse and tiller steering to the single front wheel. The construction of 4-wheelers began in 1903. By 1909 the Knox-Martin appeared, a 3-wheeled articulated tractor powered by a 40hp 4-cylinder ohv engine in two sizes for pulling either 5 or 10 ton loads. The single front wheel was placed well in front of the engine and had a lock of almost 90 degrees while the two rear wheels were duals with solid deeply grooved rubber tyres. Power was transmitted by shaft with the final drive by double chains.

The production of the 3-wheeled cars and vans lasted until 1910 while the tractors were in production until 1915. A 4-wheeled version saw service during the First World War while ex-army vehicles were still in use well into the late 1930s.

Knox-Martin　　　　　　　　　**1909-1924**　　　　　　　　　　　　**USA**
The first Knox-Martin tractors were produced after the return of former Knox employee, Charles Hay Martin. He had patented a system of attaching a 2-wheeled trailer to a tractor known as the Martin Rocking Fifth wheel. In 1913 a new firm, Knox-Martin Tractors, was formed and moved in to new premises 200 yards up the road from the parent company – the range increased to a 5 ton and a 10 ton 3-wheeled Tug. The 10 tonner had a longer wheelbase but both were able, by changing sprockets on the chain-drive, to attain a top speed of 10mph or 33mph.

By 1915 they had added a fourth wheel but so sturdy were the 3-wheelers that many were still running into the late 1930s. More information under Knox.

Kohler 1922-1928 Germany

This was a trike with a difference. A pipe platform chassis starting with a motorcycle front wheel, handlebars and hand controls, a walk-through platform, footrest, and tandem seating for two (in padded armchair-type comfort) located over the engine bay, and chain-drive to a live rear axle. The passenger straddled the engine and had footrests, motorcycle style.

Kreibich 1949 Czechoslovakia

Designed by a brilliant engineer, Vaclav Krejbich, this was a 2-seater experimental vehicle with a cabriolet body. Powered by a variety of engines including 200cc, 250cc and 300cc built by Jawa driving the single rear wheel. Top speed 80km/h.

Kroboth 1951-1955 Germany

Using a 200cc Ilo fan-cooled single cylinder 2-stroke engine, fitted just in front of the single rear wheel in a wishbone chassis, and clothed in an open 2-seater side by side body, with a pram hood as an option. Side curtains cost extra. Claimed top speed was 80km/h. Various engine sizes were reported including a 174cc Fichtel & Sachs single cylinder with an electric starter operating from a 12 volt battery.

KRS 1918-1930s Japan

Built by Yamanari Motors with either English JAP engines or one of their own engines, this was a cargo trike with the carry box between the two rear wheels.

Kurier 1948 Czechoslovakia

Kurogane 1928-1962 Japan

Like most Japanese motor manufacturers, name changes of vehicles occur. The Nippon Jidosha Co, Ohmori, Tokyo, was no exception. They built a 3-wheeled commercial with a typical motorcycle front end with a car-type back axle carrying a truck body. The first vehicles used a single cylinder engine but by 1936 V-twins were used. Its original name New Era was changed to Kurogane in 1937. In that year 1,786 commercial vehicles were produced. The vehicles had a shaft-drive through a 3-speed and reverse gearbox. Production ceased at the start of the Second World War in favour of a 4x4 military scout car but was resumed in 1949 with the introduction of a 10cwt 3-wheeled truck, retaining the original style of shaft-drive and 3-speed gearbox. The range continued to diversify with capacities up to 2 tons and an engine range up to 1.5-litre 4-cylinder water-cooled, petrol or diesel. The line kept the single cycle-type front wheel with handlebar steering on the lighter models but had steering wheels and normal automobile controls on the larger vehicles. Cabins came in either fully enclosed steel 2-man versions or soft top convertible. Body styles varied but included deep sided utilities, drop-side tray, vans of all sizes or bodies made to special order.

The firm went bankrupt in 1962. More information listed under New Era.

Kusi-Car 1919 Japan

Unusual for a Japanese 3-wheeler this vehicle was a passenger only vehicle. The two side by side seat was a bit of a squeeze, the body was enclosed to waist height with a pram hood but had no windscreen. It had one side opening door with the single front wheel tiller steered, elliptical springing and electric lighting. The engine was placed under the seat over the back axle,

Kyma　　　　　　　　　　**1903-1905**　　　　　　　　　　　　**GB**
Located at Peckham, the New Kyma Car Company built a twin cylinder 6hp engined 3-wheeled cyclecar alongside a 4-wheeled version. Production of the 3-wheelers were few and lasted only until 1905 though the 4-wheelers continued until the company closed in 1935.

Kyoho　　　　　　　　　　**1937-1941**　　　　　　　　　　　**Japan**
Kyoho Automobile Co, built a truck along conventional Japanese 3-wheeled lines. Two rear driving wheels and a single front wheel motorcycle style with handlebar steering. 2,050 vehicles were built until they turned to war production in 1941.

Lacre　　　　　　　　　　**1904-1952**　　　　　　　　　　　　**GB**
Long Acre Motor Car Company began in the late 1890s, generally known as truck and body manufacturers. In 1919 it launched its L-type 3-wheeled road sweeper which became mainstay of the company. It was offered with either a 12hp 4 cylinder or 6 cylinder engine. The vehicle had two steerable front wheels and a chain-driven rear wheel. The driver sat in a central position towards the rear of the vehicle. With continual improvements the vehicle was streamlined and an Austin engine added to the range. By 1939 a new Lacre sweeper/collector called the T-type mounted on the 3-wheeled Opperman Motorcar chassis was offered. Various mergers and takeovers ended of the 3-wheeled versions in 1952. Bedford chassis were used for all future Lacre products.

Lacroix de Laville　　　　　**1898**　　　　　　　　　　　　　**France**
This was a long four passenger tiller steered cyclecar with a single front wheel and a single-cylinder stationary-type engine, mounted low down between the front wheel and the passenger compartment. Power was transmitted from the large flywheel on the engine, via belts to a transmission case and then chains to the rear axle. Wire wheels and rubber pneumatic tyres completed the vehicle.

LAD　　　　　　　　　　　**1901-1905**　　　　　　　　　　　　**GB**
A simple cycle-like creation typical of the 1900s, a single front wheel and a single cylinder air-cooled 2-stroke engine, slung outside on the offside of the body driving one rear wheel. Kick starter, tiller steering and a windscreen were standard.

La Durance　　　　　　　　**1908-1910**　　　　　　　　　　　**France**

La Fleurantine　　　　　　　**1906**　　　　　　　　　　　　　**France**

Lagonda　　　　　　　　　　**1897-1907**　　　　　　　　　　　**GB**
Wilbur Gunn built his first tricar in the greenhouse of his Middlesex home and went on to supply an order of 12 to the Post Office. These had a load carrying compartment between the front wheels and had a capacity of 4cwt. Power was from a V twin engine with chain-drive to the single back wheel. A number of passenger conversions were also offered where the passenger sat in a plush seat between the front wheels while the driver sat in an equally plush seat located over the engine. A steering wheel, elliptical springs and large rubber tyres and rear parcel carrier were supplied as standard. All three wheel production was dropped in 1907 when the Lagonda firm went over to 4 wheels and on to the production of the luxury cars that the firm is known for today.

Lamar   1950s   GB
A road-going vehicle built mainly for invalids, similar to the Carter.

La Marne   1930   France
A parcel van based on motorcycle components and powered by a 2-stroke engine with a Staub gearbox in the typical 3-wheel configuration.

Lambda   1988 to date   GB

Lambert (1)   1891-1895   USA
Believed to predate the Duryea as the first petrol driven car in America, the Lambert built in 1891 by John Lambert in his Ohio City workshop, had the conventional small single front wheel, extra large buggy style rear wheels with a passenger compartment to match. A 4-stroke single cylinder engine was modified from a 3-cylinder engine by John B Hicks, was located under the seat and drove the live rear axle. The first vehicles were offered for sale in February 1891 for $550. An 1894 version of this car is in the Smithsonian Museum.

Lambert (2)   1912   GB
3-wheeled cyclecar built in Thetford, Norfolk, with distinctive oval-shaped radiator.

Lamb-Kar   1950   GB
Manufactured by the Lamb-Kar Company of Fordham in Cambridgeshire. Built as a body/chassis in stressed skin aluminium and available in a choice of blue, silver grey or maroon the vehicle could be mistaken for a Bond. A choice of 197cc or 250cc engine was mounted in combination with the single front wheel and, like the Bond, was chain-driven. A steering mounted gearchange provided 3 forward speeds with car-type pedals for clutch, throttle and foot brake. Reverse was probably get out and push! A single headlight, one piece windshield, removable side curtains and a foldaway cloth hood completed the vehicle. Top speed was claimed at over 50mph with 80mpg from a 3 gallon petrol tank. The cabin could hold two adults and one child. It is believed that production was limited.

Lambretta   1948-1972   Italy
The Milanese steel-tube firm of Ferdinando Innocenti, founded in 1931, started making a very successful motor scooter soon after the end of the Second World War, it was not long before a passenger sidecar and then a cargo box were included. His first commercial 3-wheeler featured a front box between two wheels taking the place of the scooter's single front wheel. A new line of commercials called 'Lambretta' were introduced in 1956 adopting the conventional configuration of a single front wheel with a 150cc single cylinder 2-stroke engine with driveshaft and a 3-speed (no reverse) gearbox supplying power to the two rear wheels. Hydraulic brakes were on the rear wheels only. A basic cabin with handlebar steering was standard but the variety of trays, vans and boxes including an articulated truck could meet most customers demands. A more sophisticated machine now selling under the name of Lambro was introduced having a 2-seater fully enclosed cabin with steering wheel and car controls, a 197cc 2-stroke engine, and a greater variety of van and tray bodies with a cargo capacity of 11cwt. Another popular version was the articulated truck, taking the Lambro and replacing the parcel tray with a towing plate. A long fibreglass van body was added as a trailer, perfect for long loads.

Lambro 1952 Italy
See Lambretta for more information.

Lambretta Rickshaw 1950 to date Italy/India
Built in both Italy and India, the Rickshaw is based on the Lambretta chassis. See Lambretta and Bajaj for more information.

Landgrebe 1921-1924 Germany

Langham 1924 GB
Auto Electric Co Slough, Bucks, were making electric motors, dynamos and similar then went into the motor trade for a short time with a 3-wheeled electric van. The 1.5hp Langham electric motor drove the single rear wheel with the driver sitting behind the cargo box, similar to the motorcycle-based vehicles of the day. A load of 8cwt could be carried but the range was limited.

La Nef 1899-1914 France
La Nef, a fancy French word for ship, was a long 86 inch wheelbase 3-wheeler with seating for four. La Croix, an eccentric inventor and sometime photographer, established the firm of La Croix de Laville in Agen, France in 1899 and went on to build more than 200 of the sturdy but strange looking vehicles that became known as the 'doctors car'.

Using a single cylinder De Dion engine ranging in power from 2.75hp to 8hp and placed well up front on the wooden curved chassis. The single front wheel was steered by a 63 inch tiller that would have taken some dexterity to manipulate in a sharp turn. Power was transmitted to the right rear wheel through a Brazier gearbox via a long flat belt. The brakes, operated by a foot pedal, acted on the rear wheels only. Access to the rear seats of the 2+2 body were by way of a rear door.

Vehicle was also known as the Larcroix De Laville.

Lansing ET 1980s GB
ET has arrived on the Beeston, Notts site of the Boots Company Ltd. For many years the mail was delivered to the principal buildings by Boots own postman. He then progressed to a shiny red, 3-wheeled postal van. This had side and rear doors, single front wheel and an electric drive adapted from a Lancing Electric truck – part of a fleet of 3- and 4-wheeled Lancing trucks used by Boots in their Beeston complex.

Larcroix 1899-1914 France
More information listed under La Nef.

Lasshaft 1925-1926 Germany
A trivan with a single front wheel built by Lesshaft & Co of Berlin and powered by a 131cc Rinne 2-stroke engine.

Latta 1852 USA
A B and E Latta of Cincinnati made a 7 ton, 3-wheeled fire engine, powered by steam to the two rear wheels. However, auxiliary propulsion and steering was provided by horses hitched to a shaft attached to the single front wheel. A number of vehicles were produced as well as a tram car, all were noted as having steam up within three minutes of firing the boiler.

La Torpille   1912-1913   France

La Va Bon Train   1900   France
Larroumet et Lagarde of Agen, Lot-et- Garonn, in France built this two passenger, single front wheel car, powered by a single cylinder 8hp engine (housed under a bonnet just behind the front wheel) and driving the two rear wheels via a series of belts and chains. For 1900 this was a very modern vehicle with steering wheel, foot and hand controls, a fold down hood, rear wheel brakes, parking brake, and a luggage locker behind the seat. A solid steel chassis, elliptical springs and pneumatic tyres made for a very sturdy vehicle, of which a number still survive today.

Lawil A4   1984   Italy
Lawil Construzioni Meccaniche e Automobilistiche SpA, Variz, built mini-cars from 1973 with a 3-wheeled 350kg cargo van listed in 1984.

Lawson Motor Wheel   1899   GB
A self-contained propulsion unit produced by Mr H J Lawson. A single cylinder engine was mounted in a frame with a single wheel powered through reduction gears. This combination was used to power a trike (taking the place of the single rear wheel) or could be placed in the shafts of a dog cart to replace the pony. The principal was later used by many for the single front wheel passenger and commercial vehicles that were to follow.

LDV   1949-1952   GB
LDV stood for Light Delivery Vehicles Ltd, of Wolverhampton, a division of the Turner Manufacturing Company. They built a tri-van which had a 148cc single cylinder 2-stroke engine driving the single front wheel. The cargo box placed over the two rear wheels had a capacity of 3cwt.

An improved passenger version was announced in 1951 for the taxi market, it was on the same tri-van chassis with the front wheel engine increased to 168cc. It was known as the Rixi, but it is understood that sales were few. A by-van, on motorcycle lines, using the same engine driven front wheel with a cargo box of 1.5cwt located under the drivers seat was also offered. Disc brakes were common to most vehicles.
More information under Turner.

Lean Machine GM   1980   USA
General Motors Experimental Division produced a futuristic 3-wheeled prototype aptly named the 'Lean Machine' after its unique steering method of leaning the cockpit pod over in the direction one wishes to go, rather like cornering a motorcycle. One could call it a 3-wheeled motorcycle that sought to combine the refinement of a car. It is basically a teardrop shaped, Lexan-canopied driver's pod which rotates horizontally and separately in relation to the 2-wheeled rear power section. Steering is by handlebars connected to the motorcycle style front wheel, with the degree of lean controlled by foot pedals. Power comes from a 185cc Honda engine reputed to give a top speed of 80mph and a fuel return of 120 mpg. Transmission is 5-speed semi-automatic courtesy of Honda, major controls are mounted motorcycle fashion on the handlebars, and disc brakes are on all wheels.

This was another machine built for evaluation only and motor show publicity – production was restricted to just a few prototypes.

Le-Cab　　　　　　　　　　1972 to date　　　　　　　　　　France
A boxy little French people mover. A product of V.E. La Voiture Electronique of Paris. This is a 2-seater battery powered car with joystick controls. The squarish fibreglass body has side opening doors with plenty of windows. The single front wheel is based on a castor principal as each of the back wheels have their own electric motors and are slowed down to allow a turn to be made. Top speed is 25km/h with a range of 40 to 60km per charge.

Le Favori　　　　　　　　　　1921-1923　　　　　　　　　　France
Built in Paris, a tiny 3-wheeled cyclecar using a 987cc twin cylinder engine.

Le Monocar　　　　　　　　　　1936-1939　　　　　　　　　　France
Built in Paris, this was a cyclecar seating one person and powered by a 175cc 2-stroke engine and 2-speed gearbox, mounted as one unit with chain-drive to the single rear wheel. A robust steel tube chassis frame was covered with a neat body without doors. It had a well padded seat because the car had no springs and was designed to run on smooth roads. Large low pressure tyres gave it some bounce. Intended for suburban use it became popular with office workers – it was affordable which made it preferable to cycling to work. It had a big steering wheel, old fashioned bulb horn, single electric light and a hood that took ages to erect. The Monocar tootled along at 28mph. Production stopped with the start of war in 1939.

Lem　　　　　　　　　　1970s　　　　　　　　　　Italy
Designed by Giovanni Michelotti, one of Italy's greatest automobile stylists, the Lem was an electric powered city car in a stylish enclosed cabin for two. The doors and roof were combined as one and lifted to allow entry. The batteries and motors were located over the rear wheels and under the seating. Steering wheel and pedal controls completed the unit.

Lenoir　　　　　　　　　　1863　　　　　　　　　　France
The many advanced technical features of this vehicle were let down by the limited power of the three phrase operating cycle gas engine. The single front wheel was equipped with elliptical springs and a steering wheel. Power to the rear wheels was transmitted via chains from the underslung engine. The timber body had space for both passenger and cargo.

Leon Bollée　　　　　　　　　　1895-1933　　　　　　　　　　France
Leon Bollée built a very fast tricar that won many races. Built in the usual style of passenger seat between the two front wheels, the driver sat in a padded chair above a 650cc single cylinder engine which, by leather belt, drove the single rear wheel. The vehicle was also available with a delivery box in place of the passenger seat. Early vehicles were supposed to be temperamental but later models were exported all over the world. Leon Bollée changed to 4-wheeled cars at the turn of the century with the 3-wheelers fading away soon after. On Bollées death the business was taken over be WR Morris in 1924 but changed hands again in 1931.

Lepoix Ding　　　　　　　　　　1975　　　　　　　　　　Germany
A fantasy from Louis Ding (French born engineer Louis Lepoix) of Baden Baden, and shown at the Frankfurt Motor Show. A large pipe chassis made of a couple of arches and welded into a 'T' formation with a plastic tray and seats slung from the overhead pipes. The two rear wheels on the end of the rear arch were powered by

1.5kw 24 volt motors. Top speed was reputed to be 16km/h and thankfully there are no reports of any other examples. However, he did produce one of the smallest runabouts called the Shopi, a 2-seater with tiller steering and the unusual feature of two wheels bolted together around the steering arm and still rated as a 3-wheeler. It used the basic tub and electric motors of the Ding.

Leprechaun   1923   **Ireland**
McLysaght and Douglas in Dublin took over the production of the Leeds-based Autogear and built a number of cars under the new name. See Autogear. (2)

Lesshaft   1925-1926   **Germany**
Lesshaft and Company of Berlin built a small number of single front wheel, tiller steered trivans, with a 131cc Rinne 2-stroke engine chain driving the back wheels.

Leuchters   1899   **GB**
Built in Leeds this was a De Dion-type motor tricycle advertised as 'entirely locally made' but probably using imported parts.

Levis   1928-1930   **Japan**
A cargo trike built in Japan from components supplied by English manufacturers.

Lewis Airmobile   1937   **USA**
Information under Airmobile.

Leyat Heliocycle   1914   **France**
With a body resembling an aeroplane minus the wings and tail but powered by an aero engine complete with propeller up front in a protective housing, this vehicle had a single rear wheel used for steering. The all metal prototype was streamlined but the vehicle was prone to accidents in the 3-wheeler form.
   A modified version with four wheels was put into production and sold in limited numbers.

Lincoln   1920   **GB**
From Lancaster Gardens, Ealing, London, came the Lincoln powered by a 1000cc 2-stroke Blackburne engine with chain drive to the single rear wheel. The engine was fitted under the 2 place bench seat in a car-style metal body.

Linday   1900-1906   **GB**

Lifante   1952-1960   **Spain**
Juan Lifante of Barcelona added a delivery tricycle to his motorcycle range and called it his 'Mot-Auto-Lifante', using an Hispano-Villiers 200cc 2-stroke engine with shaft-drive to the rear wheels. A tubular frame carried a van body with an open sided driver's cabin, and a single front wheel, motorcycle style.

Light   1913-1914   **USA**
First built by Light Commercial Car, Marietta, Pa. This firm was soon taken over by the Wane Light Commercial Car Company of New York. They built a 3-wheeled parcel van with a single rear wheel, over which the driver sat looking over a 750 pound capacity cargo box. Early units used a 6hp single cylinder air-cooled motor, soon replaced by a 14hp 2 cylinder engine. Drive to the rear wheel was by chain.

| Lilla | 1920-1925 | Japan |

Built in Japan by the Jitsuyo Automobile Company of Osaka, a Gorham twin cylinder light 3-wheeled car that sold as the Lilla from 1923. It also came in a 4-wheeled version.
See Gorham for more information.

| Lince | 1954-1962 | Spain |

The Lince (also called the Lynx) was built by Industrias Cerza in Barcelona. A delivery trike where the driver sat in front on what could be described as a motor scooter with its back wheel replaced by a 2-wheeled utility tray. A metal frame and canvas cover converted this to an enclosed van. A single cylinder Hispano-Villiers 2-stroke engine drove the rear wheels via an open shaft. Payload was 450kg and hydraulic brakes were active on all three wheels.

| Lister | 1899 | GB |

From Keighley in Yorkshire it was reported that a oil-engined 3-wheeled car had been completed and was to be marketed as the Lister. No further details found.

| Little Tyrant | 1958-1974 | Netherlands |

For more information see heading under Cock.

| Liwaba | 1930-1931 | Germany |

| Lomar Honey | 1985-1986 | Germany |

| Lomax | 1988 to date | GB |

A sporty 3-wheeler based on the Citroën 2CV components and housed in a fibreglass body. Using front wheel drive, it is a 2-seater with aero screens and full car controls. A sporty little vehicle that can be pushed to 80mph. Since its introduction, the Lomax has gone through many changes and is now available with a spaceframe chassis, a V-twin engine and is sold in that configuration as the Lambda. With production past the 2,000 mark it has a thriving export to Germany, Holland and Belgium, with vehicles also finding their way to Spain, Denmark, America and Greece. It also has a thriving club scene.

| London | 1781 | GB |

For more information see Murdock.

| Long Steam Car | 1875-1882 | USA |

Patented by A G Long in 1883, this was a 3-wheeled 2-seater vehicle with a 5ft single rear wheel, a friction 2-speed drive from a 90 degree twin cylinder steam engine, located under and slightly to the rear of the seats. First built and seen on a public road in 1875 in Morthfield, Massachusetts. Unique was the twin side mounted tiller steering that allowed either seat to be the driver's seat. The original vehicle still survives in the Smithsonian collection of Automobiles in Washington and was believed to have been built at Hinsdale, New Hampshire. Long later moved to Northfield, Massachusetts.

| Lozier | 1899 | USA |

George A Burrell, while working for the Lozier Cycle Company at Toledo designed a 3-wheeled motor carriage: it is believed a prototype was built. He formed the Lozier

Motor Company with E R Lozier in 1905 and they went on to build 4-wheeled cars until production ceased in 1918.

LSD 1919-1925 GB
Built in Huddersfield the LSD is reported to have stood for cheap motoring but more likely signified Mr **L**ongbotham who designed this 3-wheeler car; **S**ykes and Sugden's ornamental gas lamp works, who produced more than 600 variations powered by JAP, MAG and Blackburne engines; and Mr **D**yson who put up the money for the venture. A few appeared under the name 'Oak' in 1919 and under the name of 'Blackeleigh' in 1925.

In 1979 the remains of the LSD Motor Co Ltd were rescued from various lockups around Huddersfield, and 5 almost complete vans along with enough parts for another 20 vehicles, as well as a prototype 4-wheeler were found. The vehicles were available as a lock up van, a car or pick-up. The van sported a long bonnet somewhat similar to the bullnose Morris, a vertical windscreen, and full car controls with chain-drive to the single rear wheel.

Lucciola 1948-1949 Italy

Lurquin-Coudert 1905-1907 France
Lurquin et Coudert of Paris built a commercial tricar using a vertical 4.5hp single cylinder engine with a 2-speed gearbox and chain-driven single rear wheel. Load capacity was 3cwt. They also built a Sociable tricar with tiller steering to the single front wheel and powered by a 9hp water-cooled twin cylinder engine.

Luther & Heyer 1933-1937 Germany
Fahrzeugbau Luther & Heyer GmbH, Berlin were manufacturers of a small 3-wheeled van powered by a 200cc DKW engine.

Lynch 1980s(?) GB
A home-built special using a 22cc industrial engine.

Lynx 1954-1962 Spain
For more information see under Lince.

M3 1980s USA
A space-age version on the Morgan trike produced in kit form by Ross Vick Automobile Corporation, Des Moines. Kit is adaptable to use almost any motorcycle from 250cc and upwards.

Mackenzie 1874 GB
Built by H A O Mackenzie of Scole in Norfolk. This was a very advanced 3-wheeled closed Brougham accommodating four passengers and driver in an enclosed cabin. A top speed of 12mph came from a Field Tubular Boiler with chain-drive to the rear wheels. After two years of trouble-free motoring the vehicle was forced off the road by the draconian road laws of the day.

Magirus 1903 Germany
Normally associated with the production of fire fighting equipment, buses and heavy trucks, Magirus-Deutz A.G. (as the firm is known today) introduced a line of 3-wheeled street sweepers after the Second World War complimenting its other municipal vehicles.

Magnet   1907-1924   Germany

The Berlin-Weissensee firm of Magnet-Motoren AG, produced 2-, 3- and 4-wheeled vehicles with the 3-wheeled passenger and delivery vehicles being fazed out in 1913 in favour of the 4 wheeled cars.

Magnum   1988   USA

Information under Quincy Lynn.

Mammut   1928-1929   Germany

Mammut-Werke A.G., Nuremberg, built a tri-van along the usual motorcycle lines of a single front wheel and the cargo box between the rear wheels. A variety of the firm's own engines, 200cc, 250cc and 300cc, were used to power the rear wheels.

Manchester Gnu   1973-1975   GB

The Nigel Engineering Co Ltd of Swinton built a 3-wheeled truck based on Ford components, with a payload of 1 ton. The wide cabin could seat two and was supplied with the usual automotive controls with a steering single front wheel. Engines were a choice of Ford Escort 1300 or Cortina 1600 mated to the appropriate Ford gearbox, propshaft and back axle. Bodies included van, truck or 3-way tipper with a special 2-wheeled trailer for increased load capacity. Wide section tyres could be used for farm and grassland use.

Manderbach   1946-1954   Germany

A light 3-wheeled cargo carrier from the factory of Louis Manderbach of Wissenbach who had been producing 3-wheelers before the Second World War. There was also a 34bhp Ford powered 4-wheeled 1-tonner added before closing down in 1954.

Manocar   1952-1953   France

Built by the Manom Company at Sait Ouen, this was a 2-seater with an enclosed cabin. The single front wheel was a combined unit with the 125cc single cylinder 2-stroke motor. Top speed was reported as 55km/h.

Manulectric   1948-1969   GB

Sidney Hole's Electric Vehicles, of Brighton, Sussex, started building electric pedestrian-controlled cargo carriers mainly for the milk trade. They came in 10cwt, 17cwt and 21cwt capacities and intended for use in narrow streets. These were all 3-wheeled vehicles, a fourth wheel was added in 1954 with the driver riding or rather standing in a cabin overhanging the front wheels.

Marie De Bagneux   1907   France

The Marie De Bagneux's 3-wheeled car was advanced for 1907. Weighing in at 100kg, it had a 1.25hp De Dion engine slung between the two front wheels and drove the single rear wheel by a long belt. The driver sat in a wraparound padded seat with metal footrests either side of the wishbone chassis. A steering wheel completed the very open driving compartment. A small personal luggage box was over the engine and a parcel tray located over the rear wheel.

Marocchi   1900-1901   Italy

Marold   1951   Austria

Hans Marold built his 3-wheeler from scrap vehicles parts. The open sports 2-

seater body moved along at a healthy 85km/h by a 350cc motor coupled to the single rear wheel. Unable to get financial backing, Marold remained as a one-off.

Marot-Gardon 1899-1904 France
From Corbie in the Somme, a line of racing trikes that did well in time trials using a 2.75hp engine.

Mars 1904 GB
The Mars Carette used a 4.5hp engine with chain-drive to the single rear wheel. The passenger sat up front in a substantial seat complete with weather proofing covers and sprung comfort.

Marsh 1904-1905 GB
From Kettering a tricar with a 3.5hp engine and the option of either a tiller or a steering wheel.

Martin 1920-1922 USA
Martin Motors Company of Springfield, Mass. built this unusual 3-wheeler using the principal of the Scott Sociable with the front wheel in line with one of the back wheels. A pressed steel chassis was offset to allow the single front wheel to turn on a pivot, while at the back it was underslung with a 616cc air-cooled V-twin driving both rear wheels. The side-by-side 2-seater body resembled a motorcycle sidecar and was sprung from the chassis in a similar manner – a pram hood, steering wheel and the usual car controls completed the outfit. Also called the Scootmobile.

Martin & Campbell 1926 GB
Martin & Campbell Ltd of Perivale in London had a 3-wheeled van running on solid rubber tyres exhibited at the 1926 Motor Cycle Show. It had an engine driven single front wheel and the enclosed van body was listed as able to carry 3cwt. The vehicle was believed to be a prototype and did not go into production.

Martin Stationette 1954 USA
J V Martin was the designer, and the Commonwealth Research Corporation of New York were the builders of the 3-wheeled passenger vehicle. Another vehicle from the same designer is the Bassons Star. More information under Bassons Star.

Maserati 1940-1948 Italy
Famous for the sports and racing cars, Maserati also built 3-wheeled electric trucks from 1940. The E10 'Tipo' had a fully enclosed 2-man cabin with the usual motorcycle-style single front wheel, steering wheel and automotive controls. A dropside tray body with a canvas covered metal frame gave a van appearance with a $1/2$ ton capacity. The electric vehicles were available until 1944 with petrol and diesel vehicles lasted until 1948.

Massey-Harris 1900-1902 Canada
Believed to be the first petrol engined vehicles to be built in Canada in quantity. They were tricycles powered by a De Dion engine. Quadricycles were also available.

Matchless 1903-1929 GB
Builders of both delivery trikes and cyclecars, the Matchless Motor Cycle firm was located at Plumstead in Kent. They had a 3-wheeled cyclecar powered by a Fafnir

engine at the Stanley Cycle Show in 1906 which received much praise in the motoring press but sadly not many orders.

Mathis (1) 1946 France

Emile Mathis was an early proponent of badge engineering. He added his own radiator and wheel caps to the Stoewers motor cars, selling them as the Mathis and at a premium, prior to the First World War. Between the wars he was a French aerodynamic pioneer, but it was not until the 1940s that he designed his wind-cheating petrol miser, the Mathis 333 – a coupé with a 707cc flat twin water-cooled engine with a separate radiator for each cylinder. It was credited with 3 litres per 100km, had 3 seats and 3 wheels, with an aluminium body that weighed only 440kg. The first cars went on display in 1946 but did not get beyond the prototype stage because the French authorities refused to allow the car to be put into production.

Mathis (2) 1954-1958 Germany

Designed by Andreau Mathis, this was a 3-wheeler powered by a 2.8-litre flat six cylinder front wheel drive engine. It reached prototype stage only.

Mattes 1932 Germany

A Mattes & Co, Ulm, built a small truck, the engine driving the single front wheel.

Max-Kabine 1945 Germany

More information see NSU.

Maxim Motor Tricycle 1894-1895 USA

This would have been the first Maxim vehicle: a trike, powered by a 3-cylinder engine and built by the American Projectile Company of Lynn, Massachusetts, in 1894, and then moved to the Maxim Manufacturing Company of Hartford, Connecticut in 1895. The Maxim name appears on a number of 4-wheeled vehicles in various locations throughout Connecticut between 1894 and 1914 and are all believed to have been connected with Hiram Maxim.

Maxim Tricar 1911-1914 USA

Hiram Maxim built a 3-wheeled van based on the German Phanomobil with a 2-cylinder air-cooled engine mounted above the single front wheel, driven by a single chain. The whole unit was driven from the open fronted cabin using standard steering wheel and auto controls. The van was manufactured at the factory of Bushnell Press Company at Thompsonville, Connecticut, and later at the Maxim Tricar Manufacturing Company of New York. The vehicle had a 7ft 6in wheelbase and had a rated cargo capacity of 15cwt.

Mayrette 1910-1911 Germany

Mazda 1921 to date Japan

Japan has been the home of 3-wheelers with the a production run of 114,937 vehicles in 1957 and 122,505 for a 10 month period in 1959. Mazda produced many of these vehicles. Toyo Cork Kogyo Co Ltd was founded in 1921 in Hiroshima as machinery manufacturers. In 1923 the company started producing motorcycles and developing their own 250cc engines. In 1930 the first 3-wheeler, a commercial with a 500cc motorcycle front end and a light utility truck at the back was introduced. Used as a goods carrier, the use of side facing removable bench seating made conversion to a passenger carrier simple. By 1934 they were producing 114 units per month. Continual improvements and expansion of engine sizes continued until the start of the Second World War.

After the war the firm was reformed under the name of Toyo Kogyo Co Ltd and as well as starting the production of 4-wheeled cars, they continued with the 3-wheeled commercials that ranged from the Midget K360 truck (only 2.975 metres long) to the full size heavy duty trucks of 5.120 metres plus in length – a variety of bodies were available. All were for the unique home market of narrow streets where 3 wheels reigned supreme.

With the growth of the export market, 4 wheels were required and the production of 3-wheelers to stop. The no longer required factories were sold off to Third World countries – 3-wheelers still flourish in India and China, both having a flourishing export market. In 1991 a group of Mazda engineers built the ultimate in small cars; a 3-wheeler built in a suitcase. Weighing 35 kilos it was able to be stored in the back of a car, a 30cc 2-stroke engine allowed it to zip it along at 30 km/h using a half-litre tankful of fuel to travel 15km. Using motorcycle handlebar steering and hand controls, this little vehicle could be folded up on arrival at the office and parked by your desk. Production run was one only with no plans for more. Other fun 3-wheelers have been built on a one-off experimental basis and more can be expected. Translators sometime labled the marque as Mazuda.

MB (Merrall-Brown) 1919-1921 GB

Built in Bolton, Lancashire, a 3-wheeled cyclecar using a 10hp V-twin and later a water-cooled 1,498cc 4 cylinder Precision engine with shaft-drive to the twin rear wheels, just 8 inches apart. The semi slab-sided body ended in a curved tail and came with a pram hood and normal car controls. The spare wheel was located between the front mudguards and the engine bay. A 4-wheeled car was also built.

McLachlan 1899-1901 GB

Powered by a 2.5hp motor and available as either a 3- or 4-wheeler. *The Autocar* gave it a great build up without much detail but did state that it ran on petrol, paraffin or benzoline. Production numbers not known.

McDowell 1867 Ireland

Daniel McDowell, a railway engineer, built one of the few Irish motor carriages, a 2-ton 3-wheeler powered by a fire tube boiler with an engine of 3 inch bore and 7 inch stroke and able to maintain a speed of 20mph. It spent much time in the grounds of the Trinity College, Dublin.

Megola 1900s Germany

This company built a line of 3- and 4-wheeled cars where the engine was within the wheel, similar to the Smiths Motor Wheel.

Meilong 1949 to date Taiwan

A light truck with a 4.99 Perkins diesel engine using conventional drive to the two rear wheels. A sheet metal cabin, modified from the Ford Thames Trader with seating for two, with the single front wheel located where the radiator of the Trader would have been. The engine was under the seat.

Meiwa 1952 Japan

Meister G5N 1969 Austria
A metal framed open cabin, with power from a Puch Moped engine, tandem seating for two, motorcycle steering to the single front wheel and canvas curtains which gave limited protection to the open sides and hatchback rear.

Meray 1926-1930s Hungary
The firm of Meray were better known as the manufacturers of sturdy motorcycles, however, in the 1920s they produced a lightweight van, the usual box between the two front wheels and driver with steering wheel at the back. Production had been in quantity but founder Andre Meray-Horvath wanted an economical car. He used the van chassis and the end result looked like a car with a dicky seat, only that it had one rear wheel and a JAP 500cc engine tucked inside the boot. In 1934 a 1-ton forward control 4-wheel van was built to replace the aging 3-wheelers

Mercedes 1980s to date Germany
Mercedes have been regular entrants in the fuel economy runs held all over the world and (almost) always had a 3-wheeler as an entry. Usually built by the apprentices each year they are fantastic streamlined cars with engines as small as 25cc and consumption ranging in many thousand miles per gallon.

Mercury 1910-1917 USA
Mercury Manufacturing Company of Chicago began building trucks in 1910 but it was not until 1915 that the Bulley tractor became the mainstay of the company. One of the earliest 'mechanical horses' this 3-wheeled towing tractor was in two configurations, with a single front wheel and double chain-drive to the rear axle, or with two front wheels and a single driven rear wheel. The most popular model was the single front wheel unit equipped with a steering wheel, automotive controls, electric lighting and a folding hood as standard. Shod with solid rubber wheels the engine was placed directly over the back axle with the driver's compartment over the front wheel.

Merkur 1929-1931 Germany
Fahrzeugfabrik Quickborn factory built a tri-van with a single rear wheel and either a tray or box cargo space. Depending on the model's cargo capacity (300kg–850kg), engine sizes were either 200cc, 300cc or 440cc, all rear wheel chain driven. The driver sat in an elevated position over the engine, looking over his cargo box.

Merrell-Brown 1920s GB
Started life as a 4-wheeler then was changed to a 3-wheeler, probably to take advantage of the tax savings that 3 wheels gave in the 1920s. Powered by a Coventry-Simplex engine and 2-speed gearbox, it had crude drum and cable steering.

Messagate 1970 France
For more information see Citadine.

Messerschmitt 1953-1962 Germany
Originally designed by Fend, this 3-wheeler did extremely well on the market and was exported all over the world. Dubbed 'Snow White's Coffin' by some members of the motoring press, the first KR175 had motorcycle handlebars and sold as a motor scooter with a roof; almost 20,000 were produced. The KR200 had more refinements, a Sachs 191cc single cylinder 2-stroke engine able to achieve a speed

of 100km/h either forwards and backwards because reverse was just a change in the direction that the motor ran. The KR201 enjoyed a soft top convertible in its roof styles. Seating was tandem for two adults and some luggage or even a youngster. The advent of the Mini Minor with seating for four at a similar selling price put an end to this popular little vehicle though it still has a large world wide following in car clubs. More than 30,000 of the KR200s were built.

Metropoli   1953-1957   **Italy**
Information listed under Doniselli.

Metz   1909   **Netherlands**
An Amsterdam company that built motorcycles and 3-wheeled commercial vehicles from proprietary components.

Mevea   1970 to date   **Greece**
Mevea SA of Athens built the British Reliant under licence. Later they built their own ultra light vehicles using a 50cc single cylinder engine developing 5.6hp, with a fibreglass cabin, car-type controls, and a single front wheel – load areas could be either a van or tray body. Another version had an open rickshaw taxicab body and tiller steering - later improved to a steering wheel. This model was exported to the Middle East and Asian countries.

Meyra   1948-1956   **Germany**
With side-by-side seating for two, the Meyra of 1950 had the single front and two rear wheels layout, a near vertical windscreen and a canvas hood for weather protection. The 1955 version, the Meyra 200-2, had reversed the trend and now had a fully enclosed slab-sided body, a single rear wheel and a lot of overhang in front of the two front wheels. Entry was by a single front opening door and the rear mounted 198cc Ilo 2-stroke engine was underpowered for the size of the vehicle. In excess of 550 of the 200 and 200/2 models were produced.

Miari e Giusti   1896-1899   **Italy**
SA Miari e Giusti of Padau, manufactured the 3-wheeler designed by Professor Enrico Bernardi, the trike was also sold under that name. It had a horizontal single cylinder engine of 624cc with hot tube ignition and chain-drive to the single rear wheel. Listed as Italy's first petrol driven car. Information under Bernardi.

Microcar   1979   **USA**
For more information see Tri-Ped.

Milde et Mondos   1898-1909   **France**
Charles Milde, of Milde et Cie, Levallois-Perret, Seine, built some of the best known electric cars in France at the turn of the century. The 3-wheeler had an unusual metal chassis, with its single front wheel housed in a triangle frame with elliptical springs – it was turned by cables from a vertical steering wheel. The chassis was upswept at the rear to form the seat base and the rear axle was underslung with petrol-electric motors driving both of the rear wheels. In 1907 a 4-wheeled car called the Milde-Gaillardes was introduced and the 3-wheelers discontinued.

Mileage Marathon   1960s   **Worldwide**
From an almost light-hearted beginning in Britain in the 1960s the Mileage Marathon has been picked up and now competes all over the western world with

backing from the major oil companies and car manufacturers. With engines as small as 25cc and petrol consumption reaching 4,000km per gallon, 90% of the vehicles are 3-wheelers.

Miles   1910-1912   GB

Millet   1888-1892   GB
Felix Theodore Millet built a radical prototype using a Stella engine (the forerunner of the Rotary aero engine) built into a wheel with five radial cylinders and a fixed central crankshaft driving the wheel direct. Rotation was supposed to cool the cylinders, which had no fins. Patents were taken out in 1888 and it was fitted to a tricycle. The 'Pudding Wheel' – as it was derisively called – made history by winning many races when it was adapted to both 2- and 3-wheeled machines.

Mini Comtesse   1950   France
Information under Comtesse.

Mini-Cat   1978-1980   France
Designed by racing car builder Serge Aziosmanoff in 1978 as a basic 3-wheeler. The rights were bought by Janneau (one of Europe's leading pleasure boat manufacturers) and converted to a 4-wheeler which sold in numbers as the Microcar.

Mini-El   1987 to date   Denmark
The Mini-El is a battery powered 3-wheeler that has been designed as a second car, not as a family car. It is used as a vehicle to get to work, do the shopping, or wher all weather economic motoring for one or two is required. The manufacturers, El-Trans, is reported to have built in excess of 2,000 vehicles with a further 4,500 expected to be sold in Switzerland and Germany. The car has a transparent canopy hinged at the nose over the single front wheel. Canopy opening is aided by springs to show a comfortable seat in tandem for a driver and one child – this can be converted to a parcels area. The three 12-volt batteries with electric motors and the automatic drive are fitted in the engine bay between the two rear wheels. A top speed of 40km/h and a range of 50km between charges is adequate for the commuter as this vehicle will be competing with the multitude of bicycles in use each day. The body/chassis has been built from an inner and outer shell extruded from acrylic polymer and a high impact alloy. Running costs are claimed at one cent per kilometre.
    The Mini-El has a nice wedge-shaped body and is equipped with the luxuries of much larger and expensive 4-wheeled cars. Rover objected to the name Mini so the name was altered to City-El on example imported into the UK. More information available under that name.

Minima   1911   France

Minneapolis   1911-1913   USA
A commercial trike of very stylish lines using the box in front between the two front wheels. Power came from a long-stroke single cylinder engine located under the driver's seat, with shaft-drive to the rear wheel. Although the engine was powerful, pedal assistance was required to start and possibly used in an emergency if one ran out of petrol. Load was rated at 300lbs but larger vehicles with chain-drive have been noted.

Minnow 1951-1952 GB
Built by Bonallack & Sons of Forest Gate, London, a firm of commercial vehicle coachbuilders. A 3-wheeler with the single rear wheel powered from a 250cc Excelsior Talisman twin cylinder 2-stroke engine able to top 75 mpg at 45mph. A slab-sided body with a bench seat for two, small wheels and a distinctive single headlight placed in the centre of squared nose which had a hinged lid and doubled as a luggage boot. Vertical windscreen, pram hood and side curtains gave reasonable weather protection.

Minutoli-Millo 1896 Italy

Minicar 1971-1972 Greece
Built by Zamba, SA, Athens, using an unitary fibreglass body with a 2-seater slab-sided cabin. The 50cc engine was under the rear cargo space and drove the rear wheels via a chain and live axle. Car controls and a small steering wheel fitted out the cabin while the payload was 150 kilos.

Mink 1968 Bermuda
Called a UFO with wheels, the open 2-seater Mink had an almost circular fibreglass body with a an occasional pram-type hood and a rear mounted Lambretta 198cc engine and fittings. The two front wheels were well back giving a long overhang that had space for a small amount of luggage. This unique vehicle weighed just 530lbs and was able to reach a heady 55mph returning 70mpg. The prototype was built in England and still turns heads at car rallies. It is unknown if or how many may have been built in Bermuda.

Mira 1957 Spain
Information see Villof.

Mirage 1976-1985 Italy
Information see Automirage.

Mitsubishi 1920 to date Japan
Mitsubishi was better known for shipbuilding but they also built trucks along with the 3-wheeled commercials so popular in Japan of the 1920s. Reorganised after the war, they continued to build light trucks on the 3 wheel configuration, one in front and the rear usually a tray or van body with capacities of 2cwt up to 2 tons. 3-wheeled production was phased out in favour of 4 wheels about 1961.

Mi-Val 1950-1960 Italy
Mi-Val was an extra from a motorcycle factory when they mated the rear of one of their motorcycles to a cargo box between the two front wheels. The engine was a 172cc 2-stroke single cylinder from their own factory, with chain-drive to the single rear wheel. As usual, the driver was exposed to the weather. Another venture in 1959/60 was the construction of the Messerschmitt bubble car built under licence.

Mivalino 1954 Italy
The Messerschmitt range was to be built in Italy under a licence agreement and using the name of Mivalino, a number of prototypes were built to test production facilities. It appears, however, that a number of problems nipped the project in the bud before it was able to get under way.

Mizung   1930s   Japan
A cargo carrier with the freight box between the two rear wheels, and a choice of engines: 500cc, 750cc and 1000cc. Production figures for 1937 were 362 units.

Mizushima   1936-1950s   Japan
Using a pressed steel frame, the usual single front wheel treatment, the cargo box was located between the two rear wheels and sported mudguards. A steel frame covered with canvas for driver protection and a flat windscreen.

MMC   1897-1908   GB
The Motor Manufacturing Company was part of the H J Lawson empire and among the many cars made was a range of trikes powered by British-made De Dion engines of 1.75hp and 2.25hp.

Mobilek   1979   GB
An electric powered single-seater motor scooter from Dudley-based inventor, Doreen Kennedy-Way, that never got past the prototype stage. Grounded by Ministry of Transport classifications.

Modulo   1988 to date   Italy
Powered by a BMW K75, this was a tandem seating futuristic power machine, designed and built by engineer Carlo Lamattina from his motor works near Milan. Built of fibreglass over a steel tube and aluminium sheet spaceframe chassis, featuring disappearing headlights, roll over bars and available in single or tandem seating. Open or closed body was optional. Power to the single rear wheel (from BMW) produced 75bhp and a top speed of 125mph.

Monet-Goyon   1921-1931   France
Well-known motorcycle firm, Monet et Goyon, Saone-et-Loire, built a number of cyclecars. The first 3-wheeler was called the Auto Mouche with a single cylinder engine mounted over the single front wheel. The layout was soon reversed and the 3-wheeled Monet-Goyon, had a 500cc Villiers rear mounted engine driving the single wheel. The 2 seater had a bench seat, a vertical windscreen, car type controls and a large steering wheel. Monet built a number of cars in both 3- and 4-wheel configuration with both front and rear mounted Villiers engines of 269cc, 350cc and 500cc, as well as MAG engines of 750cc. Along with the cars a range of commercial vans and trucks were built using the same engines and chassis. Production ceased in 1931.

Monocar   1936-1939   France
Built in Paris, this was a cyclecar seating one person and powered by a 175cc 2-stroke engine. More information under Le Monocar.

Monoto/Monto   1935   France
More information under Poirier.

Mopetta   1951-1958   Germany
Information listed under Brütsch.

Monos   1928-1930   Germany
A 3-wheeler deseigned by Fritz Gorke with a side mounted engine driving one of the two rear wheels.

Mops   **1925**   **Germany**
Built by Schmidt & Bensdort GmbH, Mannheim, this was a small snub-nosed 3-wheeler powered by a 350cc engine mounted just in front of and driving the single rear wheel, with final drive by chain. The body shape was pleasing with step in (no doors) to the bench seating for two, normal car controls and a large steering wheel. A pram hood was available but would make entry awkward when up. A spare wheel lay outside the body over the rear boat tail.

Morette   **1903-1905**   **GB**
Built in Birmingham by a Mr B E Dickinson this was an odd-shaped 3-wheeler with the single front wheel driven by a friction roller from a choice of 2.5hp or 4hp engines mounted over the wheel.

Morford Flyer   **1993**   **GB**
Though built like a box on 3 wheels, this was a front wheel drive, sporty-looking car using a Renault 5 engine and bits and pieces. Body was in aluminium glued over a steel frame and generous seating for two. After the prototype was built, further development was planned.

Morin Aerocar   **1948**   **France**

Morland Flyer   **1994 to date**   **GB**
A kit-based 3-wheeler (Renault 5 as a donor car). The engine and front suspension are bolted directly to a ladder frame chassis while the all aluminium bodyshell panels are fixed with urethane adhesive to frames that bolt to the chassis. It has a slab-sided appearance concealing its sports car performance of 120mph plus.

Morgan   **1909 to date**   **GB**
H F S Morgan built his first 3-wheeler using a tubular chassis into which he fitted a 7hp V-twin Peugeot engine intended for a motorcycle. He finished the vehicle in 1909 and many of the ideas he used in that first vehicle were still in use when the last 3-wheeler was made in 1952, more than forty-three years later. The Morgan Motor Company is still family owned ands always has a waiting list for its vehicles.

    Over the years the vehicles have been available in 1-, 2-, 3-, and 4-seater versions and even a utility and panel van has been produced. Exported all over the world the cult of the Morgan is enshrined in clubs, books and publications. Wherever a Morgan is seen it will always draw a crowd. The 4-wheeled Morgan was introduced in 1934 and is still in production.

Morrison   **1904-1905**   **GB**
Under the name of A E Morrison & Sons, Leicester, was built a variety of cycles, tricars and electrical equipment. A range of 3-wheelers followed the pattern of a single rear wheel powered by the firm's own engines, a large cargo box in front with the latest Ackermann steering to the two front wheels. They were also sold under the name of Trilec. A 6hp front wheel drive 3-wheeler was shown at the Crystal Palace in 1904. The firm still exists building milk floats.

Morrison Krupkar   **1904**   **GB**
Built by Krupkar Ltd in a small workshop in Lancelot Place, Brompton Rd, London. Front wheel drive with a 6hp engine. With identical specification to the Morrison and also shown at the Crystal Palace in 1904 we can assume that they are the same vehicle.

Mors 1880-1926 France

Emile Mors was one of France's leading electrical engineers who, in the 1880s as a Member of Parliament, became interested in transportation. He built a light steam-driven 3-wheeled carriage exhibited in the 1899 Paris Exposition. One of the first steam vehicles to have a vertical oil-fired boiler with a rear mounted engine, driving directly from a crankshaft to the rear wheels with rack and pinion steering to the single front wheel. He went on to produce petrol engined cars but started straight off with four wheels.

Mosquito 1970s GB

Information listed under Triad.

Motivator 1976 USA

The 3-wheeled 48,000hp rocket powered SM1 'Motivator' gave Mrs Kitty Hambleton the Land Speed Record (by a woman), 524mph on 6 Dec1976 in the Alvard Desert.

Motocar 1920-1924 France

Motocarri 1952-1958 Italy

Information under Moto-Guzzi.

Motocart 1953-1959 GB

Formally known as the Opperman Motorcart from 1947 until taken over by Transport Equipment (Thornycroft) Ltd in 1953, the Motorcart was developed as an agricultural carry-all. An 8bhp JAP single cylinder petrol engine was mounted beside the single front wheel. A later version was produced as a passenger vehicle in kit form under the name of Unicar Mod T during 1958/59.

Motocor 1921-1924 Italy

About 50 Motocors were built in the factory of Armino Mezzo, Turin. The vehicle came in a variety of bodies that included a 4.5cwt tip truck, a 2-seater taxi, and a private car. The engine was mounted amidships and drove the single rear wheel via a chain. Power was an air-cooled flat-twin engine of 575cc or an ohv version of 745cc using a 3 speed and reverse gearbox.

Motoemil 1967 to date Greece

From new and reconditioned 1.2- and 1.5-litre VW engines, the factory of K & A Antoniadis, Stauroupolis, Thessalonkia, produces a very successful 3-wheeled vehicle with a variety of uses. The front cabin is in either metal or fibreglass and can be fully enclosed. Steering is through a single front wheel. Payload is 350 kilos.

Moto-Guzzi 1928 to date Italy

A long time producer of 3-wheeled commercial vehicles, the Moto Guzzi SpA, Mandala del Lair, Como (1928-1967) later changed to Societal Esercizio Industrie Moto Meccaniche SpA, Mandello del Lario, Como (1967 to date) began the manufacture of the 'Motocarri' motorcycle-type delivery vehicle with two driven rear wheels using a single cylinder 500cc engine mounted horizontally. Later models from 1938 were shaft-driven and had 4 speeds to cope with the 1 ton payloads. During the war production continued with the Trialce supplied to the Italian army. Civilian use resumed in 1945 with the 1500kg Ercole featuring a five speed and reverse gearbox. A number of variations were made with engines ranging from 65cc (Rickshaw) 1948. The Ercolino of 1956 with 192cc and load capacity of 350kg later upped to 590kg. A variety of cabins, trays and vans were available. Between 1959 and 1963 there were 220 examples of the 3 x 3 power cart made for the military and powered by a 750cc transverse V-twin engine, its all wheel drive allowed it to almost climb up a brick wall. Current production is the Ercole; fully enclosed cabin, 500cc horizontal engine with shaft-drive to the two rear wheels, handlebar steering and brakes to all 3 wheels.

Moto-Kar   1938   USA
A 3-wheeler built by Moto-Skoot Manufacturing Company of Chicago, Illinios.

MotoKart   1913-1914   USA
Tarrytown Motor Car Company of New York built a small delivery van in which the driver sat behind the cargo box. Power was from a 4-stroke 2-cylinder water-cooled engine connected through a friction transmission and a single chain to the rear axle. Engine was under the driver's seat. Pneumatic tyres on wire spoke wheels this compact vehicle had a wheelbase of 5ft 9ins and a load capacity 400lbs.

Motom   1952-1966   Italy
This was an ultra-light commercial 3-wheeler coming from the motorcycle factory of Motom SpA, Milan. Using a motorcycle front end, the 48cc 4-stroke engine powered the two rear wheels via a chain. The payload was 3-cwt. Early models were sold under the name of Gavonis.

Moto Morini   1937-1943   Italy
Based on a motorcycle this was a light commercial 3-wheeler with a 600cc engine driving the two rear wheels. The Fabbrica Italiana Motocicli Moto-Morini, Bologna was closed in 1943 following heavy air raids. When it reopened in 1945 the 3-wheelers did not reappear.

Motoporteur ARM   1919   France
This is a very interesting conversion from France. Take an all metal motorcycle sidecar and attach couple of wheels and a rear mounted single cylinder Anzani motor (with a very short belt drive to one wheel), seating for two at a pinch, a windscreen for weather protection, then remove the rear wheel from your trusty bicycle and attach it to the front of this contraption. A couple of cable controls to the handlebars and one had family transport.

Motorcar   1967-1970   Greece
Motorcar Ag, Ioannis Rentis, Athens, built a variety of 3-wheeled trucks using a method pioneered in Greece of using reconditioned VW or Ford engines with drive to the rear wheels. The cabins were fibreglass and normal car controls were used.

Motorette (1)   1898-1900   GB
For more information see under New Courier.

Motorette (2)   1910-1912   USA
C W Kelsey was a pioneer in the American Motor scene having built his first 3-wheeler in 1898. This was a commercial delivery van and came in two sizes only. The single rear wheel was driven by a chain from a 2-stroke, 2-cylinder engine believed to have been made by Lycoming. Both models had the cargo box placed between the two front wheels. In the case of the smaller version with a capacity of

200lbs, the driver sat in front of the engine. The 500 lbs version had a larger cargo box and had the driver in a seat over the engine for better visibility. Both vehicles used tiller steering. The Kelsey Motorette of 1911 was a quality car with side-by-side bucket seating, a double opposed 10hp motor under the seat driving the single rear wheel through a 2-speed planetary transmission with reverse. Tiller steering was maintained. An option was an extension front top (or bonnet) containing a folding glass windshield: other extras included lights, spare wheels, repair kits, speedo and a pram hood. A commercial version had a 250lb capacity cargo box placed between the two front wheels.

Other 3-wheelers built by or designed by Kelsey were the Auto-Tri in 1898 and the Kelsey in 1921-1924.

Motorette (3)　　　　　　　　　1912-1919　　　　　　　　　GB
For more information see Premier.

Motor Wheel　　　　　　　　　1899　　　　　　　　　　　GB
Information listed under Lawson Motor Wheel.

Mototric-Contal　　　　　　　1907-1908　　　　　　　France
This was an elaborate tricar built in Paris. During its short life was to become famous as an entry in the 1907 Peking-Paris Road Race. It was the lack of roads that forced the Contal to withdraw after only a few days into the journey. With the usual configuration of the engine in the centre of the vehicle driving the single rear wheel by a chain, the driver's saddle was well back over that wheel. The passenger compartment was as usual in front between the wheels and had leaf springs underslung on the beam axle to soften the ride. The vehicle was offered with a deluxe coachwork body for passenger use or with a box body for delivery of parcels.

Motosacoche　　　　　　　　(?) to date　　　　　　　Switzerland
Motosacoche SA, Geneve, were motorcycle makers who built a number of commercial parcel vans utilising many of their own motorcycle components. By replacing the front wheel of their standard 350cc model with an enclosed parcels van or open cargo tray, a sturdy delivery vehicle was produced.

Moto Scooter　　　　　　　　1951-1959　　　　　　　　　Spain
Moto Scooter SA. Madrid built a delivery van utilising the Ronline Motorscooter. Sold under the name of Titano the factory was taken over by the well-known Trimak firm – the vehicle was renamed and sold as the Trimak.

Motovetturetta Vaghi　　　　1920s　　　　　　　　　　Italy
For more information see MV Bambina.

MPHW Special　　　　　　　1950s(?)　　　　　　　　　GB
The MPHW (Michael Pollock Howell Williams) Special was a competition 3-wheeler used in motor sport and raced by ex-Connaught employee, Peter Wolse, in his shirt sleeves! It was powered by a 650cc Triumph motorcycle engine with a Norton gearbox, with a peculiar Ford front end and a single rear wheel of Citroën origin.

MSA　　　　　　　　　　　　　1928-1930s　　　　　　　Japan
A cargo trike built by Motor-Shokai using their own brand of 675cc engine or an English JAP engine of similar size.

MSR3   **1992**   **GB**
Another dream that did not get off the ground. Based on a Renault 5 with a heavy cruciform ladder chassis, complete Renault front end with a classic boat tail style body with the spare tyre let into the sloping rear, Morgan style. A 2-seater with aero screens and an exposed engine, cycle guards and large headlights made a classy front end. One prototype was made before the project faded away.

MT   **1940-1962**   **Spain**
In 1955 a 2-seater 125cc powered open touring car was built. It was really a 4-wheeler trying to be a 3-wheeler: the rear driving wheels were placed close together. The body was small so only two very slim people could be accommodated.

Mumford Musketeer   **1971 to date**   **GB**
Brian Mumford of Nailsworth, Gloucestershire built the first Musketeer featuring a Vauxhall Viva engine and gearbox. Using an advanced riveted aluminium monocoque chassis and fibreglass body with a long wedge shaped snout and concealed headlights, the vehicle was sold as a kit. A number of improvements have been made but production is believed to be low.

Murdock   **1781**   **GB**
William Murdock was an assistant to James Watt when he made a working model of a steam powered road vehicle. Watt was not impressed. The principals were later used by Richard Trevithick when he built his 'London' steam carriages.

Musashi   **1956-1960**   **Japan**
Mitaki Fuji Co of Tokyo built a 3-wheeled light truck along conventional lines with a 359cc vertical twin 4-stroke engine and 4 speed gearbox driving the rear wheels.

MV   **1948-1973**   **Italy**
M V Agusta was another motorcycle factory that added a 3-wheeled commercial vehicle to their production line. Built by SpA Meccanica Verghera, Gallarate, this orthodox motocarrier had two driven rear wheels and a enclosed cabin up front.

MV Bambina   **1920**   **Italy**
Built by Italian coachbuilders Lodovico Boltri di Mezzi Ganna & Cia, in their workshop at Porto Valtravagia on the banks of Lake Maggiore. This car has a substantially built tubular chassis, a single front wheel supported on minute elliptic springs, car type controls and steering wheel, a shaft-drive (from a forward sitting 8hp V-twin 1,077cc engine of the maker's design) to a 3-speed and reverse gearbox in unit with the engine which was kick started motorcycle style. The open curved-tail body was metal sheeting over a wooden frame with a vertical wind-screen and plenty of luggage space behind the bench seat. A number were exported to England and chassis No. 2 turned up brand new, still crated, at a 1980 Sotheby's auction.

Mymsa   **1955-1961**   **Spain**
As well as producing motorcycles and sidecars, the Motores y Motos SA factory in Barcelona built a fully enclosed light van along car lines with the single front wheel sitting snugly under a long bonnet. It had a 125cc engine, and payload was 200kg.

Mytholm   **1897-1902**   **GB**
Thomas Potter and J W Brown owned the Mytholm Cycle Works at Hipperholm,

Halifax, where they built their first 3-wheeled car in 1897, soon followed by a 4-wheeled prototype. By 1900 a number of cars had been built using 1357cc engines and a steering column gearchange.

Nairn Pioneer 1870-1872 GB
Andrew Nairn of Leith built a 3-wheeled 8hp steam tractor, then a 50 passenger omnibus with a single front wheel and very ornate body – he called it the 'Pioneer'.
For the four summer months of 1871/1872 it plied a regular timetable between Edinburgh and Portobello with about 20 minutes for the trip at a speed of 12mph (not much faster today!).
The 'bus' was apparently exported to New Zealand.

Naniwa 1947 Japan
A short-lived cargo trike with a pressed steel frame and cargo box between the two rear wheels. An innovation at the time was its canvas covered cabin and bench seating for two or three.

Napier 1931 GB
D Napier & Sons Ltd started building commercial vehicles in 1902 but it was not until 1931 that they developed a 3-wheeled 'mechanical horse'. It was the standard rear two wheel drive and single front wheel steer on a truck type layout. The engine under a bonnet at the front, drove through a heavy duty gearbox and shaft-drive. A turntable coupling allowed a variety of trailers to be engaged and it was developed for factory and wharf use. The single front wheel allowed the vehicle to turn in almost its own length.
  Napier did not continue past the prototype stage and sold its design and construction rights to Scammell. More information under Scammell.

Narcla 1954-1966 Spain
Industrias Narcla, SA, of Barcelona was a motorcycle manufacturer who also made a delivery tricycle using a 6hp single cylinder engine and a 4-speed gearbox.

National 1902-1906 GB
Coming from a factory in Manchester, the National was a tricar with a coachbuilt body, powered by a 4hp engine bought in from the Motor Manufacturing Company (MMC). A steering wheel was used along with automotive controls.

NCB 1945-1965 GB
Northern Coachbuilder Ltd, Newcastle-upon-Tyne, manufactured a line of battery-electric delivery vehicles. In 1949 they introduced a 3-wheeler called the 'Percheron', a walk-through delivery van with a cargo capacity of 1.25 tons.

Neander 1934-1939 Germany
This company built a series of prototypes designed by Ernst Neumann. It appears that none went into serious production. More information under Neumann.

Neckar 1963-1964 Germany
The German company built a small number of 3-wheeled commercial vehicles with a choice of van or pickup bodies. Using a small 2-seater forward control cabin, steering wheel and car instrumentation, power to the rear wheels came from a 25hp 2-cylinder under floor engine of 500cc. Vehicle was also known as the Pulley.

Nefag   **1919 to date**   **Switzerland**
Neue Elektrische Fahrzeuge AG, manufacturer of battery/electric trucks and buses went through a number of name changes since its start in 1919. After the Second World War it concentrated on 3- and 4-wheeled battery-electric delivery vehicles with a load capacity of up to two tons. With 6hp traction motors they have a range of 56km. More information under Tribelhorn.

Nef La Nef   **1899-1914**   **France**
Built at Agen by Lacroix et de Laville, the La Nef car was a sturdy vehicle and became known as the country doctor's car. Built with a wooden chassis and tiller steering, the vehicle used a variety of De Dion engines ranging from 2.75hp to 8hp. More details under La Nef.

Neimann   **1931**   **Germany**
Abram Neimann was the designer of a number of stylish 3-wheeled cars in the early 1930s. All had the wheel configuration of two in front and one at the back, the method of applying power to those wheels differed in almost all models. The Neimann Stromer had an underslung backbone chassis with a 600cc front wheel drive engine, a long bonnet ending in a duck tail coupé cabin. The Neimann-Entwurf had a similar backbone chassis but with a rear mounted engine with chain-drive to the single rear wheel and the lot clothed in an open sporty 2-seater body with cycle mudguards, aero screens and a pram hood. Many of his cars were built by or in conjunction with DKW. His work includes the Framo Piccolo, the Hercules, Goliath Pioneer, as well as design work for Opel, NSU, Hanomag, Hansa and others.

Neimann was made bankrupt and his firm Nationalised in the late 1930s. He survived the war but died an embittered man in 1967.

Nelco   **1950s**   **GB**
A 36 volt electric car built for the disabled, 35 miles per charge, single armchair seating with tiller steering to the single front wheel. A pram hood and weather sheeting for winter protection. It was also known as the Nelco Solocar.

Nemo   **1948-1950**   **Netherlands**
With a load capacity of 15.5cwt, the Nemo was built by the Nemo Nederlandsche Motorrijturigfabriek, at Jutphaas. The Coventry Victor 749cc flat twin engine was mounted over and drove the single front wheel via chains.

Nestoria   **1931**   **Germany**
A victim of the depression years, the Nestoria was built in small numbers by Bischoff & Pedall, Nuremberg. It was of the usual European format with the driver sitting over the single rear wheel with a 200cc (later 500cc) engine under his feet. A cargo box or open tray was placed between the front wheels.

New Courier   **1898-1900**   **GB**
The New Courier Cycle Company built a convertible motor tricycle in their Wolverhampton factory. During the week a tradesman's box was situated between the two front wheels while at weekends this could be changed in a few minutes for a passenger's seat. Another speciality was the 'patent starting gears', probably the forerunner of the kick start.

Vehicles were also sold under the name of Motorette.

New Eagle 1907-1913 GB
Information listed under Eagle.

New Era (1) 1911-1912 USA
The New Era Auto Cycle Company, Dayton, Ohio built just one 3-wheeled van in limited numbers. It had a single-cylinder air-cooled engine that drove the single rear wheel with the driver sitting behind a 400lb capacity cargo box and over the engine. Handlebar steering was used.

New Era (2) 1928-1937 Japan
What looked like the mating of the back end of a small truck to the front end of a large motorcycle, the New Era cargo carrier was built by Nippon Jidosha Co Ltd Ohmori, near Tokyo, and powered by single cylinder engine (later changed to a V-twin using shaft-drive and 3-speed and reverse gearbox). The driver sat motorcycle style out in all weather.
The vehicle had a name change in 1937 to Kurogane and with later changes in ownership went on to build 3-wheelers until 1962.

New Hudson 1913-1924 GB
Starting life as a 4-wheeler, the New Hudson became a 3-wheeler in 1919. This 2-seater car was built by a Birmingham motorcycle factory and was powered by a V-twin MAG engine to the single rear wheel. With no door on the driver's side and with the hood erected, it was a very awkward car to get into.

Nihon Tsubasa 1930s Japan
A cargo carrier with the choice of either a single cylinder engine of 650cc or a twin cylinder of 750cc, it had an unusual feature of 'air brakes'. The cargo box was between the two rear wheels. Production figures for 1937 was 474 units.

Nimrod 1899-1900 GB
Advertised as a 'Roadster Motor Tricycle' and built by a Bristol cycle manufacturer, this 3-wheeler was powered by a De Dion engine.

Ninon 1928-1939 France
A motorcycle firm who built a number of commercial trikes using engines ranging from 100cc to 500cc.

Nipper 1947-1948 GB
The Nipper was a speciality vehicle used by the milk industry, built by Northern Dairy Engineers Ltd of Hull. There were two models: 8cwt, with a speed of 16mph or 10cwt and a speed of 10mph. The JAP air-cooled engine, mounted at the rear had a short drive through a 2-speed gearbox and centrifugal clutch. The driver stood on the rear platform and used a long tiller to steer the single front wheel.

Nippy Carrier 1954 GB
See Auto Mower for more information.

Nisshin 1930s Japan
A cargo trike based on the front end of a motorcycle with a 600cc engine. About 182 units were built in 1937.

Nobel   1959-1961   **GB**

The German Fuldamobil built in Britain under licence. It was more car-like and came in a 2 door plastic body with seating for two or a slightly longer version as a 2+2. Powered by a 192cc engine it had coupled mechanical brakes, a 4-speed gearbox with electrically operated reverse, was 126 inches long and claimed 100 mpg. The British version was built by Lea Francis where about 260 vehicles were produced.

The original German vehicle was first manufactured in 1950 while a version called the Alta was built in Greece in 1970. With the exception of a few built as 4-wheelers, all came with two front wheels and a powered single rear wheel. Standard car type controls were used. Several body variations were offered in kit including an open utility-styled vehicle. Total production around 1,000 units.

Nobeletta   1955   **Germany**

A batch of open beach cars with a frontal treatment similar to the Mini-Moke was built by the Fulda factory on the Nobel chassis and destined for the South African market. Production was limited.

Northcote   1907-1908   **GB**

Built by the Northcote Manufacturing Company of Battersea, London, this was a tri-van using the rear of a Chater-Lea motorcycle, mated to a cargo box of 3cwt capacity slung between the two front wheels. The engine, driving the single rear wheel through a 3-speed gearbox, was a 6hp or 9hp JAP V-twin.

NSU   1904-1931   **Germany**

Well known as the builders of sturdy motorcycles, Neckarsulmer Fahrradwerke A.G. produced a tri-van from motorcycle parts with the cargo box slung between the two front wheels. Power to the single rear wheel was from the company's own 2 cylinder 10hp engine. An unusual feature was the use of a steering wheel instead of the normal handlebars or tiller normal for that era.

Nuova Amica   1971 to date   **Italy**

Information listed under BMA Amica.

Oak   1919   **GB**

This was a LSD sold under a special marketing deal, believed to be with a Co-op company. More information under LSD

Oben Lanoy   1943   **Germany (?)**

A fully enclosed single seat, electric powered car with a small single front wheel exposed under a long nose. Batteries and the motors were placed over the rear axle and driving the rear wheels.

Obus   1912-1914   **France**

Details noted under Souriau.

Ocma-Devil   1953-1957   **Italy**

The Devil Moto Factory of Milan built the usual style of 3-wheeled commercial vehicle but differed from other manufacturers in using a powerful 245cc single cylinder 2-stroke engine. This was coupled to a dry-plate clutch, along with 3 forward speeds and shaft-drive to the two rear wheels.

OD 1933 Germany
At the OD-Werke, Willy Ostner in Dresden built a trivan along the lines of the much copied Hanomag, A DKW 200cc engine powered the single front wheel. It came in tray and van bodies and in 1933 was offered as an articulated tractor with a custom-built 2-wheeled trailer. In 1935, a 4-wheeled version with a 600cc engine was introduced but the 3-wheelers were discontinued when war broke out.

Odin 1980s USA
From Cambridge in Iowa came plans for converting a motorcycle into a 3-wheeled 2-seater sports car. It was available in kit form from $1400 or as a completed vehicle, price depending on the donor motorcycle. The prototype had a vague resemblance to a '30s Morgan. It was also advertised as the Cyclecar by Odin.

Ogle & Summers 1820s-1830s GB
Nathaniel Ogle, an amateur steam enthusiast and engineer, William Alltoft Summers, are reported to have built their first steam coach in 1829, able to carry 10 passengers and weighing in at 2.5 tons plus water, fuel and passengers. After testing it was found to be underpowered and heavy on fuel. A newer version was announced in 1831 as a 3-wheeled (single front and powered rear wheels) 'treble bodied phaeton' with open coachwork. Plying in the Southampton area it was reported to have travelled over 800 miles without serious trouble at an average speed of 10mph. The partners went on to build a larger 4-wheeled coach with capacity for 28 passengers. The names of Ogle & Summers appeared in the press for another 8 years, then faded away with a record of only three coaches actually being built but with pages of exaggerated claims as to performance and reliability.

Oldsmobile 1891 USA
See R E Olds steam car.

Olympia 1900s GB
More information see Humber.

Omega 1925-1927 GB
Built by W J Green Ltd of Swan Lane, Coventry and powered by a lusty 980cc JAP water-cooled engine, it had a roomy(!) 2-seater body with good weather protection. The engine, situated up front under a normal car type hood, was driven through a cone clutch via a long tailshaft to a bevel box, just ahead of the single rear wheel with final drive by chain to sprockets on either side of the wheel - this gave variable gearing. Reverse was get out and push or pick up the tail and walk. Brakes were optional on front wheels, there was no spare wheel but excellent electric lights. Top speed was about 60mph and the Omega is recorded as the holder of a number of world speed records of the period.

Omer to date Italy
The Fabbrica Italiana Motocarri Omer are still building an ultralight 3-wheeled delivery vehicle. It has a 48cc single cylinder 2-stroke engine with shaft-drive to the two rear wheels. Using hydro-mechanical brakes the vehicle comes in a variety of body styles with a capacity of 200kg.

Omnium 1911-1914 GB
The Omnium Motor Co of London had their very popular 3-wheeled parcel's carrier

built by Premier Motor Co Ltd of Birmingham. Following the usual format for delivery vans of the day, a 6hp or 7hp water-cooled engine was placed just in front of the single rear wheel and under the driver's seat, with a chain-drive to a 2-speed epicyclic gear on the rear hub. A 6cwt capacity cargo box was slung between the two front wheels. It had tiller steering and a canvas canopy style cabin for the driver. London and North Western Railways had a fleet of these vehicles for parcel delivery. With the advent of the First World War the Birmingham factory went on to war production. The Omnium did not reappear when hostilities ceased.

Onnasch 1924 Germany

Opperman-Motorcart 1947-1953 GB
Built by S E Opperman Ltd until 1953 when the design was sold to Transport Equipment (Thornycroft) Ltd, these vehicles were originally designed as a farm trucks. Powered by an 8bhp single cylinder JAP petrol engine mounted with the front wheel on a single steering arm. The driver stood on a platform in front of the load and steered the tractor-tyred wheel using a large steering wheel. Bodies could be adapted to a variety of farm or factory uses and a number of chassis were supplied to Lacre Lorries Ltd as a basis for its T-type road sweeper.

Orbus 1912-1914 France
For more information see under Souriau.

Orient 1899-1909 USA
Located in Massachusetts, the Waltham Manufacturing Company built a very popular bicycle before introducing a rear-engined tricycle to their range in 1899. Powered by a De Dion engine (Waltham were appointed importers of all De Dion products to the United States in 1895), it was unusual as it could be converted to quadricycle simply by removing the front forks with the wheel attached, then replacing it with a frame carrying the two front wheels with a cargo box or passenger seat located between the sprung wheels.
 A number of steam cars were built in 1897 and the factory started with a 4-wheeled Voiturette in 1902

Orient-Express 1895-1903 Germany

Ossa 1954-1962 Spain
Motorcycle firm, Orfeo Sincronic SA, Barcelona built a number of delivery tricycles using a 175cc single cylinder ohv engine with a choice of commercial bodies.

OTI 1957-1959 France
Sporting a Bugatti grill as proof that it was made in the old Bugatti works at Molsheim, this was an attractive 2-seater with car controls and powered by a 125cc Gnome-et-Rhone 2-stroke engine. The designer was M. Villeple. It had a top speed of 45km/h, and in France could be driven without a licence.

Otis 1970-1975 USA
Information under West Coaster.

Oxford 1899 GB
Named after the street in which the company's sales office was located, Oxford

Street, London, the Oxford was a light 3-wheeled vehicle with belt drive to the single rear wheel from a 2.25hp engine.

P54 1957 Spain
Information under Sava.

Padwin 1950s GB
A road-going car built mainly for invalids, similar to the Carter.

Patterson 1862 GB
A Mr A Patterson built a unique 1 ton 3-wheeled passenger vehicle unique. Its boiler was mounted over and drove the single front wheel, also used for changing direction. This odd contraption proved roadworthy but Mr Patterson was frequently stopped by the police for being in contempt of the road laws.

Pan Kar 1968-1990s Greece
P Karavisopoulos, Peristeri, Athens are pioneer builders of 3-wheeled trucks in Greece. Along with other manufacturers they have based their vehicles on the use of new or reconditioned VW engines and rear wheel assemblies. A forward control 2-seater fibreglass cabin with car-type controls and a range of cargo compartments. Payload is 350 kilos.

Pappenberger 1953 Germany

Parcel Car 1919-1920 France & GB
See Trident for more information.

Paris-Rhone 1947-1950 France

Pargo to date USA
Built by the Columbia Car Corporation of Charlotte, North Carolina. A large range of electric vehicles for both passenger and freight movements within large factory and amusement park complexes and airports. Cargo range up to 960 lbs capacity and passenger from 2 to 8 plus.

Pashley 1953-1962 GB
A large side-opening delivery box, mounted between two small wheels with a motorcycle (minus its front wheel) tacked on behind, could best describe the Pashley. A unique feature was the steering wheel sticking straight out from the end of the delivery box. Power came from a Villiers 6E 197cc 2-stroke engine driving the single rear wheel by a chain. A Bond lookalike minicar was introduced with a 197cc engine in 1953 but did not get past the prototype stage.

Other listings from this company were the Pelican (see p.114) and a utility styled vehicle with a motorcycle front end powered by Royal Enfield with a half-ton capacity tray between two rear wheels. A canvas canopy over the tube frame gave weather protection.

The company W R Pashley Ltd hailed from Birmingham.

Pasquil-Rhone 1947-1950 France

PB 1955 France

Pecori 1891 Italy

Enrico Pecori of Casino d'Erba in Italy built a steam tricycle in 1891. A vertical fire-tube boiler with a central fire box was mounted in an attractive metal tray attached to a tubular underslung chassis, driving a live axle to the two rear wire wheels. The driver and passenger sat behind the axle with tiller-type steering to the single front wheel. The vehicle is now in the Biscaretti Motor Museum in Turin.

Peel 1962-1966 Isle of Man

The Isle of Man based Peel Engineering were pioneers in fibreglass mouldings. It entered the car field with the Peel Manxman, a 3-wheeler with a steel tube chassis, rear mounted 250cc Anzani engine and a coupé body. A speed of 50mph and 80 mpg were claimed.

In 1962 they were to produce the world's smallest car, the Peel P50, 4ft 5ins long with a 49cc DKW engine able to push things along at 40mph and 100 mpg. This was followed by a larger version in 1965, the Peel Trident, still a mini-mini car built of fibreglass with a clear wrap-around plexiglass dome, it was just 6ft long (see front cover). The engine that drove the single rear wheel was placed under and to the rear of a bench seat that would fit two at a pinch. Potholes had to be avoided at all costs as the wheels were minute – if stuck, the remedy was to get out and carry the car to safer ground. For reverse, you picked up the rear of the car by the handle provided and pointed it in the direction you wanted to go.

Peka 1924 Germany

Pelican Rickshaw 1953-1957 GB

The Pashley Pelican is a five seater rickshaw built along motorcycle lines; the bike up front and a tandem seating 2x2 straddling the back axle. Built with a sturdy steel pipe chassis, they were one of the first British production vehicles to use fibreglass bodywork. Most Rickshaws were for export. Information under Pashley.

Pennington 1894-1902 GB

The New Pennington Autocar was built by Mr Edward Joel Pennington at the Motor Mills, Coventry. He called it the Torpedo. As well as having an inventive flair, Mr Pennington was a publicist and realised the power of the press. It was a curious vehicle designed to carry four people with the driver standing on a platform and steering from the rear. Publicity photographs (see p.176) show as many as nine people standing or sitting wherever they can find a foothold on vehicle!

Percheron 1945-1965 GB

Information listed under NCB.

Perfecta 1899-1903 Italy

Perkins 1871-1902 GB

Built by Perkins & Sons, London, to take the place of the horse on a wagon or coach. A 3-wheeled steam tractor with a water tube boiler and a compound engine carrying power to the single front wheel, mounted with the boiler in a circular subframe within the main chassis thus allowing the whole unit to turn when a change of direction was required. A prototype was built and successfully tested and was listed in the company's catalogue for many years. It is doubtful, however, if many vehicles were actually built.

Perry   1899-1900s   GB
From the Birmingham factory of Perry & Company Ltd, a motor tricycle with a wheelbase considerably longer than normally offered in 1899. The single front wheel is carried on strengthened duplex forks. The engine used was 3.5hp.

Pestourie Et Planchon   1921-1922   France
Technically this was be a 4-wheeled car but as the two rear wheels were only a few inches apart it was able to be registered as a 3-wheeler at a usual lower rate. The rear wheels were driven from a 4-cylinder 904cc engine.

Petite   1953   GB
A direct descendent of the original AC Sociable and built at Thames Ditton. More information see AC.

Petit Puce   1976   France
This was originally built in America as the PPV, a plastic tub for two with a small rear mounted engine. To save space the lot could be lifted up and parked on the squared end. The wheel arrangement was single in front and two rear wheels located at the extreme end, just behind the seat. Extras included a lift-up canopy body with wing mirrors and traffic indicators.

Petrocar   1896-1897   GB
Information listed under Roots and Venables.

Petrol Pony   1935-1936   GB
The 3-wheeled Petrol Pony was another mechanical horse built on a tubular backbone frame, with a single cylinder petrol engine mounted behind the rear wheels. A second prototype was built using a Austin 7 engine and said to be capable of hauling a trailer with a 1.5 ton load. These two units were designed and built by a Frank Waring. It appears that no further vehicles were produced.

Peugeot VLV   1941-1945   France
A wartime runabout from Peugeot. Battery electric power to an apparently single rear wheel (which was actually two wheels very close together). There was side-by-side seating for two, a pram hood and side opening doors.

Phanomen   1899-1939   Germany
Better known for bicycles at the turn of the century, Phanomen-Werke Gustav Hiller AG, Zittau, built their first 3-wheeler in 1907. With a substantial pressed metal chassis, the V-twin 880cc air-cooled engine sat over the front wheel driven by a series of chains. The lot, engine and front wheel turned as one and was controlled by a tiller from the open 2-seater body. After 1912 the engine was upgraded to a 1,536cc 4 cylinder and the vehicle acquired a steering wheel and a cabin. The new engine was to remain in service on the 3-wheeler until 1927. Continually improved, the Phanomen was available as a covered van, an open truck and a taxi. They were also exported. During the Great War, many hundreds were used as German army ambulances. In 1911 they produced a car and though not built in great numbers it remained until all production ceased in 1939.

Phebus (1)   1899   GB
A trike of the usual design with a single front wheel and the major part of a bicycle

frame. A De Dion engine mounted level but behind the back axle supplied the power, with pedal assistance for starting and getting up hills. A few of these solidly built trikes are still in existence.

Phebus (2)   1898-1899   France

A 3-wheeler with a long pipe chassis and a one cylinder 6hp engine up front supplying power to the rear wheels by means of long belts. A two person armchair seat was fitted over the rear axle between the wheels. A vertical steering column allowed the single front wheel to be turned by a series of cables and pulleys.

Phelon and Moore   1900   GB

A single rear wheel trike with the power coming from a single cylinder water-cooled engine of 3.5hp, driving the rear wheel through a 2-speed gearbox. The passenger sat in the usual seat placed between the front wheels.

Phelps Tractor   1901-1905   USA

Possibly one of the earliest pieces of powered farm machinery, the Phelps Tractor manufactured in 1901, was designed for many uses and came in many body styles. Powered by a small steam engine it was advertised as a 'Tractor of Universal Applications'. It had a boiler with automatic fuel and water feed, required no attention and would run half-a-day without refilling. The small steam engine delivered up to 10hp and was capable of a speed of over 20mph towing a 4-wheeled farm cart or, in one of its many uses, hitched to the family Surrey. The driver controlled the tractor with reins, a throw back to the horse it was replacing. Drawing back the reins would cut the speed of the tractor, a little harder and it would stop. If the pressure was maintained the tractor would start to backup. To stop, one only had to drop the reins as this was supposed to stop the engine instantly. The driver also steered the single front wheel with another set of reins as if he were handling a team of horses. From 1903-1905 there was a Phelps 3-wheeler of orthodox design, driven by a 3-cylinder motor coupled to a 2-speed gearbox and driveshaft to the two rear wheels, all incorporated in a backbone chassis. The body was detachable to allow access to the motor. The Phelps Motor Vehicle Company was in Stoneham, Massachusetts.

Phoenix-Trimo   1903-1905   GB

Built by Phoenix Motors, advertising for this machine emphasised its reliability by a Gold Medal win in the 1,000 Mile Autocycle Club's Trial – the only machine in its class to do so in 1903. Built along motorcycle lines by a Mr J. Van Hooydonk, a fourth wheel was added in 1905 and a new name, the Quadcar. Further improvements and the vehicle was to become a true light car in 1908. Production ended in 1925 but the odd machine was still produced from spare parts until 1928.

Piaggio   1947   Italy

For more information look under the listing of Vespa Piaggio.

Piccolo   1927-1940   Germany

Information listed under Framo.

Pierce Steam Tricycle   1895   USA

It was reported that a Mr W A Pierce built a steam tricycle in the town of Sisterville, West Virginia in the year 1895. No reports of any further vehicles.

Pilain 1890-1898 France
Francios Pilain opened a factory at La Buire, near Lyon, to build the Serpollet 3-wheeled steam vehicles under licence. He did this until 1893 when he began building his own brand of tiller-steered phaeton. He closed shop in 1898 and joined the firm of Vermorel as Director General.

Pioneer 1870-1872 GB
Information located under Nairn Pioneer.

Pioneer-Borgward 1929 Germany
Information listed under Borgward.

Pinguin 1954 Germany
Originating from the Passat project for a 4-wheeled coupé, the Pinguin was built as a 3-wheeled 2-seater coupé in 1953 with a central tube frame clothed in a modern looking metal body and a rear mounted Fichtel & Sachs 197cc, 9.5hp engine, able to propel the vehicle at a steady 85km/h. In 1954 it became a larger 2+2 but by 1955 a lack of capital saw the project fold after about 10 vehicles had been built.

Pininfarina 1961 Italy.
A sleek 5-seater from the house of Pininfarina built in 1961. It had a bodyline resembling the Davis (USA) but with a much shorter nose, was rear engined, four door and had Cadillac-style rear fins, labelled the 'Y'. It never got past prototype. A two door version labelled the 'X', sporting a Fiat 1100 engine was shown at the 1960 Turin Motor show – was this the same vehicle with some modifications?

PMC 1912-1913 GB
For more information see Premier.

Poinard 1951-1956 France
Builders of sidecars for the motorcycle trade, the Poinard establishment branched out with a 2-seater car in 1952. The single front wheel was hidden under a pointed nose while either a 125cc or 175cc single cylinder 2-stroke engine was located just above the rear axle, behind the bench seat. Production was limited.

Poirier 1928-1958 France
Etablissements G Poirier, Fondettes, Indre-et-Loire started production of invalid carriages that were soon offered with modifications for highway use. In 1935 they introduced the Monoto, a single or tandem-seated cyclecar with a motorcycle front end and steering assembly. A tubular chassis was clothed in an open slab-sided metal body. Pre-war power came from a 175cc Train or Sachs engine with Peugeot or Gnome-et-Rhone as alternatives, all with chain-drive to the rear wheels. Post-war engines were 98cc Sachs or 125cc Ydral with shaft-drive.

Pokorney 1905 USA
For more information look for listing under Tricolet.

Polywog 1976 USA
The Polywog was from Southern California with a amphibious body constructed of two layers of fibreglass with a foam sandwich in between, weighing in at 425 lbs and classed as a motorcycle in its home country. Though the Polywog was street

legal it could not be used on the freeways. Powered by a 8hp Briggs and Stratton air-cooled engine, it had a land speed of 45mph and was able to do 3.5 knots on water. The amazing ability of the Polywog to traverse both land and water came from its unique wobble action designed into the rear wheels and axle. A pull control on the hub caused the rear wheels to cant over on the axle; as this rotates, the wheels created a sculling motion eliminating the use of a separate propeller when in water. The single front wheel worked as a rudder. Production was limited.

Pony 1946-1963 GB
Information listed under Brush.

Power-Drive 1956-1958 GB
Seating three abreast, the Power-Drive was a low, wide, modern-looking car with a single rear wheel powered by a 322cc 2-stroke Anzani engine. The contoured body made from aluminium had a soft hood and side curtains. With the hood down it had a very sporting look. After production ceased in 1958, the vehicle reappeared in Denham with modifications as the Coronet. The original vehicle came from Powerdrive Ltd, Wood Green, London.

PPV 1973 USA
A plastic bodied tub for two that could be powered by a small petrol engine, or pedal! Its feature was parking: just lift up and stand on end. Many were exported to Australia as pedal-powered only but proved a traffic hazard; too small to be seen by trucks and too large to be called a bicycle. The concept was taken up by the French and renamed the Petit Puce. More information under that name.

Praga 1952 Czechoslovakia
Formed in 1910, Auto Praga is one of the oldest of Czechoslovakia's Automobile factories, well-known for its heavy trucks. In 1952 it is understood that they had built a number of 3-wheeled light trucks.

Premier 1912-1919 GB
Premier Motor Company Ltd, Birmingham, built a 3-wheeled parcel carrier based on their PMC Motorette. Powered by a JAP 7hp single cylinder engine, it had a 2-speed gearbox and chain-drive to the single rear wheel. Load capacity was 5cwt and it had a close resemblance to the AC Autocarrier. It was also sold under the name of Omnium.

Primus 1899-1904 Germany
Built by Kaiser, who at that time was a manufacturer of sewing machines and bicycles, this was a 3-wheeled car using one of their own engines, fashioned after the De Dion. A fourth wheel was added in 1904.

Progress (1) 1899 GB
The Progress Cycle Co Ltd of Foleshill, Coventry, exhibited a De Dion powered tricycle with a frame and body of their own design at the 1899 Cycle Show in London. The verdict was that it was a solid and well-finished machine.

Progress (2) 1930-1934 GB
From Percy Street in Hulme, Manchester, the home of the odd-shaped Seal Sociable, the first Progress commercial was based on the Seal but with the driver

beside the load and controlling the vehicle from a bucket seat. Three engines, a 343cc Villiers, a 680cc JAP and a 980cc JAP were used. In 1932 a new line of more conventional single front-wheel-drive commercials were introduced. These had a 680cc JAP with a Sturmey-Archer 3 speed gearbox and motorcycle style controls. In 1933 a longer wheelbase with a 750cc engine was added.
See notes under Seal.

PTV   1956-1962   Spain
PTV stood for Perramon, Tache and Vila, the owners of Automoviles Utilitarios SA, Barcelona, who built light cars and vans powered by Ausa 250cc single cylinder 2-stroke engines mounted at the rear, both 3- and 4-wheeled models were made with independent suspension all round and equipped with hydraulic brakes.

Publix.   1947-1948   USA & Canada
A single front wheel convertible with a tube frame chassis clothed in an aluminium body. Power came from an engine range from 1.7hp that went up to 10.4hp. With an aluminium engine, weight was given as under 250 lbs. The manufacturer was the Publix Motor Car Co of Fort Erie, Ontario, Canada, and Buffalo, New York.

Pulley   1964   Germany
The Neckar built for a special market and renamed. Information under Neckar.

P-Valle   1952-1957   France
Information under Valle-Chantecler.

Quadrant   1903-1907   GB
First models of this famous make were built on bicycle lines with widely spaced front wheels and a variety of 2hp and 3hp engines. Improvements soon followed with the introduction of a 'luxurious, high-powered, all-weather Carette', along the standard format of passenger closest to the traffic. The Quadrant had its engine slightly behind the front axle driving the single rear wheel via a chain. The driver sat in a luxurious padded seat, with a steering wheel comfortably placed at an angle with foot and hand controls within easy reach. However, as the passenger seat was placed in front of the axle this made entry an adventure... should the driver not be in his seat the rear wheel simply left the ground!

The Quadrant Tricar was built by the Quadrant Cycle Company Ltd of Birmingham. The production of 3-wheeled cars and commercials was halted in 1906.

Quincy-Lynn   1978-1985   USA
Founded by Robert Quincy Riley and David Lynn, Quincy-Lynn Enterprises were experimenters in all forms of DIY transport. They built a number of 3-wheeled vehicles: the Urba trike started the line in 1978, followed by the Trimuter in 1980, then the Tri-Magnum in 1983. All were sold in plan form only after at least one prototype had been built and tested. Builders, however, had a habit of adapting the plans and adding their own refinements. Quincy-Lynn production ended in 1985 but their names do pop up from time to time in specials built by other parties. Robert Quincy Riley formed Robert Q Riley Enterprises, Scottsdale Arizona and went on to better things. He still produces the plans for the Tri-Magnum and the Trimuter as well as other 3- and 4-wheeled vehicles and has embraced the Internet as a sales outlet.

Raleigh 1900-1936 GB

Raleigh, the Nottingham bicycle manufacturer ventured into car and motorised trikes for a short time in 1901.

The next venture was not until 1933 with a commercial van and a car built to carry four passengers. The Raleigh car of the 1930s was a long bonnet 3-wheeler that was actually the van with an extended chassis, fitted windows and one side opening door. The single front wheel and a 742cc V-twin engine was totally enclosed under the long bonnet. A solid channel chassis carried the rear axle underslung on elliptical springs. The engine was built up in unit with a single dry plate clutch and a three forward and one reverse gearbox, and the drive was by an open propeller shaft to a spiral-bevel rear axle.

As well as the panel vans and the family 4-seater, a sporty 2-seater was available. The commercial van, a basic design by T L Williams, who later formed the Reliant Car Company, had a motorcycle-style front wheel located in front of the closed van body. The driver straddled the engine, a 742cc V-twin. Production ceased in 1936 when Raleigh reverted to making bicycles.

Raleighette 1907-1908 GB

A Sociable using a 6hp twin cylinder water-cooled engine, believed not to be connected to the Raleigh Cycle Company.

Rana Mymsa 1957 Spain

Information noted under Rana.

Randall 1903-1905 USA

J V & C Randall & Company of Newtown, Pennsylvania built a number of 3-wheeled vehicles over a period of two years.

Ranger Cub 1974-1976 GB

Built as a kit car in Leigh on Sea in Essex, the Ranger Cub used the Mini as a donor car and proved a successful vehicle for a number of years. It had a stylish 2-seater body.

Rapid 1899-1900 Switzerland

Rata 1953-1956 Spain

For more information see notes under Cresma.

Raymar 1952-1970 Spain

For more information see R.O.A.

RC-600-L 1952-1970 Spain

Information under R.O.A.

Reese 1887-1899 USA

The S Reese Machine & Tool Works of Plymouth, Pennsylvania built a quantity of 3-wheeled vehicles over a 12 year period.

Regent 1899-1900 GB

As well as building bicycles this Birmingham company also built a number of motor tricycles using an Accles-Turrell engine.

Regina (1) 1903-1908 France
Building a variety of motorised vehicles the Societe I'Electrique of Paris included the Gallia and Galliette electric cars as well as cycles, motorcycles and tricars.

Regina (2) 1921-1925 France
This was a small 3-wheeler with a single front wheel. A 902cc Ruby engine was placed behind the seat driving the rear wheels.

Reid 1895 USA

Reiju 1954-1956 Spain
The Reiju came from the motorcycle maker Reira & Juanola SA, of Figueras, Gerona, who built a small number of delivery tricycles that used a single cylinder 4-stroke Fita engine made locally.

Reliant 1934 to date GB
Reliant, the firm that won't go away. T L Williams was the designer of the original Raleigh Safety Seven, a light delivery wagon with a single front wheel mounted motorcycle style outside the enclosed van body. It had a 742cc V-twin engine with shaft-drive to the rear wheels through a 3-speed gearbox. Raleigh, the Nottingham bicycle manufacturer, decided in 1934 that they had had enough of engine powered vehicles and closed down the production line in favour of bicycles. Williams decided to go it alone and set up Reliant Engineering in an old bus garage in Tamworth, Staffordshire, where he built his first Reliant, a 7cwt van powered by a single cylinder air-cooled JAP driving the rear wheels by chain through a 3-speed/reverse gearbox.

By 1936 the vehicle had been upgraded to a 10cwt and power came from a JAP twin cylinder using driveshaft to replace the chain final drive. The following year a 747cc Austin engine was used to power 8cwt and 12cwt vans. 1951 saw the introduction of the Regal, the company's first passenger vehicle.

Continually improving, Reliant went on to give modern car comfort with the economy of 3-wheeled motoring with the following vehicles available in both passenger and commercial variations. Reliant Regal, 1951-1963. Regal 3-25 and 3-30, 1962-1973. Reliant Robin, 1973-1981. Reliant Rialto, 1981-1990 with the updated version from 1991 to date. The Reliant Ant, 1970 on, was a commercial cab and chassis unit where you could have a body of your own design fitted.

In 1990 Reliant went bankrupt because of its dealings in the property market. Beans Engineering, who had been supplying the engines stepped in and rescued the 3-wheeler part of the company only to have the receivers move in four years later when their engineering side folded.

With a continuing and full order book for the 3-wheelers, the Avonex Group, a motoring and aviation supplier, quickly moved in and plan to enlarge the export market.

Remmington 1897 USA
Well-known for its rifles, Remmington were also the makers of bicycles and built a number of 3-wheelers powered by kerosene engines.

Renaux 1901-1902 France
For more information see notes under Energie.

R.E.Olds Steam Car   **1886-1891**   **USA**
Ransom E Olds, later of Oldsmobile and REO fame, built a 3-wheeled steam car in 1886. He was employed in his father's firm, P F Olds and Sons, building small portable steam engines – these were very sturdy and successful, over 2000 had been built. Ransom was born in 1864 and grew up a natural engineer, starting work on an experimental 3-wheeled self-propelled carriage in 1886. It was not until 1891 that he had a steam carriage ready to show the public. It was a sturdy, if somewhat crude and cumbersome vehicle, with the engine was rated at 2hp. It had very large rear wheels on a live axle while a small front wheel was tiller steered. Using a vertical boiler to supply steam to a diminutive engine, the single front wheel was soon replaced by two, placed very close together as an aid to steering. A number of vehicles were built, though it was not long before the wheels were moved to the same track as the rear. With the advent of the combustion engine the Curved Dash Oldsmobile was born.

Repton   **1904**   **GB**
The Repton was a small single seater with a large steering wheel, with the engine up front under the longish bonnet. Built by the Repton Engineering Works, Repton. Derbyshire, it was powered by a 4hp water-cooled engine through a 2-speed epicyclic gearbox with shaft-drive to the single back wheel. Speed was 25mph and, unusual for a trike, had front wheel brakes.

Resello Solocar   **1940s(?)**   **GB**
A single seat cyclecar with a single front wheel, engine under the seat, vertical windscreen and a pram hood. Registered for road use and aimed at the invalid car market.

Revelli   **1941**   **Italy**
Count Gino Revelli built and sold a very successful lightweight racing motorcycle; the GR. To maintain his passion for racing he built commercial cargo trikes under the Revelli name until the war put a stop to production.

Revolette   **1905**   **GB**
Built in Birmingham by the Revolution Cycle Company, a 3-wheeled car that appears not to have been built in any quantity.

Rex/Rexette   **1899-1933**   **GB**
The Rex name started in Birmingham in 1899 as manufacturers of motor cars but soon switched to tricars. Moving into the 1900s a range of vehicles were available, the Rex Forecar improved from the early models with saddle seating, the engine was low down in front of the driver and passenger sat in a wicker armchair between the two front wheels. 1903 had the driver in a padded chair, a 550cc engine, heavy duty car-type wire wheels and the passenger's padded seat was a timber and metal unit that, when not in use, folded up to form a neat box able to be interchanged with a delivery box. The Rexette of 1906 had a steering wheel with a lot more creature comforts for the driver and passenger. Rex had started making 2-wheeled motorcycles in 1901 and these gradually took the place of 3-wheelers, replacing the trikes by 1908. As war production took over in 1914 a 3-wheeled fire car was produced (actually a Rex motorcycle with a ridged sidecar-type frame with hoses and fire fighting equipment and a crew of three).
    Rex disappeared in 1933.

Revolution   **1970s**   **GB**

Rheda   **1897-1899**   **France**
Built in Saint Cloud and advertised as a tricycle carriage powered by a 2.5hp horizontal engine.

Rhodes   **1900s**   **GB**
Built in Southport with a 5hp Forman or a 8hp MMC engine, these 3-wheeled cars were soon sporting a fourth wheel and power from 10hp and 16hp 4-cylinder engines. Another vehicle from the same stable was the Ribble of 1904 to 1908, using the same engine combination – this also became a 4-wheeler.

Riboud   **1974-1980**   **France**
Information listed under Vitrex Riboud.

Richard   **1900s**   **France**

Rickett   **1858-1865**   **GB**
This started as an experimental road vehicle more akin to a mobile steam engine. It had a timber chassis, with a boiler resembling a steam train with high flue. Twin pistons were mounted each side of the boiler and between the large rear steel wheels, with power transmitted to a live axle and transferred to the rear wheels by chains. The driver and passengers sat in a comfortable armchair in front of the boiler, protected by a phaeton hood – a tiller was used to steer the single front wheel. A number of vehicles were built before the Highways Act of 1865 restricted production.

In 1860 one of these vehicles successfully completed a journey of 150 miles from Inverness to Thurso. Rickett vehicles were reported to have averaged 10/12mph with speed bursts of 16mph on long flat stretches of open road. On 9 January 1860, a vehicle was demonstrated to the Queen, Prince Albert, Prince Edward and other members of the Royal Household at Windsor Castle. One vehicle built for the Earl of Caithness had many improvements including a metal chassis frame that doubled as a water tank. The rear wheels were driven through gears, not chains, as in the early models while the front wheel was sprung. The 2-cylinder engine had a bore of 6 inches and a stroke of 9 inches. It delivered 9hp with a top speed of 19mph and a range of 15 miles between water stops.

Rikscha   **1952**   **Germany**
A prototype of a motor scooter type 3-wheeler and the first collaboration between Fritz Fend and Willy Messerschmitt, which lead to the vehicle that would eventually bear Messerschmitt's name. Information: see Fend and Messerschmitt.

Rickshaw (1)   **1946-1950**   **GB**
More information listed under Turner (1).

Rickshaw (2)   **1948**   **Italy**
For more information see Moto-Guzzi.

Rideabout   **1950s**   **Australia**
From the Lightburn factory in Adelaide came a number of micro cars that included a little 3-wheeled electric car which was known to sometimes double as a golf cart.

Rikuo 1933-1956 Japan
A motorcycle-type delivery van with a capacity of 400kg – the front end a copy of the 750cc V-twin Harley Davidson motorcycle. Available in a number of body styles and built by Rikuo Motorcycle Co Tokyo. Production for 1937 was 230 units.

Riley 1896-1907 GB
The Riley family were originally 19th century weavers and weaving machine manufacturers who turned to the construction of petrol-powered tricycles in 1896. Built in Coventry, the Riley Tricar had become a sophisticated 3-wheeled competitor to the crude motorcycle and sidecar outfits of the day. At the front the passenger was seated in a comfortable bucket seat, wrap-around water-proofed cover to keep the legs warm and dry; to the rear but well in front of the single wheel, the driver was in an equally comfortable bucket seat situated over a 6hp or a 9hp water-cooled engine. With a low centre of gravity, these machines were capable of out-performing most similar machines in comfort, speed and hill climbing. With each year, their performance and comfort was improved – the driver was now seated beside the passenger, the luggage capacity increased and the vehicle became a favourite for touring. In 1907 a fourth wheel was added and the marque went on to producing cars. The firm was taken over by William Morris in 1938 and the Riley name appeared on quality cars until 1969.

Rinspeed UFO 1983 Switzerland

Rixi 1949-1952 GB
Built by the Turner Manufacturing Company Ltd of Wolverhampton. A taxi rickshaw with the unique 168cc Turner engine mounted over the front wheel and just in front of the handlebars of the motorcycle front end. Drive was by chain and the lot turned as one. Behind the driver was a 2-seat open-sided but otherwise enclosed 2-seat cabin. All were built for export. The factory also built 3-wheelers under the names of Tri-Van, L D V, and Turner: see these for more information.

ROA 1952-1970 Spain
Better known for their motorcycles and sidecars, Industrias Motorizadas Onieva, SA, Madrid, manufactured a large number of light vans powered by a 197cc single cylinder Hispano-Villiers engine. Load capacity was 250kg and they were also sold under the name of Raymar. A 600kg version was listed as R C 600L.

Roadable 1946-1947 USA
This was a 3-wheeler that went places! Built in Garland, Texas, by the Southern Aircraft Division of Portable Products Corp. By adding 30ft wings, a tail assembly that included a propeller, this conventional looking sedan had a configuration of two front wheels and a single enclosed rear wheel powered by a 130hp six cylinder air-cooled engine, with an air speed of 110mph and a claimed range of 600 miles. The designer of this experimental vehicle was Ted Hall.

Robertson 1915-1916 GB
From Manchester came the Robertson cyclecar with a choice of 965cc JAP or Precision V-twin engines.

Roc 1903-1915 GB
Apparently funded by the author, Sir Arthur Conan Doyle, the Roc was built and

designed by A W Hall. This motorcycle was available as a long low 2-wheeler, a trike with the usual passenger seat between the two front wheels, or as a cargo trike using either a bought in Precision engine or their own designed Roc engine.

Rochet   1907   France
A number of 3-wheeled cyclecars using different body styles and followed by a very solid built 4-wheeled car along conventional lines were produced at the French factory at Albert in the Somme region. There could be a connection with the car makers of Rochet-Schneider (1894-1932) or Rochet-Freres (1898-1901).

Roger-Benz   1888-1896   France
Assembled in France by Emile Roger, the Benz 3-wheeled cars were later manufactured under licence. He was later to persuade Benz to allow him to introduce a 4-stroke engine and high tension electric ignition for the magneto system which gave a much improved quality to the French built cars.

Rogers Rascal   1980   Canada

Roland   1907   France
Built in an Albert Cycle works in the Somme, a tricar made in small numbers.

Rollera   1956-1958   Germany
Information noted under Brütsch.

Rollfix   1933-1936   Germany
The Rollfix was metal bodied coupé, powered by a 200cc Ilo engine driving the single rear wheel and built by Rollfix Eilwagen GmbH, Hamberg-Wandsbek. Steering wheel and normal car controls with a 2-seater bench for the office area while the engine and rear wheel were housed under a boat-tail with access doors for inspection and maintenance. A 3-wheeled estate car was built about 1934 that had a single front wheel and a rear mounted engine driving the back wheels.

Romanazzi   1953   Italy
Based on the Piaggio Ape chassis this was a custom-built vehicle destined for the Taxi trade. 3 passengers could be accommodated in enclosed comfort in the rear compartment while the driver sat in the doorless front end. A few prototypes were made.

Romi-Isetta   1955   Brazil
The Isetta-BMW built in Brazil under licence – about 3,000 units were produced.

Rondine   1955-1963   Spain
A delivery trike built by Compania Iberica de Transported SA. Madrid. It was powered by a 200cc 2-stroke single cylinder engine.

Ronline   1951-1959   Spain
Information listed under Moto Scooter.

Ronteix   1905-1914   France
This Paris firm manufactured tricars and forecars before branching into conventional 4-wheeled vehicles that were of a high technical quality. The tricar of 1905

was an original design: a chassis of two paralleled tubes fitted with traverse stays that extended the length of the vehicle. A vertical water-cooled single cylinder 3.5hp engine was carried beside the single rear wheel with direct drive to a pinion on the hub, with a built in 2-speed gearbox. An armchair passenger seat was fitted between the two front wheels and steering was by handlebars on a vertical stalk. A delivery vehicle was also offered on the same chassis but used a Buchet twin cylinder engine with chain-drive to a Rivierre 2-speed hub.

Roots & Venables   1895-1897   GB
The Roots Tricar was tiller steered to the single front wheel located in front of a box-like body for two. The engine used was a 2.25hp vertical single cylinder oil engine (the term then for engines that ran on kerosene) – this was located under the seat and drove a live axle. The prototype ran for in excess of 2,000 miles before a 4-wheeled version was built.

Rosenbauer   1950   Austria
The firm of Konrad Rosenbauer was established in Linz in 1908 making gas motors under licence from Benz. In 1950 they produced a 3-wheeler coupé on a pipe chassis with a 250cc 10hp engine driving the single back wheel, hidden under a long sloping tail. Side opening doors gave access to a bench seat for two with full car-type controls. A roll-back sunroof topped the fully enclosed fibreglass cabin.

Rousabout   1962-1964   USA
Information listed under Trivan.

Rouxel   1899-1900   France
A tricycle powered by a De Dion engine. There was also a Voiturette with an Aster 2.25hp engine produced but it appears that both were built in limited numbers.

Rovena   1960-1963   Spain
From Barcelona, the firm of Talleres Sanglas SA. built delivery trikes with 12hp vertical twin 2-stroke engines and with a load capacity of 500kg. This was also sold under the name of Sanglas.

Rover   1900   GB
The company started as J K Starley and Company in 1877, building the first true safety bicycle in 1888. This firm that was to become the famous Rover Car Company built a number of battery/electric powered tricycles followed by a De Dion engined bathchair-type vehicle. The first 'proper' car was built in 1904 with the Rover name established in 1906. For more information see Starley.

Royal Enfield (1)   1899-1905   GB
Starting with a De Dion engined tricycle in 1899, advertised as being built with the precision of a gun, this firm also built a substantial quadricycle. A 4-wheeled car was manufactured in 1904 using a 6hp single cylinder engine. A 10hp twin was offered shortly before the firm ceased production in 1905.

Royal Enfield (2)   1935-1939   GB
The Royal Enfield Cycle Company, Redditch, built a parcel carrier using the rear portion of their 225cc single cylinder, air-cooled, 2-stroke motorcycle. A strong beam chassis allowed for a load capacity of 3cwt with the front wheels and cargo

box pivoting on a central axis. Top speed was 30mph. The war brought a halt to production.

Royal Ruby   1927-1940   GB
This company first built cyclecars in their Altrincham factory near Manchester in 1913 to 1914. They had another go with the introduction of a 3-wheeled car and a parcel van in 1927, powered by either a 2.5hp or a 5hp single cylinder engine and came with a 3-speed and reverse gearbox. War again put a stop to production.

Royal Scott   1923   GB
Built in Glasgow by Knightswood Motors, this was a light 3-wheeler with the load carrying area in front of the driver, who sat over the 350cc Barr & Stroud single cylinder sleeve valve engine. Power to the single rear wheel was through a Burman gearbox. Its chassis was a channel steel frame with load capacity of 2.5cwt.

Rumi   1952-1958   Italy
Fonderie Officine Rumi, Bergamo, were the builders of a 3-wheeled light truck with a payload of 300kg. Power came from a flat 125cc twin 2-stroke, mounted under the drivers seat, that drove through a 4-speed gearbox to the two rear wheels.

Rushabout   1920-1925   GB
Information listed under Santler.

RW Kit Cars   1980   GB

RWN   1928-1929   Germany

Rytecraft   1950s-1960s   GB
Built by the British Motor Boat Company. A 3-wheeled micro car.

SAF   1908-1915   France
A tricar built by Ste des Ateliers du Furan, Rue Barrouin, St Etienne (Loire).

Sadrian   1930s-1962   Spain
Adrian Viudese Hijos built small motorcycles during the Spanish Civil War. These were improved until he was able to add a small delivery trike to his list. Powered by Hispano-Villiers 125cc engines, later upgraded to 197cc. In 1956 he built an unusual articulated 1 ton vehicle with a 3-wheeled tug as the prime mover with a matching trailer. A spartan metal cabin, no doors and no protection below the seat line did give plenty of ventilation to the underseat low slung air-cooled motor.

Salisbury   1895-1896   USA
Built by Wilber S Salisbury at the Horseless Carriage Company of Chicago, this was an ungainly looking vehicle with three 48 inch wagon wheels. Power was supplied to the single rear wheel from a 'double cylinder, double acting engine, producing an explosion at every revolution' and rated at 3hp. Designed to carry four persons at a top speed of 24 miles per hour. Alternative power was a battery electric engine with a much lower speed and range.

Sam   1924-1929   Italy
From an old chicken factory the Sam 3-wheeled cyclecar was built from the plans

of the Vaghi (1920-1924), powered by a 546cc twin cylinder engine. The factory went on to upgrade and build 2-, 3-, and 4-seat sporting style cars using a 1056cc 4-cylinder side-valve and overhead-valve motors of their own design.
More information under Vaghi.

Samca Atomo   **1947-1951**   **Italy**

Samson   **1923-1939**   **GB**
The James Cycle Company of Birmingham had been building a range of 3-wheeled commercials when they introduced the Samson in 1933, a departure from the light carryalls produced during the previous ten years. Using a 1096cc V-twin of their own design, this vehicle boasted a sturdy steel welded chassis, a steering wheel, 3 speed gearbox and spiral bevel final drive to the two rear wheels. A basic cabin was provided for the driver. In 1935 all was updated, the load capacity increased to 12cwt and the cabin enlarged to seat two people, but it still remained austere and without doors. Production ceased with the start of the Second World War.
More information under James.

Sanchis   **1906-1912**   **France**

Sanford   **1922-1939**   **France**
Using the Morgan as an inspiration, Malcolm Stuart Sanford, an Englishman living in Paris, built a large number of sporting 4-cylinder ohv Ruby-engined 3-wheelers with 900cc, 1,075cc and 1,100cc capacity all available with superchargers. They were popular in the racing events of the day. Some 3- and 4-wheeled versions were built with a 950cc Ruby engine.
   Come the Second World War the factory closed.

Sanglas   **1960-1963**   **Spain**
For more information see listing under Rovena.

Sankar   **1955**   **Japan**
This was a light truck with a 750kg payload, a utility-style body with a hint of streamlining to the flared mudguards and frontal treatment that had headlights in a flared section over the well-sprung single front wheel. A three piece windscreen supported the canvas hood and top-to-floor side curtains.

Sanson   **1954-1960**   **Spain**
The firm Talleres Arau, Barcelona, built delivery tricycles with a 600kg load capacity. Power was a single cylinder engine with chain-drive to the single rear wheel.

Santler   **1920-1925**   **GB**
Just up the road from the Morgan factory in Malvern, Worcestershire, the Santler factory built motor ploughs. In 1920 they launched the Santler-Rushabout with a choice of air- or water-cooled M.A.B 10hp engines. A limited number, believed to be 12, were produced with a close similarity to the Morgan Runabout of the day.

Saporo Jetz Zaz   **1954**   **Russia**
A 2-seater side-by-side open coupé powered by a 400cc 2-cylinder engine with kick starter mounted over the rear axle. It had a single front wheel, side opening doors and a soft top.

Sauerbronn-Davis   **1883**   **Germany**
A steam engine, fired by petrol, powered this velocipede. The boiler and cylinders were underslung at an angle between the two front wheels and drove a live axle. The driver sat above this contraption with the rear directed steering column between his legs controlling the direction via a small rear wheel.

Sautel et Sechaud   **1902-1904**   **France**
Built in a factory at Gentilly, a 3-wheeled Nouvelle Voiturette which combined such advanced features as a pivoting steering wheel with column gearchange. Another feature was the braking and clutch levers also attached to the steering column. A 3.5hp single vertical engine was mounted behind the driver's seat, driving the single rear wheel via a 2 speed gearbox with a column mounted gearchange.

Sava   **1957 to date**   **Spain**
Soc Anon de Vehicules Automoviles, Valladolid, are truck builders who started with a 3-wheeler, the P.54 with a 2000kg payload. Usual configuration of two rear powered wheels and a single steering front wheel. Power came from a 673cc single cylinder engine with shaft-drive to the rear axle. A large fully enclosed cabin fronting a variety of bodies, van, tip-tray, or customer's own design were available.

Scammell   **1919-1970**   **GB**
The Napier Aero Engine Company decided to diversify in order to use the mechanical capacity built up during the war. Realising the horse was on the way out, they decided on a replacement for use in railway yards and factories. A prototype was built featuring a single front wheel, conventional engine and gearbox, driveshaft to rear axle and wheels shod with pneumatic tyres. Once finished they sold the project, lock stock and barrel, to Scammell Lorries Ltd. Refining the vehicle and working with engineers from the major railways, the Scammell Mechanical Horse was released to the public in 1932. Continual improvements, coupled to a variety of trailers that included tray tops, tankers and refuse carriers, they were exported all over the world. After the Second World War a facelift gave the Scammell a new look, streamlined cabin, larger vehicles with weights up to 6 tons and construction licenced to many countries.

Late in 1960 bureaucracy brought the construction of the 3-wheeled mechanical horse to a halt. They continued as 4-wheelers though a few 3-wheeled vehicles were built overseas. Their sturdy construction allowed many to continue running for as long as spares held out and even today a few are still pottering about in strange places.

Scarab STM   **1980s**   **USA**
The Scarab from Fiberfab Inc, Bridgeville, Pennsylvania, could be classed as two vehicles in one. Using a square steel chassis with VW front suspension, steering, pedals and master cylinder, a motorcycle (minus its front wheel), and clothed in a streamlined beetle-shape 2-seater fibreglass body, we have an all weather coupé. A flip-top roof opens to expose the whole cabin. About 40 minutes (it is claimed) is all it takes to remove the motorcycle and revert to 2-wheeled motoring.

Scarsdale   **1904**   **GB**
This was a tricar built with many advanced features for the period. A pipe chassis housed a 5hp water-cooled engine driving the single rear wheel, the driver sat behind the passenger who was in the usual position between the two front wheels.

A steering wheel and car controls were standard. This sturdy machine was built by the Scarsdale Cycle & Motor Co Burton on Trent.

Schilling Tricycle   **1894-1895**   **USA**
Built by A Schilling & Son of San Franscisco, California.

Schuckert   **1899-1903**   **Germany**
Schuckert & Company of Nuremberg built a number of electric powered vans with a choice of either a single front or single rear wheel. These vans were built for postal the services in Germany. After 1903 they were manufactured under the name of Siemens-Schuckert Company. More information see Siemens-Schuckert.

Schwammberger   **1950**   **Germany**
A very unusual vehicle. A single pipe backbone chassis had its front wheels on outriggers on a fixed beam axle, it then went through the body to end above the single rear wheel with the engine slung onto a frame to the rear of the wheel. The lot turned by a series of cables from a half-moon steering wheel. Two bucket seats either side of the pipe chassis were built by A W Mantzel in Stuttgart.

Scootacar   **1957-1965**   **GB**
An odd-looking single or tandem seating 3-wheeler bubble car that used Villiers engines of 197cc and later 324cc, driving the single rear wheel. A fully enclosed body and handlebar steering. One of the few all-British attempts at building a 'Bubble Car'. Continually improved, the Mk 3 had a top speed of 68mph from the twin cylinder 16hp 324cc engine. The fibreglass body gave an all-up weight of about 500lbs with a length of 7ft 7ins. About 1,000 were built when production ceased in 1965. This was a product of Hunslet Engineering.

Scootavia   **1950s**   **France**
A delivery trike with the platform placed between the 2 front wheels and usual motorcycle treatment at the rear. At least one vehicle had an enclosed passenger compartment but the driver remained exposed to the elements.

Scootmobile (1)   **1920-1923**   **USA**
For more information see notes under Martin.

Scootmobile (2)   **1947**   **USA**
A prototype 3-wheeler built by Norman Anderson of Corunna, Michigan, who had plans for cashing in on the shortage of transport after the war.

Scorpion Grinall   **1994 to date**   **GB**
Information see under Grinall Scorpion.

Scott (1)   **1897-1956**   **GB**
Alfred Angus Scott was born on the 5th October 1874. He built his first 2hp twin cylinder 2-stroke engine about 1898 which he attached to the frame of his Premier bicycle. Allowing for modifications and improvements, he finally registered this machine in December 1903 for use on the public highway. During the following years Scott designed a motorcycle with a walk-through frame and had six units built by an outside firm of W & B Jowett. 1909 saw the firm of The Scott Engineering Company Ltd building motorcycles in their own factory at the Mornington Works at Manningham, Bradford. It was not until 1915 that Scott

ventured into 3-wheelers with a gun carriage of unusual design. This was to be carried into peacetime as the Scott Sociable (see under that name). In 1930 came the 3-wheeled tradesman's van marketed under the name of Trivan. An unusual feature was the front axle was pivoted in the centre allowing the whole delivery box and attached front wheels to turn as one unit. Sold under the banner of SAV Light Cars Ltd, the units were underpowered and gradually faded away from the scene. Some Scott engines were used to power Morgan 3-wheelers and other specials.

Scott (2) 1952 GB
Scott Electric Vehicles Ltd were well-established manufacturers of industrial and railway platform trucks when they introduced a 1-ton battery electric delivery vehicle in 1952. This was a 3-wheeler van with its single front wheel coupled to a 2hp traction motor with the whole unit steering, as was the practice with most battery/electric vans.

Scott-Sociable 1921-1925 GB
The Scott-Sociable, derived from the Scott Gun Carriage, was a sturdy 3-wheeled motorcycle and sidecar-type combination but with the driver and passenger sitting side-by-side in the wide sidecar It had a steering wheel and standard car controls.

In 1915 a number of prototypes were submitted to the War Office. Despite receiving good reports, the contracts were withheld because production costs were going to be high. Details of this novel 3-wheeler appeared in the *Motor Cycle* on 28 July 1916 and production of the civilian version began at the end of the First World War. Power was from a twin cylinder 578cc in-line engine of Scott's own design through a 3-speed gearbox and shaft-drive to one rear wheel. The vehicle was equipped with a pram hood, windscreen, lights and full instrumentation.

Seal 1912-1934 GB
Looking very much like a large motorcycle and sidecar, the Seal predated the Scott-Sociable. Built by Haynes & Bradshaw of Manchester until 1920 when the firm became Seal Motors Ltd of Manchester. The motorcycle side of the vehicle used a 770cc JAP engine in 1912 that was updated the following year to a 980cc 8hp from the same firm, driving one rear wheel by chain.

By 1924 the chain had been replaced by a driveshaft. The sidecar section was a 2-seat side-by-side with room for luggage behind the seat. It had a full set of car controls, steering wheel, vertical windscreen, pram hood and permanently fitted side curtains. Later versions included 3- and 4-seat family models. In 1922, commercials using the same chassis included a van, pickup, and convertible – all with the same engine as the passenger vehicles. In 1930 these commercials upgraded and sold under the name of Progress. More information under Progress.

Secretand 1891 France
A steam powered trike on show at the Henri Malartre Collection at Lyon.

Securus 1906 Germany
Built by a Max Ortmann in Berlin, this was a 2-speed tricar that had a very small production run.

Seetstu 1906-1907 GB

Serin 1899 France
Similar to the Bollée 3-wheeler, the Serin was powered by a 4hp horizontal engine.

Serpollet   **1883-1907**   **France**
Leon Serpollet built his first steam powered tricycle in 1883, a spindly creation made of bits and pieces from his workshop. In 1885 he persuaded Armand Peugeot (then an ironmonger and cycle maker) that self-propelled vehicles had a future – he should build a strong 3-wheeler to his (Serpollet's) design. It was not long before practical 5-seater coachbuilt road vehicles appeared, all steam powered, using twin cylinder engines of 4hp to 6hp, able to propel these heavy 3-wheelers along at 16 mph. They came in a variety of shapes and sizes, including a 12-seat bus. By 1891 a fourth wheel was added. Leon took the World Speed Record at 75mph in 1902 in Nice. Steam power stayed until Serpollet, and his company, died in 1907.

Sertum   **1938-1940**   **Italy**
Officine Meccaniche Fausto Alberti SA, Milan, were already successful motorcycle builders when they built delivery vehicles with a single front wheel, motorcycle style, with an enclosed van or open tray placed between the two rear wheels. Power came from a 500cc ohv vertical twin engine located under the van floor.

SGS   **1983**   **Switzerland**

Shanghai   **1957 to date**   **China**
The Shanghai Motor Vehicle Plant manufactures a range of 4-wheeled trucks and cars but also turns out a 3-wheeled truck known as the Shanghai 58-1, powered by a 27hp V-twin air-cooled engine. Payload is 1-ton and speed about 20mph. This vehicle has been built in large quantities and exported to Nepal and Tibet.

Sharpe   **1900s**   **GB**
Using an unorthodox triangulated framed chassis with a V-twin cylinder engine powering the single rear wheel, the whole unit was supported on the patented Sharpe Pneumatic Spring Buffers.

Sharps   **1953-1955**   **GB**
The Sharps Mini Truck was the forerunner to the Bond light car, built in Preston, Lancashire. Power came from a 197cc single-cylinder Villiers engine mounted as part of the single front wheel, hidden under the long bonnet that was to become part of the Bond range. With a rear loading van body, the vehicle was built of fibreglass, though the driver sat under a canvas hood with an extra large steering wheel taking up much of the 'office' space.

Shell Valley Apollo   **1980s**   **USA**

Shell Mileage Marathon
See under Mileage Marathon.

Shelter   **1954-1958**   **Netherlands**
Designed by a Mr Van de Groot in 1947 as a small, closed 3-wheeler with a boxy-type body. Powered by a 200cc Ilo engine, although later versions had a special 228cc engine. Promised finance from government coffers never materialised and a few prototypes only were built over an 8 year period.

Sherpa   **1954-1960**   **France**
The Sherpa looked comfortable as a 3-wheeler, its single front wheel located under

a long car-type bonnet in unit with a 850cc Dyna-Panhard 2-cylinder engine. A central tubular frame chassis ended in widely-spaced, independently sprung, rear wheels. The cabin was wide enough to seat three abreast with the large cargo body available in either a van or a bus configuration. Unusual was its 3-speed gearbox fitted with a high and low range.

Sherrin 1887 GB
Ralph Sherrin of Ramsgate, Kent, exhibited his first electric tricycle at the 1887 Cycle Show – by 1891 it was in full production. With a name change to Vaughan-Sherrin, the company added invalid carriages to its range of vehicles offered.

Showa Fujiya 1930s Japan
A motorcycle-based cargo carrier using a 675cc engine rated at 9hp. 530 units were built during 1937.

Shuttle 1984 to date USA
Try Trylon for more information.

Sibrava 1920-1923 Czechoslovakia
Jaroslav Sibrava from Prague modified the discontinued Walter 3-wheeler and began production under the name of Sibrava-Trimobil using a 1.75 litre 9hp V-twin engine with driveshaft to the single rear wheel. Available in both passenger and commercial variations and also sold under the name of Walter-Trimobil or just Trimobil. See notes under both those names.

Siemens-Schuckert Electric 1904 Germany
Built for the Royal Bavarian Postal Service of Munich this was a battery powered vehicle capable of 9.5 miles per hour and was used for the delivery of mail and small parcels around Munich. More information noted under Schuckert.

SIM 1953-1955 Italy
Societa Italiana Motorscooters, Reggio Emila, adapted their 125cc scooters and 150cc shaft-driven motorcycles to 3-wheeled delivery vehicles by adding two wheels and a box where there had formally been the one front wheel. Both vehicles used single cylinder, 2-stroke, air-cooled engines with 3- or 4-speed gearboxes.

Simms 1899-1908 GB
Frederick R Simms first imported the Daimler Benz engine into England and went on to build his own engines. His only venture into 3-wheeled motoring was the 'Motor Wheel', a strange little vehicle steered by its single rear wheel and powered through the two front wheels (an early attempt at front wheel drive), it had a bad habit of tipping onto its side when cornering, something it did on numerous occasions during the 1900 One Thousand Mile Motor Trial. However, the Simms 4-wheel car was successful and was built until 1908. F R Simms went on to form the English Daimler Company.

Simo 1924-1959 Spain
Formerly a motorcycle maker, Miguel Simoa built a few delivery vehicles between 1924 and 1936: these were basically one of the firm's motorcycles attached to a delivery box with two wheels mounted where the bike front wheel would normally

be. From 1952 a larger version was introduced, powered by a 197cc single cylinder Hispano-Villiers engine under the driver's seat and powering the single rear wheel through a 3-speed gearbox, with final drive by chain. A vertical column and handlebars controlled the steering while the driver sat exposed in all weathers.

Simplex 1902-1968 Netherlands
This was a bicycle company that moved into motorcycle production in 1902. They used a variety of engines to power both motorcycles and the trike popular in the first decade. A number of commercial vehicles were built along the 3-wheeled layout of the box in front and a standard motorcycle to the rear.

Sinclair C5 1985-1986 GB
London-based Sinclair Vehicles launched Sir Clive Sinclair's C5 Electric Tricycle onto the world with an initial run of 6,000 vehicles. This was supposed to become the bicycle of the future, an electrically assisted 3-wheeler with an aerodynamically designed shell made of tough thermoplastic resin. Powered by a conventional lead-acid battery and electric motor drive it was claimed to be both economical and pollution free, with a top speed of 15mph and a range of 20 miles per charge (estimated to equal 1000 miles for the average price of one gallon of gasoline). Pedal power was also included to help get up a steep hill or get one home if the battery runs out of charge. Ideal for shopping, running messages or pottering round the village the vehicle was to be sold for about £500 and could be legally driven by 14 year olds.
  The project folded after only 8,000 were produced of the estimated 100,000 that were going to be built. They are now becoming a collector's item.

Singer 1900-1907 GB
George Singer of Coventry started manufacturing bicycles called the 'Xtra-Ordinary', propelled by a peculiar system of foot operated cranks. In 1901 he acquired the rights to the 'Perks and Birch' motor wheel, a hollow metal wheel with a rotary engine situated between the spokes, and began production of both front and rear driven tricars. By 1904 he had a line of tricars fitted with a 5hp 90 degree V-twin cylinder fan-cooled engine, a countershaft 2 speed epicyclic gear and chain-drive to the single rear wheel. As an option you could have your car fitted with either a 6hp or 9hp water-cooled engine.
  The first 4-wheeled car was introduced in 1906 and the 3-wheelers fazed out by 1907. Singer is credited as one of the first to introduce time payment. Vehicles also sold under the name of Forecar.

Singer Governess Car 1903 GB
This unusual vehicle was similar to the tricycle but had a 2.5hp engine enclosed within the single front wheel. The 'Governess' passenger compartment had face to face side mounted seats with entry through a single rear door while the driver sat in front bicycle style with handlebar steering. See Singer for more information.

Skip 1990 to date GB
This is one 3-wheeler that was built for a purpose: to win trials. Built by Jeffrey Carver and based on the Mini; its engine, floorplan and many other bits and pieces are used. The engine is totally exposed and with cycle wings looks threatening when seen head on. Built at the Carver factory in Durham, the car is road legal and has been very successful. A number are already road registered.

SMZ	**1956**	**USA**

Sno-Pony	**1980s**	**USA**

For summer months we have a 3-wheeled all-purpose all-terrain passenger carrying vehicle and for winter with the addition of a few add-ons it can be converted to a snow mobile. All power is to a single rear wheel via a 16.6hp Solo Engine. Vehicle was advertised by Sports Pouri Inc.

Snuggy Tobrouk	**1980s**	**Italy**

See All Cars Charly for more information.

Solar Challenge	**1987 to date**	**Australia**

The inaugural World Solar Challenge was first held in 1987 as a race for solar powered vehicles over 3000km from Darwin to Adelaide through Central Australia.

Twenty-one cars, mostly 3-wheelers, made the first trip in 5 days, 4 hours and 54 minutes. Held annually, the entries have passed three figures with cars ranging from the ten million dollar experimental from Honda Japan to backyard efforts put together from recycled parts that have halved the time taken in that first race and actually achieved speeds of over 100km/h. 3-wheeled single seated cars are now dominating the event.

Solocar	**1950s**	**GB**

See Nelco for information.

Solomobil.	**1921-1922**	**Germany**

Built by Hugo Mitzenheim at Chemnitz, a 3-wheeled car powered by a 12hp V-twin engine that soon progressed to four wheels.

Solyto	**1970s**	**France**

Has a front resembling a forward control truck in miniature with the single front wheel tucked in, well behind the louvred grill and under the cabin built for two. Full car-type controls and side opening doors with sliding glass windows but no roof. The cargo tray has pipe hoop frame and is canvas covered that can be rolled out to cover the vehicle, including the driver. Power comes from a 50cc to 125cc engine with auto clutch attached to and driving the front wheel. It can still be seen in rural France on market days loaded with produce. Some fully enclosed panel vans with a supposed 5cwt capacity were produced using the larger engine.

Something Special	**1980s**	**GB**

Probably based on the Stimson Scorcher but with some improvements. The tandem seating is for two and stepped, it has a wind deflector that started life as part of a telephone booth. A small luggage box is located over the single rear wheel.
See the Stimson Scorcher for more information.

Souriau	**1907-1915**	**France**

From A Souriau et Cie, Montorie, Loire-et-Cher, came an unusual 3-wheeler where the engine and single front wheel were combined within a subframe that both drove and steered the vehicle. The first prototypes were built in 1907. Engines could be either 5hp 625cc single cylinder or 8hp 4 cylinder engines of 1,460cc.

These vehicles were also sold under the name of Orbus.

Sparnobill   1983   Germany
See VW Scooter for more information.

Spartan   1911   USA
A prototype from the C W Kelsey Manufacturing Company that was to become the Kelsey Motorette. More information under both Kelsey and the Kelsey Motorette.

Spatz   1954   Germany
Information listed under Brütsch.

Speedy   1905-1906   GB
Built by the Jackson Brothers and Lord of Salford's factory in Lancashire. Had a 4hp engine. The passenger sat behind the driver in a 'comfortable and cosy seat'.

Spiegel   1932-1950   Belgium
Founded about the turn of the century in Antwerp by G van der Spiegel, this company built pedal-powered delivery tricycles. It was not until 1932 that they added an engine and updated the vehicle to carry 500kg. All vehicles had a single rear wheel and a cargo box between the two front wheels. Improvements included a steering wheel coupled to a 2CV Citroën Cloverleaf built front axle and wheels. Chassis was steel with a metal body mounted on ash frames. Engines were JAP single cylinder; later versions had either Ilo 2-stroke or BSA 500cc installed. Smaller vehicles still used handlebar steering. On all models the driver sat on a sprung saddle over the engine protected by a vertical windscreen and a fabric hood without a back or side curtains. Independent front suspension was added in 1950, the last year of production.

Spider   1972-1980   GB
Look for more information under A F Grand Prix.

Spijkstaal   1930 to date   Holland
Added to their range of 4-wheeled vehicles in 1955 was an electric milk float with a single powered front wheel, vehicles were designed for local deliveries.

Spirit   1993 to date   GB
Roy Webb, a principal of Hudson Component Cars of Norwich, Norfolk England, a firm with five generations and a well-established history in the automotive industry, was the creator of the Spirit range of 3-wheeled sports cars. Sold mainly as a kit, some 150 have found homes in England, America and Australia. Using the Renault R-5 as a donor vehicle.

   The Free Spirit is a single seater with a fibreglass body wrapped around a professionally fabricated, jig welded, tubular chassis which comes complete with floor, bulkhead, and mounting brackets for engine, suspension and steering.

   The Kindred Spirit has a chassis 12 inches longer which allows for an extra passenger seat in tandem or extra luggage space for touring.

Spirit of America   1963-1964   USA
A 3-wheeled 3-ton monster powered by a J47 jet engine, shod with 42 inch Goodyear tyres, built and driven by Craig Breedlove. Aim? To break the Land Speed Record. Breedlove became the first man to take the record over 500mph with an average of 526.28mph but FIA refused to recognise records by 3-wheelers. So in 1965 he built his 4-wheel 'Sonic 1', and took the record averaging 600mph.

SP Spi-Tri　　　　　　　　　1980s　　　　　　　　　USA
Structural Plastics Inc of Tulsa, Okalahoma, developed an electric car using the basic Reliant Bond Bug shell with their own improvements. Claiming a top speed of 50mph and a range of 40 miles, a feature was extra large impact bumpers and oversize wheels.

ST　　　　　　　　　　　　　1922　　　　　　　　　　GB
Another vehicle using the layout of the Seal or Scott Sociable with a Blackburn single cylinder engine and gearbox, with chain-drive to one of the two rear wheels. It had a sidecar-type body with a steering wheel and the usual car type controls.

Standard　　　　　　　　　1933-1939　　　　　　　Germany
Standard started building trivans in Ludwigsberg using the proven methods of the Goliath and others with a single steering and powered front wheel, and a box or tray platform located between the two rear wheels. Engines were either 400cc or 500cc with a 4-wheeled version with rear wheeled drive added in 1936. These were built side-by-side until the outbreak of the Second World War when production was halted.

Stanhope　　　　　　　　　1915-1922　　　　　　　GB
A 3-wheeler built by Stanhope Motors (Leeds) Ltd of Dixon Lane Road, Lower Wortley, Leeds. The Stanhope was a ungainly affair that had an engine-driven single front steering wheel. Continually requiring improvements, production was patchy.
　　Was also sold under the name of Bramham between 1922 and 1924.

Starley　　　　　　　　　　1888　　　　　　　　　　GB
John Kemp Starley promoted the safety cycle but became interested in electric powered vehicles. In 1888 he combined the two interests and formed J K Starley & Company to build a trike with two large rear wheels, and a small front wheel placed between forks from a bicycle, and tiller steered. The batteries sat under the seat for two and drove via a live rear axle. The vehicle was also listed in the company's catalogue as a Rover and from this small beginning would evolve the Rover Car empire. More information noted under Rover.

Stevens　　　　　　　　　　1932-1936　　　　　　　GB
Stevens Brothers Ltd of Wolverhampton built a light van along the lines of the Reliant, with motorcycle front wheel out in front of a slab-sided plywood body, a 588cc engine drove the rear wheels, via a chain (replaced in 1935 by a shaft-drive).

Stevens and Croft　　　　　1933　　　　　　　　　　GB

Stevoort Steam Car　　　　1896-1899　　　　　　Belgium
This steam powered vehicle was built by A M Palmesoole Groote Stevoort, using the most common 3-wheeled configuration of a small steering front wheel and the much larger powered rear wheels. A boiler was slung low to the centre of the vehicle and space for the passenger was provided alongside the driver on a single plank seat. There was no protection from the elements in the first few vehicles built, although the feet would have been kept warm as they were placed beside the boiler. By 1897 improvements were to include a roof over the driver. A larger boiler was fitted and by 1899 Mr Stevoort had made real progress: his vehicle was very

modern for the day, the steam engine had increased in power but shrunk in size and had gone under cover in what we would today call the rear boot or trunk. Passengers sat in comfort with the driver on upholstered seats. Operating levers were situated in the centre of the floorboards and on a tilting steering arm. A headlight was fitted on the front of the vehicle.

Stimson Scorcher   1976-1981   GB
People still query, 'is it a car or a bike?' Comprising of a Mini front end, a box-like chassis body with seating for three in tandem straddling the box, a steering wheel and foot pedals, exposed engine out front, and headlights on cycle wings. It was claimed to reach 100mph – if you could hang on! There was no protection from the elements and helmets had to be worn at all times. Sold in kit form, it was built with many modifications. One, the 'Something Special' had a sheet aluminium engine cover and part of a Perspex telephone booth cover as a windshield. Though the vehicle went out of production in 1981 it still has a cult following today.

Stimula   1905-1914   France
Builder of cyclecars with three or four wheels using a variety of engines.

Stinger   1994 to date   GB
A new comer to the kit car scene, the Stinger hails from the stable of Tony Bradwell, Stratford-upon-Avon. The front end is in fibreglass and closely resembles a Lotus while the rear is pure BMW motorcycle from the front of the steering pillar back. Comfortable seating for two, safety harness and aero screens make this a potent machine.

Story   1941-1944   Netherlands
A battery powered electric 3-wheeler built in the Hague during the Second World War.

Stoewer   1897-1899   Germany
From a company formed in 1895 to build sewing machines, they soon branched out to include typewriters and bicycles, soon to be followed by motorcycles and 3-wheeled vehicles powered by the De Dion engines. A 4-seater car appeared in 1899 and was soon followed by a 4-wheeled version. 3-wheelers disappeared while the 4-wheeled versions were built. The factory was destroyed in 1944.

Stromer   1933   Germany
Utilising a backbone chassis, the 600cc engine was up front driving the single rear wheel by shaft and through a 3-speed gearbox with final drive by chain. Clothed in a sporty coupé body, built in metal from a design by Abram Neimann. See Neimann and Framo for further details.

Stylcar   1965-1970   Greece
First built in Thessaloniki (1965-67) and later in Athens, S Karakatsanis were the first company to produce a light 3-wheeled truck in Greece. It had a sturdy steel chassis, fibreglass cabin, large steering wheel with car controls and a wide bench that would hold three small Greeks. A rounded cover was fitted over the single front wheel. Power came from a new or reconditioned VW or BMW engine, the tray back body carried loads well in excess of maker's specifications and vehicles from dilapidated to mint condition can still be seen on roads today.

Succes	1952	Belgium

Success	1928-1930	Japan

A cargo trike built by Osawa using the front half of a motorcycle and a choice of 600cc and 650cc engines from the English factories of JAP and BSA.

Sui Tong Rickshaw	1960-1980	Taiwan

Sui Tong Cub	1982-1983	Taiwan

Sulky	1975 to date	Italy

See under Casalini.

Summerscales	1917	GB

A 3-wheeled steam tractor built by Summerscales Ltd of Keighley, Yorks by J T Ridealgh. Engine was a 4-cylinder high pressure poppet valve 'Uniflow'-type with roller chains as final drive. Two believed to have been built and classed as 'lemons'.

Sunrise	1980	USA

Sunrise Badal	1978-1982	India

Built in Bangalore, this chunky roughly-finished fibreglass 4-seater was powered by a 198cc single-cylinder engine with chain-drive to the solitary rear wheel. The firm is still producing cars, currently the Indian version of the Austin Montego.

Suntera	1990s	Hawaii

Also known as the Suntera Sun-Ray, a 3-wheeled vehicle used by the Hawaiian Police for general traffic duties, mostly parking offences. This is a locally-built Solar-Electric 2-seater of advanced design. The low slung electric motor is coupled to the single rear wheel. Cabin is totally enclosed with side opening doors.

Super Kar	1946	USA

A prototype of a mini car from Louis R Elrad of Cleveland, Ohio.

Super Pratique	1978	France

The commercial version of the Arola with a pickup tray tacked on the back. See Arola for more information.

Suzuki	1981	Japan

The Suzuki CV (or commuter vehicle), was a single seat 3-wheeler powered by a 50cc 2-stroke single cylinder engine in a practical fibreglass body that boasted air conditioning and a large amount of space for shopping. The large wheels, car controls and a 20mph speed limit made it ideal for the narrow streets of suburban Japan.

Swift	1899	GB

A copy of the De Dion tricar built by the Swift Cycle Co Ltd of Coventry. However, the engine was carried behind the axle and used the same carburettor and battery as the Ariel motorcycles from Coventry.

Sycar	1915	GB

SZL	1956-1969	Russia

Tamag	1933	Germany

Tankette	1919-1920	GB

A diminutive 3-wheeler driven by a single cylinder 2-stroke Union engine of 2.75hp. The chassis consisted of an ash frame reinforced with steel strips. The front wheels could be pushed inwards to allow entry through a doorway. The rear wheel was actually two wheels bolted together with the chain-drive arriving through a 2-speed Burman gearbox with car-type controls and an almost vertical steering wheel.

Production was by Tankett Ltd of London. Sales were believed to be low.

Tatin	1898-1899	France

Built by the Societe Europeenne d'Automobile of Paris, the first Tatin was a steam-driven tricycle of simple design. It was followed by a much larger steam carriage with a single tiller steered front wheel, powered by a steam engine between the rear wheels.

Tatra	1938	Czechoslovakia

Better known for 4-wheel trucks, Tatra ventured into 3-wheelers: the type 49, an 8cwt delivery vehicle with a 528cc single cylinder engine of 7hp. About 200 were built.

Taylor-Gue	1904	GB

Probably England's first kit car, the Taylor was sold as a 3-wheel chassis leaving the buyer to fit a power unit of his own choosing. This company went on to build motorcycles under the name of Veloce, later to become the Velocette.

TB	1919-1920	GB

T B stood for Thompson Brothers of Bilston, well-known engineers of the day. Built by Bradley Engineering Works, the TB followed car lines with a tubular chassis and cantilever rear springing. Its metal body with Bugatti like radiator and longish bonnet covered a Blackburne V-twin engine of 1.097cc – or a JAP 980cc engine was also available. Drive to the single rear wheel was through a floating plate clutch and a 3-speed gearbox and propeller shaft to a conventional crown wheel. Options included gas or electric lighting and air- or water-cooled engines. A pram hood and folding windscreen were standard as were front wheel brakes. More than 750 units were reported to have been built.

The TB reappeared in the mid-1930s in the form of a 3-wheeled mobile aircraft refuelling tanker, with a rear mounted Ford engine powering the two rear wheels. A large fuel tank was positioned between the driver and the single front wheel and clothed in a curved low slung metal body.

Teilhol Citadine	1972-1982	France

For more information look under Citadine.

Teilhol Messagate	1975-1983	France

Single back wheel and car type controls, the TVE Messagate runabout had back-to-back seating in an open body and used battery power. More information listed under Citadine.

Temple-Crowsley   1906-1907   GB
This was an up-market tricar built in London. It had padded bucket seats, wheel steering and was powered by a 5hp Peugeot engine.

Tempo   1923-1935   Germany
Vidal und Sohn GmbH of Hamburg built a range of 3-wheeled commercial vehicles, starting with a van. This had its body slung between the two front wheels, while the driver sat over a 195cc Rinne engine driving the single rear wheel. Engines were updated in 1933 and the layout was changed so that the popular Tempo was born.
  The Tempo was powered by a 400cc Heinkel 2-stroke engine located above and driving the single front wheel via a massive chain. Performance was slow but the large truck or van body carried 15cwt and often much more. The cabin was enclosed with bench seating for two. Their first 4-wheeled truck was introduced in 1936 and was produced alongside the 3-wheeled version. The Tempo 3-wheeler was also built under licence in Spain.
  After a number of mergers, Tempo became part of the Hanomag range and was produced under that name but with its engine relocated and shaft-drive to the rear wheels. In the 1970s the Tempo-Hanomog 3-wheeler dies and names were sold to Bajaj Motors in India who continued production in their Chinchwad, Poona factory. The Tempo/Hanomag, under the Bajaj name, has been exported to many adjoining countries. Today, many tired looking Tempo Trike Taxis can be seen doing battle with local traffic in Bombay and other Indian towns.
  More information under Hanomag or Neimann.

Tennant   1867-1872   GB
After first building 3-wheeled steam tractors for R W Thompson under contract, Tennant decided to go it alone using the same design but with at least one engine built to their own modifications. A low standard of workmanship and a lack of finance led to their insolvency in 1872. More information listed under Thompson.

Tevere   1958-2974   Italy
A 3-wheeled light truck/chassis was exported to other countries for the fitting of the importer's own bodies and name tag.

The Petro-Cycle   1883-1888   GB
Butler's patent Petrol-Cycle design was first shown at the Inventors Exhibition in 1885 with provisional patent No.13541 granted in 1884 from designs produced in 1883. The first actual working prototype appeared in 1887. See Butler Petrol-Cycle for more information.

Thomas   1903   GB
This was an unusual looking 3-wheeler built on cycle lines, with two front wheels and seating for two. A single cylinder engine was slung between the front wheels.

Thompson   1846-1875   GB
Robert William Thompson was a brilliant inventive Scots civil engineer who saw the need for a heavy duty, road-going tractor for hauling heavy loads. Using a vertical boiler of his own design, extra-wide solid rubber tyred wheels, the two back wheels were driven from a 2-cylinder engine, with a single wheel steering at the front. These vehicles, which came in a variety of both sizes and horsepower, were very

manoeuvrable and could be hooked together to tow the heaviest of loads. Many units were exported; the largest batch going to India. The manufacture of many of these units was farmed out to nearby engineering firms. Two of these 1875 units built by Tennant and Co, Leith, were reported still in use in Glasgow in the 1930s.

| **Thrift-T** | **1955** | **USA** |

| **Thurlow** | **1920-1921** | **GB** |

From a factory in Kingston Road, Wimbledon, the first prototype was tested in 1914 but the war put a stop to production until 1920. Using a tubular chassis, power from a 10hp engine was transmitted to the single rear wheel through a Sturmey-Archer 3-speed gearbox with final drive via a wide belt. The all-metal body had bench seating, a sloping windscreen with side curtains and a pram hood. It had normal car controls and a large steering wheel.

| **Thury** | **1880** | **Switzerland** |

A tiller-steered steam trike. The driver sat over the front wheel while the passenger sat facing the rear with his legs either side of the boiler. Photographs of the Thury are on display at the Geneva Science Museum.

| **Tibicar Bella** | **1979-1985** | **India** |

| **Tinkham** | **1895-1899** | **USA** |

Designed and built by Denison & Walton of the Tinkham Cycle Company, New York. The Tinkham was manufactured at the Denison Motor Carriage Company and was sometimes sold under that name.

| **Tilli Capton** | **1957** | **Australia** |

Another microcar that was to be grounded by the introduction of the Mini Minor.
The Tilli Motor Co hailed from Moonee Ponds in Victoria and proposed to produce fifty 3-wheeled 2-seater cars per week, powered by a 2-cylinder, 2-stroke, air-cooled Anzani engine that would develop 15hp. With single rear wheel drive, fuel consumption of the prototypes was noted at 60 mpg with a top speed of 60mph. The fibreglass-bodied roadster was intended to sell at $990 while the hard top was $1195. A few prototypes only were produced.

| **Tipo** | **1940-1948** | **Italy** |

See Maserati for more information.

| **Tippen Delta** | **1950s-1960s** | **GB** |

A rear-engined single seater with a slab-sided body and sweeping curves in fibreglass. A vertical windscreen, pram hood and side curtains, a single door on the left side and a single headlight flared into the long bonnet. Favoured as a road going invalid carriage.

| **Tischer** | **1914** | **USA** |

Built by the Tischer-Linton Tri-Car Company of Peoria, Illinios.

| **Titan (1)** | **1905** | **Denmark** |

Built by Titan Maskinfabrik, Copenhagen, this was an electric van where the driver sat over the single rear wheel, chain-driven from a 1.5hp electric motor. The up front cargo area carried 250kg with the batteries under the tray and between the front wheels.

Titan (2)   1911   GB

Titano (1)   1972   Italy
Information under Intramoto-Gloria.

Titano (2)   1951-1959   Spain
For more information look under Moto-Scooter.

TMC   1930s   Japan
A cargo trike with TMC's own manufactured engines of 600cc and 750cc. They were still listed in 1937.

Toboggan   1905-1906   GB

Todd   1869   GB
Leonard J Todd of Leith designed a compact 3-wheeled steam velocipede with side-by-side seating for the driver and the stoker. A Field Boiler, feeding a 2-cylinder engine of 2.5 inch bore and 4 inch stroke, drove the rear wheels by leather belts. Many orders were received but production was stopped by the Highways Act of 1862 and later amendments.

Tomazo   1987   Austria
A motorcycle-based trike with tandem seating for two and a power plant of 1500cc.

Torpedo   1911-1920   Germany
For more information look under Tourist.

Torpelle   1914   France

Toro   1953-1962   Spain
More information listed under Cresma.

Tourette   1956-1958   GB
Made by a firm called Progress Supreme, the egg-shaped 2-seater body is topped by a flip-up hard top; remove a couple of bolts and you have a convertible. The small 197cc engine driving the single rear wheel was able to move the vehicle along at 55mph. Production run was 35 vehicles.

Tourist   1907-1920   Germany
A long 4-seat cyclecar with a single front wheel built by Tourist Automobile-Werk GmbH in Berlin from 1907-1911. From 1911-1920 it was sold by George Beck & Co, in Berlin, with a name change to the Berliner Automobilfabrik 'Torpedo'.

Up front was a V-twin, air-cooled 7hp engine. Transmission to the rear wheels was by shaft with final chain-drive. The seating was tandem with a single seat for the driver and a three seat bench for the passengers. Both open and closed bodies were available, as well as a van or tray to take the place of the passenger seat.

Townmobile   1982   Australia

A concept vehicle range designed by Australian Roy Leembruggen to be battery electric powered. The Townmobile used a unique electric motor incorporated within a twin-tyred front wheel while the battery bank was in a removable compartment under the cargo floor of this forward control van. A Government grant was given to the manufacturer to build two prototypes of this 3-wheeled delivery vehicle.

Toyota   1953 to date   Japan

From the 1890s, Sakichi Toyoda was an avid inventor and manufacturer. In 1897 he developed an automatic wooden-framed loom that revolutionised the textile industry. The first venture into the motor industry was about 1935 with commercial vehicles and his first exports were 4 trucks to China in 1936. The majority of vehicles built in Japan pre-war were commercial vehicles – and 3-wheelers predominated. In 1936 the total production of Japanese vehicles were 847 cars, 11,339 4-wheeled trucks and 12,840 3-wheeled vehicles. By 1959 more than 600,000 3-wheelers were registered for road use in Japan and many more were exported. No details are available as to whether Toyota made any serious inroads with 3-wheelers athough a number of prototypes were built.

In the 1960s they announced the EX-11 Commuter, a single front wheel bubble car. It had a fully enclosed fibreglass body with sloping front and squared rear end, with a bench seat for two. Similar vehicles were shown at the 1969 Tokyo Motor Show and again there was an electric 3-wheeled vehicle on display at the 1970 Show.

Tractavant   1951-1952   France

Tractors   1899 to date   Worldwide

Though not correctly classed as people movers, tractors have left their mark on transport over the years. Like the cars and trucks, the early tractors were 3-wheelers. The first recorded petrol-engined tractor was the Charter (1889), built by John Charter (USA) it had four wheels but the front steering wheels were only a few inches apart. In 1902-3, an Englishman, Dan Albone of Biggleswade, built a pure 3-wheeler with a single front wheel. The Gougis (1906-7) from France, again with a single front wheel, introduced the first power take-off shaft (PTO). The Bull of 1913 (GB) was unusual in that all three wheels were of different size! The Glasgow (GB) of 1923 had an offset single back wheel, similar in layout to the Scott Sociable. Even today the agricultural industry relies on 3 wheels for many of its implements.

Transporette   1925-1926   Germany

Another copy of the Goliath built by Maschinenfabrik Schwabenthau and Gormann of Berlin.

Trevithick   1796-1803   GB

Richard Trevithick was an enthusiastic inventor who built the first vehicle to run on rails – it was designed to carry coal in the Penny Darren mine in Wales. Between 1796 and 1801 he built various tricycles for the transport of light goods and passengers. His first successful steam powered carriage was called the London; this ran in 1803 but was so far ahead of its time that he was unable to get the finance for it to continue. All his vehicles were steam powered and had the configuration of a single tiller-steered wheel in front. A few vehicles had two small wheels close together, while the very large (8ft) rear heavy wagon wheels were powered by direct-drive through a live axle.

In the 1980s professional engineer, Tom Brogan, realised a 15 year dream and built a second London steam carriage from the original plans and specifications. This fantastic monster is as near authentic as it could be with the use of modern materials and minimum of additions to pass regulations for road going steam vehicles.

Triad 1992 to date GB
From the moulds of a little known trike called the Mosquito (mid-1970s, based on the Mini), which had been refurbished and modernised by Ian Browse and Rick Jones, a firm called Malvern Autocraft, based near the Worcestershire home of Morgan, began to produce a 3-wheeler called the Triad. With the front end of a Mini and single rear wheel from the same car, it had a fibreglass body and generous seating for two, clothing a jig-built steel spaceframe chassis. Extras included all-weather equipment, full-width windscreen and an external luggage rack. Production was slow and steady.

Trialce 1940-1945 Italy
Built on the commercial chassis that had been in production since 1928, the Trialce was the military version, complete with rear facing heavy machine guns, armour plating and tandem seating for the crew of two. Other versions had a variety of platform bodies adapted for military use. For more information see notes under Moto Guzzi.

Triauto 1919 France
More information listed under Godet

Tribelhorn 1918-1920 Czechoslovakia
Built by A Tribelhorn, Feldbach, this company were builders of electric commercial vehicles with the occasional 2- and 4-seat car when they had the time. In 1918, under the name of Electrische Fahrzeuge AG Alstetten, they introduced a 3-wheeled chassis with a single front wheel and a 2-seater body with batteries under the seat driving the rear wheels. By adding a commercial body they were able to supply a large order to the Swiss Post Office, this became so popular that they had to drop their passenger cars, building only in very limited numbers to special order. A gasoline-electric generator power plant was introduced to allow a larger range and the number of models increased, including a car that had a high metal body with pointed nose, exposed front wheel, side opening door and pram hood. In 1920 the company continued with both 3- and 4-wheeled commercials under the name of E.F.A.G. They had another name change in 1937 to N.E.F.A.G.

Tri-Bilda 1995 Australia
1930s style with 1990s precision. A full waist-high ladder chassis clothed in an aluminium body of superior design and finish, the Tri-Bilda has a number of novel innovations. Built by Bill Davis of Bilda Cycle Car Works, in Padstow, a Sydney suburb. It used an exposed V-twin Moto-Guzzi 1,000cc engine with shaft-drive to the single rear wheel. It is a wide and spacious car with side-by-side seating, you simply step over the side and slide into your seat. The front bonnet is side-hinged and when raised exposes the gearbox and electrics as well as spare tyre and small luggage space. A split windscreen is firmly attached to the bonnet. The rear deck is

similarly side-hinged and when raised gives access to the rear wheel, twin petrol tanks and some further luggage space. The two-tone finish, green top with the sides in natural polished metal with twin side exhausts in stainless steel and large fluted ends make this a crowd puller whenever it is stationery. Bureaucracy has sadly made this a one-off vehicle.

Tri-Car   1955   USA
Built by Lycoming Division of the Avco Corporation, Williamsport, Pennsylvania.

Tricarettes   1899-1930   GB
For more information see entries under Clyde.

Tri-Ciao   1947 to date   Italy
See Vespa-Piaggo for more information.

Tricolet   1905   USA
The H Pokorney Automobile & Gas Engine Company of Indianapolis, Indiana, built a 3-wheeler using their own manufactured engines. Also known as the Pokorney.

Trident (1)   1919-1920   France & GB
Another 3-wheeler with a difference: the usual configuration of one wheel in front and two behind, but the one in front was actually two very narrow wheels bolted together and counter balanced with a 2-cylinder engine on one side with a 3-speed and reverse gearbox and magneto balanced on the other – and this was the steering wheel as well! A long hinged bonnet lifted to expose the works. A 2-seater, it was also available as a 4-seater. Used as a taxi in France, it was also available as a 'parcel car' and an 'open tourer'. The Taxi version had the passengers in an enclosed cabin with space on the roof for luggage, with the driver sat out in the open.
    It was imported into England by a firm called Federation Exports Ltd and Vickers were reported to have looked at manufacturing it. Production is believed to have been limited to a few prototypes of each model.

Trident (2)   1965   GB
More information listed under Peel.

Triffid   1990   GB
With a construction run of four, the Triffid is a distinctive Mini-based tricar, with semi exposed engine and bug-eye headlights to give the front an unforgettable look. The single rear wheel was fully exposed from the slab-sided rear end. Comfortable seating for two made this a fun car eminating from Hopton in Norfolk.

Trihawk   1984 to date   USA
A California-based fun vehicle built at Dana Point, just south of Los Angeles. With an output of 100 vehicles a year, it proved so successful that they were taken over by the Harley-Davidson motorcycle empire. A Citroën 4-stroke, opposed four air-cooled engine, rated at 1299cc drives the two front wheels through a 5-speed full synchro box.
    The Trihawk can accelerate through the quarter mile in 17.2 seconds.

Triking   1978 to date   GB
From Marlingford in Norfolk came a kit car, that on the surface looked like a

reincarnation of a 1930s Morgan, with a strong backbone chassis, steel spaceframe and stressed alloy body panels and cycle wings. At the back, the single wheel was suspended on a swinging fork, driven by shaft from a Moto-Guzzi 844cc V-twin 68bhp engine, well up front and with outstanding results. Cabin is a tight squeeze for two and the pram hood has to be dismantled each time entry is made. Noted as one of the best trikes available, production is now in hundreds.

Cars have been sold as far afield as Australia, with agents in America, Germany, Netherlands and Japan.

Tri-Kon   1936   GB
Grandex Motor Tri-Kons Ltd, St Albans, Herts, used a tubular frame built by Accles and Pollock for their single rear wheeled motorcycle-type goods carrier. A 247cc 2-stroke Villiers engine drove the rear wheel through a Burman 3 speed gearbox with final drive by chain. The smaller front wheels were mounted in cycle type forks located outside the cargo box.

Trilec   1934   GB
For more information see notes listed under Morrison.

Trilox   1930s   GB
Trilox Trike-Works of Trowbridge, Wiltshire, built a range of folding bath chairs, hand propelled tricycles and the Trilox Invalid Motor. Using a pipe frame, a 150cc Villiers engine mounted aft of the rear wheels, the single front wheel was tiller steered. It is believed that they were available in a number of styles with both foot and hand controls.

Trilux   1986   GB
Another 1930s Morgan-like shape. Built using Citroën Ami parts on a ladder chassis with shaft-drive to the single rear wheel. Kit production was mooted but production costs made it uncommercial so only the one, very professional looking prototype was ever built.

Tri-Magnum   1980 to date   USA
A 3-wheeled bullet-shaped kit car, built of fibreglass on a tubular frame from plans featured in the *Mechanics Illustrated* magazine. Adapting the major portion of a large motorcycle complete with engine and wheel fitted to a two passenger carrying pod and sheathed in a streamlined body. More information under Quincy-Lynn

Trimo   1903-1905   GB
See Phoenix-Trimo for more information.

Tri-Motor   1896-1901   USA
Built by the Western Wheel Works, also known as American Bicycle Company, of Chicago, Illinios. This 3-wheeler was also known as the Tri-Moto.

Trimak   1952-1972   Spain
With sales of over 2,500 in one year, this could be classed as one of the better 3-wheeled commercials available. Built either as a van, a light pickup or a special refuse vehicle, it was well built with car controls and steering wheel in a comfortable cabin equipped with a heater. Power came from a 250cc Lew engine built under licence from Poland. A few vehicles were produced with diesel engines. More details listed under Moto Scooter.

Trimobil　　　　　　　　　　　**1912**　　　　　　　　　　　　　　**Austria**
Also sold as the Walter-Trimobil: see Walter for more details.

Trimobile　　　　　　　　**1903-1912**　　　　　　　　　　　　　　**GB**
Built by the Avon Motor Manufacturing Co of Narrow Wine Street, Keynsham, Bristol. A tubular framed 3-wheeler with the usual single front wheel. A choice of single cylinder 4hp or 5.5hp water-cooled engines mounted at the rear, with chain-drive to a springless live axle. The radiator was mounted on a bulkhead just behind the front wheel. To save road shocks, the 2-seater body was sprung and the vehicle came equipped with mudguards and gas lights. A commercial van was also offered.

In 1905 a 4-wheeled version was added to the production line. Also known as the Avon-Trimobile. More information under that name.

Trimuter　　　　　　　　　　**1980s**　　　　　　　　　　　　　　**USA**
Quincy-Lynn Enterprises of Phoenix, Arizona, were pioneers in eccentric 3-wheeled transport but the Trimuter could be classed as one of their most successful ventures. Concentrating solely on plans alone so that the DIY enthusiast could do everything himself. Planned as a dart-shaped 2-seater, single front wheel trike, the power plant could be either batteries or whatever engine you could fit in – a Briggs & Stratton twin cylinder engine was suggested.

Over 30,000 sets of plans were sold in the first year and a magazine was founded for the enthusiasts.
More information listed under Quincy-Lynn.

Trio　　　　　　　　　　**1993 to date**　　　　　　　　　　　　　　**GB**
This a real do-it-yourself trike. The Trio was conceived by Ken Hallett of Wareham, Dorset, utilising a Mini subframe and an 'A' series engine. The body is basic and made of wood, skinned with aluminium. To build this trike you buy a set of plans for £25 and utilise a bagful of parts available from any spare a parts warehouse or auto breakers/wreckers.

Tripacer　　　　　　　　**1994 to date**　　　　　　　　　　　　　　**GB**
The Tripacer is factory built. You leave a Citroën CV donor car at the Frome, Somerset, factory of Classic Car Panels, come back later and pick up a neat hand-formed aluminium body over a steel tube frame attached to your modified Citroën floorplan, with staggered seating for two, plenty of rivets and yards of louvres. The engine is left exposed up front and sits between neat cycle wings. All in all, an attractive car all the way to its single rear wheel.

Tri-Ped　　　　　　　　　　**1979**　　　　　　　　　　　　　　**USA**
Built by Tri-Ped Corporation of Farmingdale, N.Y. A trike with an under floor mid mounted 500cc 2-stroke engine and automatic centrifugal clutch. The wrap around metal frame formed the chassis and a two place cabin and was covered with clear plastic with side opening doors of the same material. Used for a while in New York as a shopping runabout, the pedal assisted machine was capable of 32km/h and only used 2.8 litres of fuel for 100km.

Tripod (1)　　　　　　　　**1985-1987**　　　　　　　　　　　　　　**GB**
The 3-wheeler that never was. Built by the UK importers of Suzuki, using Suzuki moped parts, this was a 3-wheeler with two wheels up front, an aluminium

honeycomb chassis and a fibreglass 2-seater body. Half a dozen prototypes, in both open and closed versions, were built with an export market in mind. However, it was soon found that the production costs did not make the project a viable one and all prototypes were ordered to be destroyed!

Tripod (2) 1986 USA
Believed to have been advance notice of the English Tripod to test the market.

Tri-Ricksha 1914-1915 USA
Built by the International Tri-Ricksha Company of New York.

Triro (1) 1962-1963 Germany
A very sturdy 3-wheeled commercial from the Goliath stable. A forward mounted engine drove the rear wheels via a driveshaft. With a comfortable cabin, it came as a drop-sided truck or an enclosed van. More information listed under Goliath.

Triro (2) 1950-1953 Germany
With a 200cc Triumph 2-stroke engine mounted over the single front driving wheel, Goliath style, this half-ton payload trivan was built by the Triro-Werke, Mockmuhl.

Trisport-Scorpion 1990 GB
The Trisport-Scorpion was unique as it was designed specifically for single seat racing in the old single seat cyclecar class. With a Formula 1 spaceframe chassis mated to a Yamaha FZR 100 super bike clad in sleek aluminium its top speed was expected to exceed 145mph. A de-tuned road legal prototype was contemplated but the designers lost interest and only the racing example was built.

Tritomibile 1926-1930 Germany
A very unusual vehicle built by Bruno V Festenberg-Pakisch of Hamburg, using the standard single rear wheel with the driver behind the cargo box. Unusual was the box placed over the engine was between the two front wheels, but only had drive to one. The lot was central pivoted and the box, the engine, and the wheels all turned as one.

Tritractor 1925 GB
A 3-wheeled tipper built by the firm, Tritractor Ltd of London. The prototype was built with two wheels side-by-side in the front with a 6.5 ton tipper body ahead of the driver. However, the production run, with almost the same wheel configuration, now had the driver sat in a one man cabin alongside the AEC engine at the front, with the tipping body to the rear. The vehicle used many components of AEC origin.

Triumph (1) 1933 Germany
A motorcycle firm that built a number of 3-wheeled cargo carriers using their then current line of motorcycles as its base.

Triumph (2) 1901-1970s GB
The Triumph Cycle Company Ltd of Coventry built a number of 3-wheelers during the 1900s using a 3hp water-cooled engine with chain-drive to the single rear wheel. They went on to build their motorcycles, with a 4-wheeled car appearing in the 1920s. In 1933 a small number of motorcycle-based cargo carriers appeared.

3-WHEELERS ALMANAC   157

Triumph Tina   1970s(?)   GB
An amalgamation of a motor scooter and a delivery tray which could be folded into a smaller size. A production run of five were believed to have been built.

Tri-Van   1949-1952   GB
See Turner and LDV for more information.

Trivan (1)   1930   GB
More information under Scott.

Trivan (2)   1962-1964   USA
This Trivan comes from the Roustabout Company, Frackville, PA. A modern-looking lorry with a forward control, fully enclosed cabin. The 32hp 2-cylinder air-cooled engine is underslung and drives the single rear wheel through a 3-speed transmission. The chassis is built from steel tubing and the suspension is by air bags. Production totalled about 150 units.

Tri-Vator   1980s   USA

Triver   1952-1960   Spain
From Bilba, Construcciones SA built delivery tricycles with a choice of 125cc or 175cc engines powering the single rear wheel. They also built an 'almost 3-wheeler' – it was a light car or a commercial van with the rear wheels just a few inches apart.

Trivette   1980s   USA
A triangular-shaped 3-wheeler making use of a Fiat 850 engine and other bits, all housed in a fibreglass tandem seating cabin. The single front wheel is well hidden under an upturned canoe-shaped nose. Designed by Robert Keys, the chassis is fabricated from steel tubing and incorporates a roll bar, side beams, and a progressive crumple front end. A large gullwing door takes up most of the right side of the cabin while a similar door in the almost vertical triangle shaped rear end allows access to the engine bay. Top speed was indicated at 60mph with 70 mpg.

Trivoiturette   1910   France
See Austral (1) for more information.

Tri-x Commuter   1980s   USA
Featuring a tubular steel chassis, independent suspension and disc brakes, a choice of engine power and available either as a complete car or in kit form from Gallati-Tenold Ent. Inc. of Rodgers, Minnesota. This was a single front wheel, 2-seater with a fibreglass body and claiming 60-80 mpg.

Trojan 200   1961-1965   GB
The Trojan 200 was the Heinkel bubble car built under licence in the UK. It was built in many countries and came with the variation of either a single back wheel or two wheels very close together. All vehicles were rear engined with the only entry being through the front of the vehicle where the front door opened revealing the steering wheel and instrumentation – a fixture attached to a short bracket protruding from the side of the cabin. A shelf over the engine bay provided a large luggage compartment, while a roll-back soft roof allowed for sunshine motoring.

More than 10,000 of the 200 model were sold in England. The Heinkel was first built in Germany by the former Heinkel Aircraft factory at Stuttgart from 1955 to 1958. It was also produced in Argentina as the 200. A 4-stroke air-cooled 198cc engine drove the single rear wheel through a 4-speed gearbox with reverse. Top speed was about 56mph with 100mpg achievable while touring. A few models were turned into small vans with the roof extended over the engine bay and a door placed where the rear window would have been. More information under Heinkel.

Tryker　　　　　　　　　　**1984**　　　　　　　　　　　**USA**
A kit car from Santa Barbara, California. Resembling a modern 3-wheeled Morgan, it could be built using parts from the Honda Accord 1977-82 series with the power coming from a Yamaha 4-stroke 75 V-twin 920cc motorcycle.

Trylon　　　　　　　　　　**1984 to date**　　　　　　　　**USA**
The Trylon was built by a Star Trek fanatic and looks like something liberated from the TV series. Coming from a factory called Star Fleet Headquarters owned by a Dale H Fox, this long (15ft 4ins) squarish body, with a wide rear end to hide a complete VW engine and powertrain combination, has a GRP bodyshell over a box section steel cage. Entry to the tandem 2-seater cabin is by a clamshell canopy, hinged to the rear. Front wheel and suspension are motorcycle components. The Trylon is offered in two models, the basic vehicle is called the 'Shuttle' while the tarted-up version was sold as the 'Viper'.
　The project is available in kit form or as a completed car. More than 250 vehicles have been built and it is known that at least seven cars have been exported to Europe.

TST　　　　　　　　　　　**1922**　　　　　　　　　　　**GB**

Tsubasa　　　　　　　　　**1932**　　　　　　　　　　**Japan**
A motorcycle-based carryvan with a 498cc engine. The usual cargo space was behind the driver. This unit had a number unusual features such as a sprung saddle with backrest, a heavy duty frame allowing larger loads, pressed steel wheels, and a hand operated gear lever.

Tuck Tuck　　　　　　　　**1950s to date**　　　　　　　**Thailand**
A backyard construction industry has grown up around the Tuck Tuck, a unique taxi, all the rage in Bangkok. Based on a home-grown design, very similar to the Piaggio, it has a single front wheel (motor scooter style) with handlebar steering. The driver straddles the engine while the passengers sit in a rear bench seat. It has a windscreen and roof but without any side weather protection. A batch was even exported to Australia for tourist industry use. In order to try and reduce pollution many new vehicles are using battery-electric or LPG as a power source.

Tung Feng　　　　　　　　**1950s to date**　　　　　　　**China**
For more information see under Dong Feng.

Turner (1)　　　　　　　　**1900-1901**　　　　　　　　　**USA**
The Turner Automobile Company Ltd of Philadelphia, Pennsylvania built a number of 3-wheeled carriages.

Turner (2)   1946-1950s   GB
The Turner Motor Manufacturing Company of Wolverhampton had close links with the motor industry since the turn of the century. After the the Second World War they produced a range of 3-wheelers called the Trivan, the Rixi and a Taxi Rickshaw, all fitted with their own Turner 168cc engines, mounted over and driving the front wheel of the motorcycle-type front end.

The Trivan had a large box mounted between the two rear wheels whereas the Rixi had an open-sided 2-seat cabin.

The Rickshaw was similar to the Rixi but was intended for export. Vehicles were later sold under the name of LDV. Under either name it is believed that only a few found customers. More information is listed under LDV.

Turbo Phantom   1978-1981   USA
Probably one of the widest 3-wheeled vehicles ever built in modern times, the Turbo Phantom from Newport Beach in California had a width of 7ft although the wedge-shaped body itself was only a mere 44ins high. This was an exotic machine, powered by the then popular mating of a Japanese superbike and accessories to a tubular steel chassis with a modified VW Beetle front end. Clothed in a GRP and Urethane hand-built body, entry to the two side-by-side seats was by raising a large canopy. Speeds of 109mph were quoted but with the high finished price of near $20,000 a handful only were completed. Later on diy plans were sold for $20.

Tuxford   1856-1858   USA
Mr William Tuxford of Boston built a self-propelled traction engine using the Boydel (UK) system of broad, flat, wooden shoes fixed to the rear wheels to spread the load. A fire tube boiler fed the 2-cylinder engine with power to the two rear wheels. A single front wheel provided the steering.

Twike   1993 to date   Switzerland
With a bullet shaped and fully enclosed cabin, the entire clear plastic canopy rises to allow entry for two seated in tandem. Batteries and electric motors are located low and between the two rear wheels. Pedal power is supplied to both the driver and the passenger in case of emergencies.

TXI & TX-GT   1950s to date   GB
For more information see Electron.

Tyseley-Unicar   1911   GB

Unicar   1956   GB
Built by S E Opperman of Borehamwood, better known for the Opperman Motorcart, designed by Lawrie Bond. An enclosed fibreglass coupé with a rear mounted 328cc British Anzani or a 225cc Excelsior engine, claiming 85 mpg with a top speed of 75mph. A sports version with a Steyr-Puch 500 engine was announced in 1958. Power was by chain-drive to the single rear wheel.

Unisport   1980s   USA
Built by Unicar Corporation of California, the Unisport was a very successful mating of a large motorcycle to a tandem-seating, all-weather cabin, with all the comforts of an up-market sports car. The cabin had a frame of steel tubing, a roll bar behind the cockpit and a steel plate in front of the driver's feet, all clothed in

an attractive fibreglass body. It had special suspension, something like a Morgan but with linear actuators controlled from the steering wheel which allowed the vehicle to tilt into corners. Disc brakes on the front wheels were linked to the donor motorcycle fixed at the back. For best results a 500cc or larger engine was needed. Soon after release, the Unicar Corporation were producing 50 units a month and unable to keep up with demand.

Universelle   1926-1929   Germany
Built by J C Muller and Company in Dresden, a trivan built along motorcycle lines.

URBA   1978   USA
See Quincy-Lynn for more information.

Utility Three Wheel   1913   USA
Built by the Utility Car Company of New York.

Utopian   1914   GB
From the Utopian Motor Works of Leicester, a firm that made bicycles, came the Utopian; a 2-seater, 3-wheeled, coupé-style body with a parcel tray. Partly under the seat was a 2-cylinder water-cooled engine. The chassis was a metal triangle with the single front wheel controlled by a vertical side-mounted tiller. A pram hood provided weather protection and a utility-style luggage box was fitted between the rear wheels.

Vaghi   1920-1924   Italy
Built originally as a 3-wheel cyclecar using a 546cc twin cylinder engine, the Vaghi had a fourth wheel added in about 1923. The 3-wheeled version was taken over and produced by SAM, another Italian manufacturer. More information listed under that name.

Valentia   1907-1908   France
A large range of tricars using a variety of different engines and built in a factory at Vernon, Eure, by a Mr Saunier.

Valle Chantecler   1952-1957   France
'Round, small, and on 3-wheels', said the reports on this vehicle. A 125cc engine drove a single rear wheel. The body was made of fibreglass with ridged front and rear windows with a cloth hood stretched between as weather protection. Could be used in Germany without a driving licence provided one did not exceed a speed limit of 60km/h. Built by Societe Colas, Loir-et-Cher.

Vallee, Paul   1950s   France
These egg-shaped vehicles were built in both fibreglass and steel using a square tube chassis derived from a delivery scooter. The single rear wheel was chain driven from a 175cc Ydral 2-stroke, single cylinder engine. They came with a bench seat, half-moon steering and bouncy rubber suspension.

Vanette   1923-1930   GB
Built by the Stepney Carrier Company Ltd of High Holborn, this was a standard parcelcar with two wheels and a box in front of a motorcycle rear end, with a 247cc single cylinder 2-stroke engine placed under the driver's seat and a 2-speed

gearbox and chain-drive to the single rear wheel. A 3-speed box was introduced in 1929 while in 1930 the name was changed to Karivan.

Vaughan-Sherrin 1890s GB
See Sherrin for more information.

Vedovelli & Priestley 1899 France
A 3-wheeled electric carriage where the steering was done by slowing one wheel.

Velam 1955-1957 France
The Isetta built under licence. A luxury version was also produced and called the Ecrin. A total of 7,000 plus cars were produced. For more information see under Isetta.

Velocycle 1886-1888 GB
Look under Butler for more information.

Velomobil 1905-1907 Germany

Velorex 1958-1971 Czechoslovakia
Built over a steel pipe frame and covered in canvas, the Velorex had one of the longest production lives of any 3-wheeler since the Second World War, from its inception in 1954 until its demise in 1971. Using the Jawa range of motorcycle engines, one had a choice of 250cc or 350cc twin cylinder motors driving the single back wheel.

Velox 1929-1930 Germany
A trivan with tiller steering to the single front wheel. Built in Nuremberg by Scharrer & Gross along motorcycle lines, the live rear axle was driven by chain from a single cylinder Velox engine, available in 350cc, 500cc and 600cc capacity.

Verbiest 1672 Belgium/China
This was a very basic experimental vehicle conceived by a Belgian missionary, Ferdinand Verbiest, while living in China. Steam from a vertical boiler was directed through a nozzle on to the blades of a turbine that drove, through a series of gear wheels, the two front wheels on a live axle. A very small rear wheel provided stability. As this was a pure experiment in the use of steam to move a wheeled vehicle, no provision had been made for steering or the carrying of passengers – remember this was 1672. It travelled in a forward motion at a reasonable speed but was limited by the capacity of the boiler.

Vespacar 1951-1973 Spain
The Spanish version of the Vespa range of light delivery vehicles. Five different models with payloads from 250kg to 550kg with both open and enclosed cabins.

Vespa Piaggio 1947 to date Italy
Built under licence in many countries, the Piaggio company are as well-known for the production of motor scooters as they are for commercial 3-wheelers. Starting with the Tri-Ciao, a 49cc powered motorcycle with a metal box in front over the two steerable front wheels, its range of delivery vehicles is extremely large.
  Better known throughout the world are the Vespa Car 50 range of delivery

vehicles: the all metal cab, bodies that cover drop-side metal trays, the enclosed delivery van, a garbage truck, a tip tray, or a chassis and cab for your own particular body – all have the familiar single front wheel with a headlight either built into the mudguard or placed in the centre of the body. Steering is by handlebars with hand and foot controls. Larger vehicles have car-type cabins, with steering wheels and normal car controls, as well as twin headlights. Depending on the model, engines range from 50cc single cylinder (placed under the front seat and driving the rear wheels through a 4-speed gearbox and chain-drive) to 122cc, 125cc, 185cc, or 216cc, placed just behind the rear wheels and under the cargo floor. All engines are air-cooled 2-stroke, brakes are hydraulic to the rear wheels, and load capacities of up to 550kg but more often than not are seen way overloaded. See Bajaj for more information.

VG3 1983 USA
After more than three years of testing, the VG3 was launched in October 1983 as a tandem-seating 3-wheeler, using the major part of a motorcycle for power to the single rear wheel. The front wheels tilt and allow the vehicle to lean into corners. A Perspex canopy slides back to allow entry but can be left open for that 'wind in the hair' motoring. Intended to be available in kit form.

VH 1961 Spain

Vi-Car 1952-1953 GB
The Vi-Car was built by Vernons Industries as an invalid tricycle, powered by a Villiers 9E engine, which was placed to the side of a roadster-type body and driving one only of the two rear wheels. The square-sided body came complete with a vertical windscreen, a pram hood and a luggage boot and was registered for road use. This vehicle could be classed as the predecessor to the Gordon.

Victoria 1934-1935 Germany
A slab-sided, no curves, utility-bodied 3-wheeler with a single front wheel, an open sided cabin, and a steering wheel and car controls. The 200cc engine was side mounted under the seat and drove one only of the two rear wheels by chain. Production numbers were believed to be low. Built by a firm that began building motorcycles in 1899 and ceased production in 1966.

Vidal 1923 Germany
For more information see listing under Tempo.

Vigilante 1970s USA
This is a Californian dream car, a wedge shape with a tubular steel frame chassis, laminated fibreglass body, gullwing doors and tandem seating. The rear engine pod was extended with squared mudguards to hide the rear wheels and also accommodate the twin front headlights and rear tail and stop lights. The single front wheel was exposed under the long bonnet. The first prototype was built in 1970 with the project laying dormant until it reappeared in 1990 as the Vigillante, with an extra 'l' in the name, supposed to be the fastest street machine. It is believed a prototype or two have been built in the 1990s but it appears to remain a dream machine.

Vikram 1960s-1990s India
A very large panel van, loosely based around the Vespa but almost double in size. Many were sold to Nepal.

Villard 1925-1935 France
M Villard of Janville, Eure et Loir, took over the design of the Colombe Cyclecar in 1925 after it went out of production. With improvements he reintroduced it under his own name. He used a Harissard engine of 346cc which drove the single front wheel through a 6-speed friction transmission and single chain for final drive. In 1931 a modern 500cc drop head sports coupé was introduced. Both 3-wheeled and 4-wheeled cars and commercial vehicles were produced until 1935.

Villeple 1959 France
Designed by M Villeple, the prototypes of these natty 3-wheelers were being tested in the Paris traffic during 1959, powered by a 125cc engine mounted over the front wheel early 'Bond' style. It was claimed to carry two people at a speed of 47mph in the luxury of a car-style body, with a curved engine bay, vertical windscreen, side opening doors and a pram hood.

Villof 1949-1962 Spain
Built in Valencia by Vincento Llorena Ferrer. A single front wheel with a tray or canvas covered van body over the two rear wheels, and a single cylinder engine under the seat in the metal cabin. Tiller steering and motorcycle controls were the essentials until 1957 when the new Mira was introduced with an enclosed cabin, steering wheel and car controls. A 3-speed gearbox was added and an improved tubular frame chassis.

Vimp 1955 GB
A mini car for two very small people, the Vimp had the two wheels in front with a single rear wheel driven by a Villiers 197cc single cylinder 2-stroke motor. A vertical one-piece windscreen had no wiper, so this was a fine weather only open tourer. Top speed was claimed as 80 km/h with petrol consumption at 3-litres per 100 km. Production was limited to a few prototypes.

Vincent 1950-1955 GB
Began as a prototype with the idea of utilising Vincent Rapide power units and gearboxes to maintain economic production after the initial post-war rush for motorcycles declined. The Vincent 3-wheeler was to have an independently sprung front axle, rack and pinion steering, hydraulic brakes and an aluminium 2-seater sports body. The engine was carried on a subframe, just behind the seat, centred between the driver and passenger and transmitting power to the rear wheel (carried in the standard Rapide triangulated rear forks). This was all fitted to a 4 inch steel tube chassis.

An unusual feature in a 3-wheeler was the popular reversible rear wheel of the Vincent motorcycle; this incorporated two different size sprockets, thus allowing a docile road car to be turned into a race car in minutes. With a wheelbase of 11ft 2ins and a track of 4ft 3ins, speeds of 90mph were achieved in standard trim. By substituting the Vincent Black Lightning engine, speeds of 120mph were possible. A number of experimental cars were made but owing to the downturn in the Vincent motorcycle fortunes the project was allowed to die a natural death. It is believed that one original car still exists in England.

Vinco 1904-1905 GB
Built in Peterborough, a tricar powered by a 3.5hp Fafnir engine.

Viper   1984 to date   USA
More information noted under Trylon.

Vitrex Riboud   1974-1980   France
This firm also produced vehicles in the same time slot under the names of Addax and Gildax. These were all basic 3-wheelers, the Riboud, designed by Jacques Riboud, used a 47cc, 2.4hp Sachs engine in a plain open-seater body. Many thousands were produced.

Voiture Electronique   1968-1976   France
A plastic tray with wheels would be an apt description of this simple two people mover. Between the seats was a single joystick, available to either passenger, that controlled everything. Each rear wheel had its own electric motor while the single front wheel was on a castor and free to move in any direction. No steering wheel, just power to one motor and you did a 360 in its own length. Top speed was 15mph with about 40 miles to each battery charge. Improvements over the years caused a name change to Porquerolles and included such luxuries as a hard top, wing mirrors and indicators. Also known as the Stil Voiture Electronique. Production stopped in 1976.

Volk   1895   GB
Magnus Volk built the first electric tram line alongside Maderira Drive in Brighton, England. Experimenting in personal transport, Mangus, in 1887, was running his first motor car; a 3-wheeled, battery-electric powered dogcart, chain-driven from a half-horsepower Acme & Immisch electric motor.

A number of 4-wheeled versions with a 1hp electric motor were built and at least two were exported to Turkey.

VW Scooter   1986   Germany
Volkswagen built a number of energy efficient prototypes including 'The Scooter'. This very stylish vehicle was 3170mm long and, athough only 1500mm wide, had side-by-side seating in armchair comfort for the two occupants. Entry was through Mercedes-style gullwing doors, with space for luggage over the single rear wheel. Flush Windows, flowed bumpers, recessed lights and handles allowed the 1.4-litre front wheel drive engine to accelerate from 0-100km/h in 8.5 seconds with a top speed of 160km/h from the VW Polo engine, returning 19.2km/l or 54 mpg. 200km/h has been claimed for a sports version. Built to meet all the then current European safety standards, this vehicle has been put on hold until further notice. Other 3-wheeled vehicles built by VW include the Sparmobile in 1983, built for economy tests, and capable of 1970 miles per American gallon but at speeds of only 16mph. A later version called the Economymobile, using the world's smallest direct injection diesel engine – just 25cc – gave an impressive 2,498 mpg!

VW Special   Since inception   Worldwide
The VW Beetle has always been a favourite with kit car specialists for 4-wheeled conversions, however, the 3-wheeler has not been left out: VWs have provided basic parts for many 3-wheeled sports car variations.

Waggenhals   1910-1915   USA
The Waggenhals Manufacturing Company of St. Louis changed its name in 1912 to Waggenhals Motor Car Company and moved to Detroit, where it built a large

parcels carrier for the US Mail. Power was from a 2 cylinder 14hp engine with planetary transmission and final drive by chain. Its long box body was slung between the two front wheels while the driver sat majestically in a cabin, with a pram hood over the single rear wheel and engine bay. From 1913 a 4-cylinder engine of 24hp was used, and a steering wheel and normal car controls. They added electric cars to their line during 1914/15.

Walco　　　　　　　　　　**1905**　　　　　　　　　　**GB**
A number of trikes were believed to have been built by W A Lloyd and Co of Birmingham and sold under the name of WalCo

Wall　　　　　　　　　　**1911-1915**　　　　　　　　　　**GB**
A W Wall Ltd of Tysely, Birmingham, built an unusual shaped body, something like a motorcycle sidecar, placed over a pressed steel chassis. It had a choice of 4.5hp Simplex single-cylinder or a 6hp twin-cylinder Precision engine, placed aft of the single front wheel and driving the two rear wheels by a driveshaft. Tiller steering was used up to 1914 after which a steering wheel was introduced. A side-opening door and a pram hood helped with weather protection but without a windscreen was a hindrance in a head wind. The Wall has also been credited with the nickname, 'Roc Egg'.

Wallace　　　　　　　　　　**1900s**　　　　　　　　　　**GB**
In 1904 the Wallace was using a 4hp water-cooled engine in a pipe frame chassis. The engine was just in front of the single rear wheel and under the driver's padded seat. A cargo box or a wicker seat was between the two front wheels.

Walmobil　　　　　　　　　　**1920**　　　　　　　　　　**Germany**
Built by Walter Loebel Maschinenfabrik of Berlin.The single front wheel was tiller steered with a twin cylinder engine mounted Panmobile style.

Walter　　　　　　　　　　**1908-1936**　　　　**Austria & Czechoslovakia**
Jos Walter was a maker of bicycles when he moved into motorcycles and tricycles. In 1908 he produced a cyclecar using a 500cc and later a 1,250cc engine, placed just behind the single front wheel in a tubular steel chassis, with shaft-drive to the rear wheels. Fitted with tiller steering, car-type controls, a ratchet lever handbrake and a pram hood and canvas cover to give some weather protection. The car was sold as the Walter-Trimobil in 2- and 4-seat variations. In 1921 the 3-wheelers were taken over by Sibrava, while Walter himself continued with a new 4-wheeled variant that he produced well into the late 1930s, until the company went over to the production of aero engines and heavy trucks and buses.
More information see under Sibrava.

Warrick　　　　　　　　　　**1911-1931**　　　　　　　　　　**GB**
Progressing from pedal powered parcel carriers, beloved by the butcher and grocer, the Warrick gained a 723cc single cylinder air-cooled engine (of their own manufacture) mounted in a heavy metal frame with power to the single rear wheel, via a 2-speed epicyclic transmission and final chain-drive. As usual, the driver sat over the engine and out in all weathers.
　Over 2,000 were made with little change in design between the first and the very last vehicles produced.

Wasp — 1983s — Australia

On show at the 1983 International Motor Show in Sydney, Australia, the Wasp was a futuristic combination of sports car and motorcycle. The wedge-shaped fibreglass front cabin for two, fully kitted out with car type controls and padded seating, but not for a girl in a tight skirt as entry was over the side and through the roof that slid sideways allowing you to drop directly into the form-fitting seat. The rear half was pure motorcycle from the engine back, within its own streamlined and matching covering. As this vehicle was tailored for the kit car market, power plant was of your own choosing. Intended as a 3-wheel sports vehicle, combining power, reliability and economy, turning a motorcycle into a highly individual 2-seater.

Produced in Western Australia, little has since been heard of the venture.

Watburg — 1896 — Germany

Established in 1896 to build military machinery, Fahrzeugfabrik Eisenach AG, with Heinrich Erhardt heading management, quickly saw the need for motor cars and built a 3-wheeled improved copy of the De Dion, intended for exhibition at the Dusseldorf Motor Show.

The prototype was successful, but there was a change of plans and instead the company built a 4-wheeler that was to found the Watburg motoring empire.

W & E — 1945 to date — GB

Wales and Edwards Ltd of Wyle Cop, Shrewsbury became W & E Vehicles Ltd in 1957. They are noted for their single front wheeled electric milk floats with capacities from 20cwt to 40cwt. Also built in 4-wheeled versions they had a special 5 wheeled model, and a 3-wheeled tug with an articulated trailer.

Weber — 1899-1906 — Czechoslovakia

A 3-wheeler made under licence from Egg and Egli, Switzerland.

Weise — 1929-1939 — Germany

The Berlin firm of Weise and Company built a trivan along the lines of the Hanomag with a single front wheel, complete with a 200cc Rinni engine mounted above the wheel and driving it via a chain. Early models were tiller steered but were soon modernised and replace with a steering wheel, enclosed cabin and car controls. In 1939 a 1-ton diesel-engined van was included in the production line but the start of the Second World War soon put the factory onto a war production footing that did not include 3-wheelers.

Weiss — 1931 — Germany

A light trivan built by the Munchen firm of Konrad Weiss, using a 96cc Sachs engine mounted in a heavy bicycle frame driving the single rear wheel, while a large enclosed cargo box was slung between the two front wheels.

Welb — 1928-1930s — Japan

A very modern looking commercial carrier with the cargo box between the two rear wheels. A 670cc JAP engine was used and production figures for the 1937 year were 740 units.

Wellan — 1900s — GB

This tricar had a tiller steering front wheel with a single cylinder engine mounted on the steering head, transmitting power to the single front wheel through leather belts. Comfortable seating for two was between the rear wheels.

Wendax   1931-1935   **Germany**
Wendax Fahrzeugbau GmbH, Hamburg, built their first prototype in 1931 but it was not until 1935 that they entered into serious production of a trivan with the standard layout of a single driven rear wheel, box up front and driver sitting on a saddle over the engine. Power was from a 200cc Ilo engine with a chain final drive.

Wendaz   1931   **Germany**

Westcoaster   1927-1975   **USA**
The West Coast Machinery Company was formed to build farm machinery that also included a 3-wheeled small truck. Built in a variety of forms over a long life, the vehicles were used in both passenger and cargo versions and powered by either 17.6hp 2-cylinder engines or 36 volt electric motors. They were used by Police for traffic duties, by the US Postal Department, and even as in-plant ambulance and first aid vehicles.
After a takeover by Otis Elevator Company in 1975, the vehicles were marketed under the Otis name.

Wesnigk   1920-1923   **Germany**

Westfalia   1950s   **Germany**
This 3-wheeler had an open bodywork, side-opening door, vertical windscreen and handlebar steering to the single front wheel. Power came from a rear mounted 125cc Ilo 2-stroke engine with self-start. A pram hood provided weather protection.

Whitehurst-Homer   1905-1906   **GB**
Built in Longsight, Manchester, a tricar using a 3.5hp engine.

Williamson   1912-1920   **GB**
Billy Williamson built luxury motorcycles as well as trikes in the early part of his manufacturing career. Engines listed were 964cc flat-twin, air or water-cooled, built by Douglas from 1912 to 1916 after which he switched to JAP 770cc side-valve twins until production ceased in 1920.

Witcar   1980   **Holland**
Designed as a shopping commuter, this strange looking car had a metal box base acting as the chassis, to hold the engine and wheels; two in front and a single rear driven from a bank of batteries and an electric motor. This was topped by a bench seat for two, a steering wheel and car type controls. For the body we had a plexiglass container that had more than a passing resemblance to a large jam jar with a white screw top! Add a windscreen wiper, a sliding door and we had a vehicle that could be parked nose to the kerb and three to a parking bay. It was supposed to reduce the pollution in Amsterdam and take larger cars off the road.
The project worked for a few years, and the odd one is still seen in the suburbs.

WMC Bug   1990 to date   **GB**
Using the original Reliant Bug moulds, Mike and Garry Webster set up the Webster Motor Company intending to build a 4-wheeled car, only to find that there was a

demand for a 3-wheeled Bond Bug lookalike. Using donor cars such as the Reliant Robin or Regal, WMC developed an improved ladder chassis and updated suspension and with the use of an 850cc engine, 100mph was said to be obtainable. Available in kit form from the factory at Braishfield in Hampshire.

Wolf 1904-1905 GB

A 3-wheeled cyclecar built in Wolverhampton by the Wearwell Motor Carriage Company Ltd, powered by a 2.75hp to 6hp Wearwell engine through a 2-speed constant-mesh gearbox with final chain-drive to the single rear wheel. Both passenger and trade models were built in limited numbers. The firm reverted back to motorcycles and continued producing these until the Second World War.

Wolseley 1895-1899 GB

The Wolseley Car Company had its roots deep in the Australian Wool trade. Frederick Wolseley left his native England to manage an Australian sheep station and, while working there, developed a mechanical shearing system. Herbert Austin, also an Englishman, came separately to Australia to work for the newly formed Wolseley Sheep Shearing Machine Company. In the early 1890s the company transferred the operation to England and Austin went with it. In 1895, as part of a plan to offset the seasonal demand for its shears, Austin designed and built a 3-wheeler with tiller steering. It was a Bolée-type machine featuring a horizontally opposed, air-cooled, twin cylinder engine of 1255cc with chain-drive to the single rear wheel.

A second car featuring a single front wheel and seating for four was exhibited at the 1896 National Cycle Show. The vehicle made many long journeys and was proved sound. Further cars were built and in 1899 a fourth wheel was added. Austin went on to form his own company in 1905.

More details will be found under Austin.

Wooler Mule 1919 GB

John Wooler built conventional motorcycles from 1911 until 1955 but he had one adventure into 3-wheeled car production with a rotary-valved, horizontally opposed, 8/19hp twin cylinder 1,022cc air-cooled motor with variable gearbox and belt drive to a single rear wheel (actually two wheels bolted together). It had a square steel box chassis with independent front suspension and a bath tub-style body and a narrow tube-like engine cover in front. A parcel carrier was placed over the rear wheel.

It seems that only a few experimental prototypes were made.

WSC 1907 GB

Wholesale Supply Company of Aberdeen built a small 3-wheeled cyclecar and parcel carrier that apparently was not very successful and few vehicles were made. They tried their hand at a larger 4-wheel cargo carrier with better results. The few vehicles built were all sold under the WSC name plate.

Wuhan 1970 to date China

Built by the Wuhan Pedicab Factory, this motorcycle-based 3-wheeler converts from a 2-seat plus driver in front taxi, to a delivery vehicle by removing the seats and canopy. The power comes from a single cylinder 12hp engine with 4 forward speeds and reverse with final drive to the two rear wheels by chain.

Xenia　　　　　　　　　　**1914**　　　　　　　　　　**USA**
Built by the Hawkins Cycle Car Company, Xenia, Ohio. This was a long and narrow vehicle (8ft 4ins by 3ft) with a single front wheel, and power from a 10hp air-cooled, 2-cylinder engine driving through a planetary transmission and belts to the rear wheels. Was also known as the Hawkins-Xenia.

XK-1　　　　　　　　　　**1980s**　　　　　　　　　　**USA**
Developed by the Quincy-Lynn stable and produced by Western Front Inc, of Texas, the XK-1 was a kit with a single front wheel and styling somewhere between a Bond Bug and a Trimuter. It had a sloping rear end, twin bumpers, a windscreen from a Honda Civic, steering column from a Toyota Celica, the rear suspension from a Datsun and a choice of engines from a Briggs and Stratton to VW Beetle. It could be purchased in kit form or as a set of bare plans.
More information under Quincy-Lynn.

Xtra　　　　　　　　　　**1922-1924**　　　　　　　　　　**GB**
The Xtra came from the Xtra Cars Ltd, Chertsey, Surrey. The single cylinder Villiers 3.75hp 2-stroke engine, with 2-speed friction rollers, was mounted just ahead of the back wheel. A bench seat was for two at a pinch, and a large steering wheel took up much of the width of the body, which itself could be mistaken for a motorcycle sidecar with wheels, two in front and one behind. Equipped with a windscreen and a pram hood that when in the 'up' position would have made entry difficult.
   Production is understood to have been limited. It has been noted that one example of the Xtra made an extensive tour of the Continent without suffering any problems.

Yatsuka　　　　　　　　　　**1930s**　　　　　　　　　　**Japan**
A motorcycle-based cargo trike using a 650cc engine.

Yamanari　　　　　　　　　　**1919**　　　　　　　　　　**Japan**
A commercial trike with the cargo box between the two rear wheels and built by a firm noted in automobile literature as KRS.

Yamata　　　　　　　　　　**1916**　　　　　　　　　　**Japan**
A commercial 3-wheeler in usual motorcycle style; the driver exposed to all the elements.

Yawmata　　　　　　　　　　**1930s**　　　　　　　　　　**Japan**
A motorcycle-based cargo trike built by Nakajima using imported JAP engines of 350cc, 600cc and 750cc.

Yeu Loong Rickshaw　　　　　　**1970 to date**　　　　　　**Taiwan**
Yeu Loong Motor Company, Taipei, built many vehicles using licence agreements with Japanese and American companies as well as trucks and buses under their own name. The Rickshaw has the driver in front, motorcycle style, and a passenger compartment for two, with both a hard and a soft roof between the two back wheels.

Yellow Peril　　　　　　　　　　**1990s**　　　　　　　　　　**GB**
Not the name of some Chinese monster, but a Citroën Dyane modified with a rear

end conversion to a single wheel and an open coupé body made in sheet aluminium.

Its claim to fame is as one of the few 3-wheelers to take part and successfully complete in the 1993 Stella Alpine Rally in Italy. It was built and driven by a Peter Hill.

ZAZ 1954 **USSR**
Prototype of a little known 3-wheeled van or car destined for export to Asian countries.

Zenette 1907-1908 **GB**
A sociable tricar with a 6hp twin cylinder engine and tiller steering to the single front wheel.

Zetgelette 1923 **Germany**

Zipper 1983 **Japan**
Japan has been the home of 3-wheeled vehicles since the first cars were built there in the 1900s. The Zipper was a one person transporter that is made of fibreglass. It had a body is almost as wide as it was long, at 2.1 metres. It was powered by a 50cc engine driving the single rear wheel. With car type controls and a steering wheel, the Zipper had a top speed of 72km/h. It was available as a closed cabin with one side opening door or as an open sports with a step-in body.

Zoe 1990s **USA**
The Reliant Robin imported from England and modified with extended rear wheel arches and bumper bars and available with a choice of either a standard petrol engine or an electric motor. See information under Zoe Zipper.

Zoe Zipper 1984 **USA**
The first Reliant imported into America in 1984 sold as the Zipper or the Zoe Zipper. Sales were slow, so moves were made to modify the vehicle and it was relaunched as the Zoe in the 1990s.

Zundapp 1928-1935 **Germany**
As a manufacturer of motorcycles, Zundapp Ges, GmbH of Nuremberg, built a trivan following the usual motorcycle lines, box in front and the driver out in all weathers at the back. In 1933, a trivan with a single front wheel, enclosed cabin and a van, or a tray, body was introduced. A 400cc or a 500cc Zundapp motorcycle engine drove the rear wheels through a cardan shaft. In 1935, the vehicle was replaced by a 4-wheeled version.

Zwerg 1954 **Germany**
For more information look under Brütsch.

MORE ODDS AND ENDS

While researching for this book I came across another side to the 3-wheeler; the collector. Starting around the same time as the combustion-engined car hit the road, toy manufacturers found a steady supply of subjects to copy, first in metal and, much later, in plastic.

The appearance of the first metal toys was in the 1700s while the first tinplate trike was probably made in the early 1900s.

Germany is believed to have been the largest producer of tinplate toys up to the First World War; they made the trike in many forms that would have filled many a Xmas stocking. Walter Stock of Silingen started production of a range of lithographed tinplate 3-wheeled cars with spring motors about 1906 – one, with some imagination, had a passing resemblance to a Benz. Lehmann of Brandenburg, established in 1881, built good quality hand-painted trikes from about 1910. Most German toy vehicles were of the single front wheel variety as were the majority of their big brothers.

Die cast models started to hit the market in crude forms after the First World War.

It was after the end of the Second World War that the model maker started to cater for the 3-wheeler in limited numbers. Brumm of Italy had a good range of collector models called the Revival that included the Morgan, Darmont, and the Sanford, their 'Old Fire' range featured the 1681 Verbiest and the Cugnot.

Mattel UK Ltd produced a number of limited editions of the Scammell. Gama of Germany had a range of 3-wheeled road sweepers, while ARII of Japan released a range of 1/32 plastic build-it-yourself classics which included five commercials, such as the Mazda T2000 truck down to the Daihatsu Midget. Another popular DIY plastic from Japan is the Morgan.

Charbens of England had a range of very small models that included a rough 1904 AC, while Corgi included the Heinkel in a variety of colours. Another English firm, Budgie Models Ltd, produced a very solid range of Scammell Scarab Articulated vehicles in a variety of colours and depicting freight lines such as the Post Office and British Railways.

The Scammell seems to have been a very popular base for many of the toy companies in the 1950s. The Crescent Toy Company of England made a very elaborate die-cast Scammell Scarab, built to scale with a 6 ton low loader complete with ramp and winch.

Lesney made a few miniatures of the same vehicle in the early years of the firm's history, while even smaller models of the Tempo, built to compliment the 00 gauge railway sets, can be found occasionally in retailers specialising in model railway accessories.

Dinky Toys, under the Meccano label, came up with a well detailed version of the Motocart. Solid enough to have survived many years of rough handling. Possibly the 'king of the range' is the Franklin Mint Benz, beautifully crafted at a price to match.

An unusual model of the 'fifties, powered by miniature engines, were those marketed under the name of Pylon. They included a range of 3-wheeler BSA's and Morgans.

Not available in great numbers are the cigarette cards and greeting cards that feature 3-wheelers. The odd cards were produced in 1908 but it was not until the 1920s that cards became popular – sadly the 3-wheelers are thin on the ground. In 1958 The 'Mills' Miniature Cars and Scooter Cars series enclosed in their filter tip cigarette packs featured 25 cars of which as many as 14 were 3-wheelers.

Post cards were very popular at the turn of the century and the Edwardian novelty card featured the odd 3-wheeler. In modern times a good collection can be made from the range from the coloured photographs of 3-wheelers exhibited in Museums. There are also the reproductions of paintings featuring classic cars that include the odd 3-wheeler put out by the likes of Metcombe Fine Art (GB).

Classics are the beautiful hand-coloured post cards of the 1888 Benz produced in Stuttgart in the 1930s. A lot of fun can be had wading through the boxes of unlabelled postcards in local junk shops, looking for that elusive card featuring a 3-wheeler possibly tucked in the corner of some distant scene.

Postage stamps of Automobilia look colourful but other than the Benz are lacking in 3-wheelers.

Another interesting source of information and a colourful addition to any collection are the sales brochures. As most of these are from Europe, both language and availability are a problem, however they still turn up at swap meets in limited quantities.

Though not strictly a motorised vehicle but can be classed under odds and ends as collectables are prams. First appearing in Britain about 1840 they were pushed and had three wheels, along with bathchairs. The 4-wheeled versions were not allowed on the footpath until 1880. In the 1990s a new version of 3-wheeled prams are now coming into vogue as the 'joggers cart'. Take baby with you when you go running. One passed me the other day with Mum on roller blades and going like the clappers!

If you want to see more of the 3-wheeled models of bygone years, I have found the toy museums to be well stocked but as they don't class 3-wheelers as a variety on their own, you have to go searching. The Toy Museum in London has a good collection.

If you are looking for the real thing, the Story Small Car Museum, in northern Germany, has one of the best collections of 'small' cars – it includes a large variety of 3-wheelers, mostly from the '50s and the '60s. In fact, most museums the world over will have the odd 3-wheeler tucked in a corner somewhere.

So good hunting!

DATA REQUIRED

List of vehicles in the *3-Wheelers Almanac* for which no information could be obtained before publication. Please write to the author or the publisher if you can help fill these gaps, or know of other vehicles that are not listed in this book.

Acam Nica	1984-1987	Italy
Aerocarene	1947	France
Albrecht	1950-1951	Germany
Aleu	1954	Spain
Alpha	1927-1936	Spain
Andre Py	1899	France
API Rickshaw	1955 to date	India
Baldet Bluebird	1950	GB
B E F	1907-1913	Germany
Bell	1920	B
Bell Motors Veleto	1976-1981	France
Bubu Cabin Scooter	1982	Japan
Bully	1933	Germany
Bunger	1947-1949	Denmark
Cheeta	1992 to date	Switzerland
Classic Images MSR3	1992	GB
Cloumobil	1906-1908	Germany
Colliday	1960	GB
Convenient Machines Cub	1982-1983	USA
Dallison	1913	GB
Dandley	1910	GB
Daulton	1950	France
DD	1949-1950	Vietnam & Morocco
De Boisse	1900-1904	France
Decolon	1957	France
Diehlmobile	1962-1964	USA
DMC	1913-1914	GB
Doddsmobile	1947	Canada
Dorran	1991	USA
Dual E Turconi	1899-1901	Italy
Egan	1952	GB
Ekamobil	1913-1914	Germany
Entrop	1909	Netherlands

Europeen	1899-1903	France
Fire Aero	1980	USA
FR	1927-1928	France
Gaitan	1950	Spain
Gashopper	1980	USA
Gasmobile	1900	USA
Gorke	1921	Germany
Grewe and Schutte	1904-1905	GB
Haargaard	1950	Denmark
Hero	1934	Germany
Horrocks	1918	GB
HSM	1913-1915	GB
Induhag	1922	Germany
Internationale	1942	Netherlands
ISSI	1953-1954	Italy
Jet	1955	Spain
Kikos	1980-1983	France
Knight	1955	Spain
Knollner	1924	Germany
Kurier	1948	Czechoslovakia
La Durance	1908-1910	France
La Fleurantine	1906	France
Lambda	1988	GB
Landgrebe	1921-1924	Germany
La Torpille	1912-1913	France
Linday	1900-1906	GB
Liwaba	1930-1931	Germany
Lomar Honey	1985-1986	Germany
Lucciola	1948-1949	Italy
Marocchi	1900-1901	Italy
Mayrette	1910-1911	Germany
Meiwa	1952	Japan
Miles	1910-1912	GB
Minima	1911	France
Minutilo-Millo	1896	Italy
Motocar	1920-1924	France
Onnasch	1924	Germany
Orient-Express	1895-1903	Germany
Pappenberger	1953	Germany